Who's Afraid of Wolffy?

A sister's struggle to make sense of her Vietnam Vet brother's reclusion and murder.

This book is a work of nonfiction. Dialogue in chapters about the author's family life when she was a young girl were recreated to the best of her recollection.

First Edition: February 2018

ISBN: 978-0692076576
Cataloging-in-Publication Data is on file with the Library of Congress.
Released for Electronic Publication and Print versions in the United States of America.

In memory of my brother,
John Charles Wolff, Jr.

May you be at peace ...

Who's Afraid of Wolffy?

Introduction

I loved all of my brothers, and I was proud of each of them and their accomplishments in life. My brother John, however, became very special to me. At times when I needed one most, he became a mentor, a father figure, and a role model.

The attention John gave me, though not constant, had a huge impact on my life. Especially during my difficult teenage years, he validated me as an individual, as my own person. He didn't treat me as simply an extraneous little sister, but as an individual who had her own mind and struggled like he did to find their way.

When John was first drafted, he made me, his 14-year-old sister, his beneficiary so that if something happened to him while in the service my college tuition would be paid. He thought that my education was especially important to lift me up and out of the kind of life we had while growing up. He made that gesture for me even though he himself had essentially been forced to drop out of high school.

While John was in the service state-side and while he was in Vietnam, we shared many private hopes, dreams and troubles in the many letters that we wrote back and forth. Those letters helped us to bond even more closely together. Unfortunately, that bonding – on his side – would be unsustainable.

It was important to me to write this book to commemorate my brother's life. It sheds light on all the details of John's life – the good, the bad, the ordinary, the extraordinary, the highs, the lows, his ultimate illness, and the horrible way in which he died. At the same time, it highlights how my own life was impacted by all that he endured.

Who's Afraid of Wolffy initially takes the reader through our growing up years amidst a dysfunctional family, one that was peppered with mental illness among family members nuclear and further out. It focuses on some of the trauma we lived through, the trauma we siblings all would need to overcome in order to live productive lives. How we who are still alive look back on all of it and how those who are now gone looked back on it, I'm sure, is and was totally different for each and every one of us.

Despite our background, I loved both of my parents dearly. Each had experienced their own traumas while they were growing up. Each had flaws, some pointed out in this book, and their flaws affected our family deeply. But, I like everyone else have flaws, too. However in retrospect we might wish it to be different, we can each only be a product of our total current environment and past learning experiences at any one given point in time.

Chapter 1

I first sat and tried to write this book in a ratty old zipped gray hoodie that I found in my brother John's belongings, struggling to find words that might make sense of his life and death. To become wearable, this sweatshirt underwent at least 10 washings before I was able to eliminate the repulsive smell of his house, an unforgettable odor borne of 20 years of heavy smoking, wood stove heating, dirty carpet, old cat urine, and thousands of mouse droppings. As a teenager I had begged to wear his beautiful clothes. This gray hoodie to me was now the epitome of irony.

Though I wrote down many notes immediately after John's estate probate was completed, the preponderance of this history of events detailing my brother's life and murder came a full two years after its occurrence, and a bit of it up to fourteen years afterwards. Thus, not every recollection will be 100% accurate. Although, even if it were written mere days, weeks, or months after the fact, my recollections would not be 100% accurate, nor would they be identical to any other person's recollections about this horrible event.

Again, I want to stress that what this book contains is my reality and no one else's. The impact my brother's murder had on my life has been great. Eventually, it was the breaking point that led to the demise of my marriage. John's murder brought everything – all past and present experiences – to a psychological head for me. It made me question everything about my life. In fact, I began questioning everything about life in general.

This experience made me know without a doubt that my life – and anyone else's - could be gone in an instant. I now understood completely that my life could be taken at any moment at the whim of someone else, and that all my taking care of my body and my mind wouldn't make one iota of difference. We see these horrible events in movies and on television shows;

it's entirely different when murder enters your own life. You can't simply turn it off and walk away.

In the aftermath of the murder, I began to see clearly that it was time to change the things in my life that I still wanted to change because our time runs out quickly. George Harrison's line in his song "This is Love" about little things appearing suddenly and changing your life forever is absolutely correct. In this case, however, it wasn't exactly a "little" thing, but a huge thing that has forever changed me. It was murder.

The impact of the murder of someone you love is truly beyond words. I have tried many times over these past fourteen years to write down the feelings it evoked and the subsequent actions I took based on those feelings. It's something that on most days still seems beyond me, but I have done my best.

There are many sources of grief support for those who have lost a family member: articles, books, on-line information and on-line grief groups, and even community grief counseling groups may be available. It is a totally different story when you lose a family member to murder, particularly if the family member was "only" a sibling. One of the articles I found on The Compassionate Friends web site shortly after John's murder hit it right on the head:

> "When a sibling dies, the world changes in a heartbeat.
> Oftentimes when such a loss occurs, others fail to recognize
> that the surviving sibling faces emotional battles on many
> fronts while working through the loss. Largely ignored,
> surviving siblings are often referred to as the 'forgotten
> mourners.'"

T.J. Wray in her book *Surviving the Death of a Sibling* expands this thought further. "For some reason, our society fails to recognize the depth of love we feel for our brothers and sisters and the consequent grief felt at their passing. Aside from our parents, our siblings are the only people who have known us for our entire life."

In the book, Wray shares a conversation that she had with an older gentleman in a doctor's office waiting room. He discovered during their talk that she had recently lost her brother. "I lost a brother in 1972 [this having been many years prior]," he said. "You never get over losing a brother, you know. You never really get over it." After 14 years since John's death and my other brothers' deaths, I can certainly attest to that.

Sibling grief, as with grief over the loss of any family member, is compounded when the cause of death is murder. Several points cited on the International Critical Incident Stress (ICISF) Foundation site by Dr. Atle Dyregrov in "A Murder in the Family" seemed to speak directly to me:

1) The murder may trigger other types of losses a family has had that may need to be reprocessed.

2) No other experience has prepared the family or its members how to deal with the homicide. And,

3) Little else competes for attention for months or years to come. Without a choice, murder becomes an unwelcome guest existing in each family forever more.

The ICISF site also elaborated on societal factors surrounding the loss of a sibling through murder. Initially, there may be a greater outpouring of sympathy from the community because of the horrible circumstances of the death. However, this rather quickly changes to avoidance by the majority of family, friends and acquaintances who now view you as unlucky. It's as if they expect your circumstances to somehow rub off on them if they talk with you about your loss. I, rather understandably, became a vision of death to many. I remember quite vividly that it was the same when I was struggling to cope with the fact that my mother was dying of Lou Gehrig's Disease. It was okay to talk about it once with someone, but it wasn't necessarily something anyone wanted to hear about a second time, and certainly not in any length or detail.

What would have helped me immensely would have been the ability to talk with my remaining siblings – two brothers – about John's life and death. Comforting conversations with them, however, never developed. First of all, one of them had never seemed to accept the fact that John was schizophrenic. He had essentially cut John off as a family member decades earlier because John had threatened him and his family (with whom he was staying at the time) when he thought they were trying to poison him. Of course, this is understandable to me – to a point. My other brother? He had issues of his own to deal with and therefore did not know how to deal with John's murder, nor did he know how, or even want, to be part of a support system for me. Since both of our parents were gone, there were no family members left with whom to discuss anything about John's life, and these two brothers would have been the only people who could have truly understood our family dynamics and helped me through my loss. The thought occurred to me that part of my grief processing of John's death has been like a huge debriefing of my entire former family life, both before and after marriage.

The Compassionate Friends' author summed up sibling loss very well. "When your parents die, it is said you lose your past; when your spouse dies, you lose your present; and when your child dies, you lose your future. However, when your sibling dies, you lose a part of your past, your present, and your future."

Barbara Lazear Ascher states this thought more profoundly in *Landscape Without Gravity*: "Siblings may be ambivalent about their relationships in life, but in death the power of their bond strangles the surviving heart. Death reminds us that we are part of the same river, the same flow from the same source, rushing towards the same destiny. Were you close? Yes, but we didn't know it then."

After my brother's murderer was convicted, I was asked to write an impact statement to the Court of Missouri. The following is my response to the statement's first question that I wrote and submitted in 2004, and it still rings true for me, even though a full fourteen years have elapsed.

How has this crime affected you and those close to you? Please discuss your feelings about what has happened and how it has affected your general well being, etc.

"Overall, I would say that John's murder has estranged me from people. This is something that no one that I personally know has gone through. How could they possibly know the feelings that I have had? It makes me angry that this has befallen MY family. We've had enough sorrow in our lives through many other family tragedies. I don't wish that it had happened to any of my friends, in-laws, etc. Just angry that I have to deal with it, and they don't have a clue what I'm feeling.

"Does it impact me that I've lost my third brother? You bet. You bet it matters that I lost another sibling – even under the circumstances of his mental illness and his hermit-like life. I still have all the memories of what John was and the potential for what he could have been. No one deserves to die like he did. MY brother did not deserve to die like he did. John did not hurt anyone.

"Because of John's illness, we did not know him through these past 25 years other than what the postmistress told us. But, in handling his probate, I had to go through each and every item that he owned. I learned exactly what his life was like: the things he did, the places he went, how he spent his hours. It was very heart rending to learn how very ill he was; how very alone he was. Not only heart rending, but disturbing.

"It was on my birthday that we went to the funeral home in Macon to view my brother's body. I had not seen my brother since approximately 1983!! How does anyone know what that felt like to see my brother as an old man and to understand that I would never, ever get the chance of talking to him again in his life. That probably wouldn't have happened anyway, but I always hoped, I always prayed for it.

It was the hardest thing I ever did – right up there with the difficulty of sitting through his trial – to see how frail he was and to know how large a person had thought it their right to hurt and kill him. My brother, who had been the kindest, most caring member of my family to me in so many ways. My brother, who had been taken away from us and shipped off to Vietnam and literally broken. If someone can explain to me why he had to suffer such a horrible death, I'd sure like to hear it.

"I sought counseling once during the course of these past two years. I searched to find a group of people mourning their murdered siblings in the Chicagoland area. I was told that I might want to start one of my own. I did not – and especially now do not – have the energy to do such a thing. When I needed it, it was not there. No one's fault. It just wasn't there.

"So has this affected my relationship with people? YOU BET! My husband has had to deal with my feelings about this for the past two years. That cannot have been easy. I've watched my son suffer through this, and that wasn't easy for me. And vice versa. He has now watched me suffer through all of this, and that wasn't easy for him. I know my friends got tired of hearing about my grief, and my anger, and the probate process. And, mainly because of all the work involved, I did not get to see much of my friends these past few years. Additionally, I put my own life goals on hold for two years while I dealt with the painstaking process of handling his probate, which was so involved because of his mental illness and how he handled his financial affairs.

"Indeed, this has put my life on hold. So now that the trial is done, I feel as if I've lost two years of my life. How do you get those two years back? Every time something had to be done for the probate, for the investigation, for whatever aspects were being dealt with, it sent me back into the mourning process.

"I was unable to complete my master's degree as planned. In fact, I have given up on it. Two years ago, it mattered a great deal to me. Right now, I'm not sure what really matters to me. It's been all I can do to get myself to work and many times that has been difficult because my concentration became very poor during the procedures I had to go through."

John's murder, to me, was like a final nail in my family's coffin that was increasingly holding far too many – those people who had made "family" a reality for me. I had lost one of my five brothers to drowning in 1958 when I was only 6; my mother to ALS (Lou Gehrig's Disease) after five cruel years in 1986 when I was 35; my nephew to a train in 1994; my father to a heart attack in 1995; my oldest brother to a heart attack coupled with lung cancer in 1998, along with his wife to COPD several months earlier; and then John's death – my third brother to die – in 2003. (Since then, my stepfather passed away in 2007 and yet another brother in early 2016.) Those people had filled a huge portion of the full pie comprising my family circle.

I understand now that what increasingly drove me away from my husband during the years following John's murder was the fact that his family – consisting of him and nine siblings, plus his parents – was still intact. Only within the past several years did he lose his parents. I cannot fathom at times why I should have been the one to bear so many, many losses (only a portion of which dealt with death from loved ones) while still so relatively young. I know in my head that people suffer far worse and lose far more, but to have to look each day at my then-husband's totally intact, large – large like my own *had* been – family seemed such an insult to me. It's as if I were part of a family that deserved so much misfortune, while his deserved so much better. Again, in my head, I know that is nonsense, but my heart still feels that it is so.

All of that in no way detracts from my saying unequivocally that I am thankful to my ex-husband for being there with me and for me during those extremely difficult days. I am also thankful that my son (a boomeranger) was living at home at that time, and that he was such an excellent support system for me. I don't know how I would have gotten through it all without their willingness to be involved. Because it does indeed take a "willingness" to get involved in a murder – and to get involved in the clean up of both physical and emotional things.

While my ex-husband shared so much of what went on surrounding John's murder and the trial of his murderer, his reality, I am sure, would sound very much different than my own. And, my son's reality would be different still. At that time in 2003, though, we were all tucked in bed, still in the same house, when the news came.

Before the story of John's murder unfolds, though, I think it's important to share how John and I grew up and the incidents that helped us grow closer together. (The conversations included are as they may have been.) Most importantly, it's important that I share the person John really was through his letters home from Army boot and training camps and from the jungles of Vietnam. And then sadly to share how his schizophrenia set in and how the second half of his life would be lived.

Chapter 2

I woke in the middle of the night again, just as I did most nights, terrified and alone. I pulled my increasingly threadbare blue and red Indian blanket up around my head and tried to hide. My mother always told me that the sound that woke me was just the pear tree, its branches blowing in the wind and scraping against my window. How could I believe her when it sounded like a boogeyman or witch with terrifyingly long nails trying to open the window? It could be a zombie or a werewolf or some frightful bad person that would snatch me up and kill me. Outside my lower level farmhouse window was the pear tree, but also a row of shrubby trees along the gravel driveway, and beyond that the lonely farm road with no near neighbors. I tried praying for God's rescue, but that didn't help either.

There were some nights when I would just crawl under my twin metal bed and hide for hours. It was pretty tough trying to go to sleep on the cold wooden floor, though, and invariably I would go running into my parents' bedroom and beg my mother to let me sleep with her.

"Please, mama," I sobbed, "There's something in my room trying to get me."

Some nights she would say, "Okay, come on in, but just for a little bit. You've got to learn to stay in your own bed. There's nothing there trying to get you."

Other nights Mama would sound annoyed and say, "Mary Lee, you've got to go back to your own bed. Your father needs his sleep. He has to get up early in the morning to go to work. And, I need my sleep, too. How many times have I told you that there is nothing in your room to be afraid of. It's just the pear tree in the wind."

I would still beg to stay. I would even offer to sleep on the rug covering the floor next to her side of the bed if I could just stay in close proximity to someone safe. A few times she relented and allowed me to do this, but many times, she would get up, take me by the hand, and lead me back to the demons terrifying me in the dark back bedroom that lay beyond the living room, seemingly far, far away from everyone else in the house.

Sometimes I would think about running upstairs to the closest of my brothers' rooms for comfort, but the stairwell was too far away and the path too scary. Besides, they would just tell me to get out of their room anyway. I was always happy when day broke, and I could actually see that there was nothing in my room that would harm me.

"Hey, Mary," Charley, the youngest of my five brothers, said. "Get up and come here and watch cartoons with me." It was very early in the morning on a Saturday, which was a great day for cartoons. I especially enjoyed Mighty Mouse, and I can still hear his boastful theme song and see his muscular little mouse body in full super hero costume flying up across the sky.

Since Charley and I were closest in age, we tended to play together. He was four years younger than the next eldest, and he was generally ostracized from the older group of three who were only a year apart in age. Johnny was seven years older than me, Jimmy eight, Ronnie nine, and Derald, thirteen. I always thought my mother had to have been super surprised when she finally ended up with a girl as her last child.

As we watched cartoons that day, Johnny and Jimmy came strolling in, but didn't stay long. I was only five years old then, so Johnny would have been 12 and Jimmy 13. They didn't watch too many cartoons anymore; they were focused on the animals they were raising for 4H, hoping for winners at the fair, and on other activities with friends – when they could get a ride to see them.

I believe that Jimmy had his eyes set on winning at the state fair some day, and this year my mother had promised she would accompany him to the county fair to watch him get a ribbon. Today was the day. All of a sudden it occurred to me that she was leaving me behind and I was terror-stricken. What if she never came back? I would be left with my father, of whom I was frightened, and essentially I would be "alone."

There had been a horrible incident a few weeks prior. We were all sitting at the dinner table, and an altercation cropped up between our father and my oldest brother Derald, who was about 18 at the time. I don't remember what the issue was, but my father seemed to be boiling with anger. He picked up a table knife and threw it towards Derald. Then, everything seemed to go into slow motion - the trajectory of that heavy silver knife flying through the air, the knife missing its mark but instead hitting my brother Ronnie on the side of his head, and the knife slicing into his ear. Blood spurted. Dinner over. Medical attention needed.

And so today, "Mama," I cried, "Please don't leave me here by myself." I clung to her legs.

"You won't be here by yourself. Your brothers and your father are here. It will be okay."

"It won't be okay. They'll go off and leave me here all by myself. They do it all the time. They just leave me in the house all alone. Please, Mama!" By this time, I was sobbing hysterically.

"I have to go soon, Mary Lee. You're going to be okay. I'll only be gone for the day, and I've asked Johnny to stay here in the house with you."

I was relieved to know that it was Johnny she asked to stay with me, and I calmed down. Charley wasn't old enough, and he could be very mean to me. His punching me had certainly not been a solitary event. One day, he had grabbed my porcelain-headed doll as I tried desperately to hug her to my chest. He managed to pull her away and then dangled her over the sidewalk, head first. He started swaying her head back and forth above the sidewalk, inching it down closer and closer until finally it hit and her head split open. He thought it hilarious. I was devastated.

Another brother would call me "Runt" and push my head into his armpit for his "BO treatment." Again, he thought it was hilarious, and there was nothing I could do about it. On a different day, one of my brothers had thrown some small boards at me from the roof of a shed as I walked by. One of them had a nail in it, and it hit me in the head. Of course, he told me not to tell my mother, but I did anyway. A lot of good it always did me as nothing really happened to them, and the damage to me had already been done.

That was why I calmed down when told that Johnny would be the one who would stay with me that day. It felt like he was my savior, at least for a day. I don't remember doing much with him when I was that young, but maybe it was that absence that made me think more of him. He, at least, wasn't around trying to hurt me somehow or make fun of me.

Chapter 3

There was some joy, but much sorrow during the years between when I was five and when I was seven. So much badness that by today's standards, all of us surely should have been in counseling.

We all went to a Lutheran school from first to eighth grade, and one by one, we all got confirmed. This was Johnny's year. I don't really remember the event itself, but looking through old pictures, it looks like we had a good time, had lots of extended family at our home to celebrate the day, and everyone looked happy.

That same year when I was six, my brother Derald, having graduated from high school the previous year and now holding a good job, was getting married. I was happy at the thought of having a sister-in-law since I had never been lucky enough to have a sister. Better yet, she herself had a sister who was just my age.

Derald and Jane got married in June in a quaint, old-timey white wooden church in rural Roselle. It was the kind of church that looked great in old photos, and it was decorated with lovely fragrant flowers for their wedding. Jane looked beautiful in her white dress, and the little church was packed with both of our large extended families.

The reception at her parents' home was great fun. Their family had essentially grown up in the same fashion as our own, so we all got along well. And again, for me with no sisters, it was such a treat to to have her sister as my companion for the event. The joy of that day was not to last long, however.

Within a few months of the wedding on a hot August day, our party-line black wall phone rang. My mother, in her floral farm wife's version of a Donna Reed belted dress, went over to answer it as usual. She was silent for a time, turned pale and cried out, "Oh, no!" She had just been told that my brother Ronnie had drowned. He had gone out with friends for the day swimming in the Fox River. The current proved too strong for him, and he had gone under. Though his friend Hugh had valiantly tried to save him by grabbing his hair, Ronnie slipped out of his grasp.

I vividly remember my mother getting that phone call, and I vividly remember Ronnie's funeral. It was held at Miller's Funeral Home in Dundee; the daughter of the undertaker, Michelle, was a friend of mine. All of our extended family was there, of course. I was only six, and I was extremely distraught to see my brother lying dead in a coffin. When we all had to sing the hymn, "I'm But a Stranger Here," I sobbed loudly. My mother told me to quiet down.

If I had felt all alone before Ronnie died, things got worse afterwards. My mother always had a huge workload having to care for six children, and therefore, she didn't always have much time for me. But after my brother's death, she still had the work, and she became deeply depressed.

My father's anger had morphed into deep sadness as well. The night after my brother's funeral, after all of our relatives had left our home, I saw my father out in the yard in the darkness crying. I decided not to approach him. I don't think I saw him cry again until he had retreated into dementia a short while before his death.

My father's grief turned inward and though he never said it, he must have blamed himself. There was a day when he pulled out his rifle and told my mother that he was going to kill himself. It was not something that a little six-year-old girl should see or hear, and it's not something that I could ever forget.

Within the year, my father's grief turned back to his usual anger, and that anger was taken out anew on my remaining brothers. Now, the oldest brother left at home would take the brunt of it.

I heard loud pounding on the kitchen door one night, which was usually unlocked. I had been at the other end of the house, but ran out to see what was happening. On that night, my father had locked the door to keep my brother from entering. My father was angry that he had either gone out when he wasn't supposed to or that he had gotten home too late. My father opened the door, they argued, my father punched my brother in the face, and my brother left. From that night on, he stayed elsewhere, and I was too young to remember the details of where.

Chapter 4

"Ma, why doesn't he come home anymore?"

"Because your father called him a 'hood' and booted him out," my mother said sadly. "I miss him so much, but I know it's best for him to be gone."

"Why?"

"Oh, Mary Lee, I can't explain it to you, you're too young to understand. Please go play."

Our household number had dwindled significantly and nothing seemed right to me. Derald was married and gone. Ronnie was gone and dead. Another brother was gone, and I hated that. I even missed his teasing. My remaining two brothers now spent as much time away from home as possible. My father, well, it was okay that he was gone working so much because too many scary things happened when he was home. My mother was different. I needed her and wanted to be with her, but she was always sad, and it seemed she didn't want me around her much.

My mother eventually started to go to "group sessions" (a new concept for us) with a psychologist (another new concept) in Elgin. At least she did this while I was in school; if on weekends or in the evening, I would have been left alone with my father. Someone must have come to pick her up, or she must have taken a cab, because my mother still did not drive.

After a time, the group sessions seemed to be working. She became more like her old self, more cheerful and more available to me. She and my father did not seem to get along much better, however.

I recall a day when she decided to have all of her new friends from her group bring their kids out to our farm for a picnic. I don't really recall the kids themselves, but I remember having fun. Something that embedded itself in my memory is that it was the first time that I had an honest-to-goodness Twinkie. And, how it made me throw up.

The year I was eight wore on, and although I cannot remember the specifics, a time came when Johnny was asked to move out as well. He was only 15 years old, but apparently my father just couldn't help taking his anger out specifically on him at the time. The only good thing was that Derald now had his own home, and Johnny went to stay with him for a time.

As an adjunct to my father's carpentry job, he farmed 80 acres on Beverly Road, which at that time was Elgin, which then became Hoffman Estates and home to Sears Corporate Center. But, it was distinctly rural with a dusty gravel road when we lived there, with scarcely any traffic and few homes along its path.

I was feeling pretty much abandoned out on the farm with four out of five brothers gone. Charley had taken a lot of the anger that had passed down from my grandfather to my father to brother to brother and so on, and there were many times he treated me badly. He was four years older anyway, and he had boy things to do that did not include me. Unless he was feeling abandoned, and then he would demand that I play with him. I did it willingly, not having anyone else to play with, but there were times when he would force me to continue to do so even when I wanted to quit.

Loneliness, for me, seemed to grow on the farm. I spent many hours in the rocking chair next to the radio listening to music and singing, one time rocking so hard that the chair flipped over backwards. For a time I had my dolls, but I never really liked dolls all that much. My stuffed animals were better friends, and better than that were the real animals on our farm. Baby pigs were fun to play with, as were the little chicks. I adored the cats, and I had one that I could dress in doll clothes and wheel around in my doll buggy. Even better than that was when there were tiny kittens, and I would play with them for hours out in the barn. Our dog Pal was fun, but he could also be mean to the cats. In fact, he would drag my favorite cat – the only one I could dress – around by the scruff of her neck.

Many kittens, though, met a cruel fate on the farm. I remember one of my brothers standing over a bucket in which he was drowning all of the little kittens. I was beside myself with grief. How could anyone be so cruel? I'm sure he learned it from our father, as I had personally seen the evidence left after he had clubbed a litter of little puppies to death. Today, people are brought in on charges for such animal cruelty. Then, I'm afraid, it was probably just a way of life on many farms, though I couldn't imagine it happening in other families.

After a year or two of counseling, my mother decided that our father's anger and cruelty were no longer to be tolerated, and she took me and Charley and moved out. She had gotten a clerk's job at Joseph Spiess in the at-that-time upscale Meadowdale Shopping Center. She must have taken a cab to work or had a friend take her back and forth because she still did not drive.

We moved to an apartment over the jewelry store in downtown Dundee, and I was absolutely elated. I felt like I still loved my father, but I did not miss him one bit. And, now I could walk to Immanuel Lutheran School that was just several blocks up the hill, walk to stores by myself, go to the library that was only a block away, and walk to my friend Jeanne's house.

"Is Johnny going to move in with us, Ma?" I felt that it was the one thing that would make everything seem complete for me again. I knew that Jimmy was now staying out with our father, and I would guess that at 16 he hadn't enough money to take care of himself. Maybe he felt sorry for our father, who had to be pretty darn lonely even though he is the one that caused everyone to move out at various times in the first place.

"No, Johnny isn't going to move in with us. He has a job now with Derald, and he's decided to stay there." I was happy, of course, that things were going okay for him, but I sure missed him a lot. And, one of the best times for me in that apartment was when he showed up to visit.

"Mary, I brought you a present for your birthday," he said, handing me a small box. It's the first time any of my brothers had given me a birthday gift that I remember. I was so excited to see it. My mother seemed to beam when he gave it to me. I opened the small hinged box and found a beautiful cross made of clear glass beads with a small blue glass stone in the center commemorating my December birthday. I still have it.

"I love it, Johnny, thank you so much!" I cried out. And, I rushed over to give him a huge hug.

Our months in the apartment that I loved were short, but I had spent all of them happily. One day in the fall, I had been able to walk through the crunchy beautiful red, yellow and orange leaves to my friend Jeanne's house for lunch. This was such a common occurrence for children growing up within a town, but a novelty for anyone having grown up on an isolated farm. It really was a special event for me.

Even in the winter cold and snow, I would walk behind our apartment building and pick up glass bottles that people had carelessly thrown about. I took these to the little store just behind us to get the deposit money. I would turn right around and buy loaves of bread that I could throw to the ducks on the banks of the Fox River,which was only a block's walk behind our building. And, I was constantly at the library, taking out as many books as was allowed, which I would then read voraciously back at the apartment.

Sadly, for me, we moved back to the farm around Christmastime. I had just turned nine, and I did not want to go back. In the spring of the coming year, we all moved to a new farm.

Chapter 5

Early spring on a farm can be overwhelmingly dismal. On some days it was warm enough to melt the remaining snow, which created a muddy mess in drives and farmyards, and on other days, flurries would still arrive amidst the gloomy gray. What I remember most about first driving onto our new, larger farm was the long line of now-leafless bushes that separated the house from the farm buildings. The bushes were flush with sparrows, and I loved seeing them hop about within the barren branches or all of a sudden swoosh out en masse.

Our new house in Marengo was huge in comparison to the old one in Dundee. To me, it seemed almost palatial. My father had bought the farm from a doctor's widow, a doctor who had been reputed to be Al Capone's doctor (Charley did find brass knuckles in the basement), and the décor and furnishings seemed very grand indeed. The sale contract included most all of the elegant mahogany furniture, which was a tremendous upgrade from what we had. The only room we had to furnish was the living room, and our old, well-used sofa now looked extremely out of place.

The huge pillars holding up the front porch roof, the beautiful fireplace, the screened in porch complete with lovely furnishings, it all seemed too wonderful. It was a home to be proud of, and I think we all felt like the newly rich. Cash flow was a different story, but the looks of it all made us feel wealthy.

I, of course, had high hopes that my brothers Johnny and Jimmy would live there with us as well. Jimmy actually did move in for a time. In fact, he took over the whole unfinished basement for himself. He had learned taxidermy back on the farm in Dundee, and he also liked capturing and keeping foxes and hawks. The basement with its concrete floors and walls made it a perfect place to bring an animal inside for a bit after he first caught it, and I do remember a small fox living there for awhile. As I think back on it, the poor thing cried and cried to get outside again, and it was only a bit happier when Jimmy built it a huge cage outside. I was happy when one night someone apparently opened the door and let it escape.

I rode the bus the seven miles to and from school each day, getting on promptly at 7:00 a.m. and dropped off fairly promptly at 4:00 in the afternoon. At that time, I always looked forward to going to school. It had been easy for me to make friends at our (mine and Charley's) new parochial school, Zion Lutheran. Class size was just over 20, so I was able to interact with each and every one of my new classmates in some fashion. I really liked seeing our pastor in the hallway. He'd tease me and call me "Foxy." Somehow Foxy seemed better than "Wolffy," or the Lone Wolf as my brother Ronnie had had embroidered on his long-sleeved denim shirt.

School came easy to me, and I always managed to get along with everyone, even my teachers. After I had acclimated and had a group of close friends, it seemed we spent a lot of time goofing off during class. I had a hard time believing that my 5th grade teacher chose me as "Best Behaved," for which I received a ribbon. Maybe she was being ironic. It still makes me laugh.

In 6th grade, I tried out for cheerleading and made it. Given that our class was so small probably had a lot to do with that, but I was very proud to have been chosen. I loved my short white swirly skirt and my pale blue fuzzy sweater. "Go Zion!" Best of all was getting together for practice and then going to the games. Somehow my mother made this happen for me that year.

It wasn't long before I had a best friend, someone that I could ask over to spend the night now and again. Mostly I remember my friend staying with me during the winter months, the cold months when we could walk down to the nearby creek and go ice skating. In the evenings, we would get into our pajamas and have hot cocoa and popcorn in front of the fireplace, where wood and flames were snapping and crackling.

Of course, I was always apprehensive having her visit lest my father do something horrible. I was always appalled when she, like me, was woken up to my father hollering at my brother Charley.

"Get up, you lazy good for nothing. You have chores to do!" This may or may not have been accompanied by a boot kick. That all depended on the day and the amount of anger our father was experiencing.

Chapter 6

The good news/bad news at that time was that my brother Johnny was coming back to join us on the farm, but it was only out of necessity. He had fallen asleep at the wheel one night while either out on newspaper delivery (my brother Derald ran a news agency for which he worked) or on his way home. He suffered a major concussion, a broken leg and a broken wrist, and we were very lucky that he did not die. He obviously needed a lot of personal care, and we put up a hospital bed in our living room.

(Recently I found information about a Danish study, highlighted in "Head Trauma May Boost Schizophrenia Risk" by Rachael Rettner, that links concussions to later development of schizophrenia. Malene Breusch Hansen also wrote about the study in a Science Nordic article that "head injuries can increase the risk of developing certain mental disorders by up to 439 percent." And, further, that out of the over 10,000 people diagnosed with schizophrenia during the study that "twelve percent of these had suffered a head trauma before being diagnosed.")

I am sure that this was not a good time for John (too old to call Johnny any longer), but I loved having him home with us no matter his condition. I was more than happy to run his errands and help be his caretaker. We set up his record player right next to the hospital bed, and he would ask me to change his 45s and LPs from time to time.

After some weeks, he was able to move around quite sprightly in his walker. He would call out, "Hey, Mary, watch this!" And, he would race around the adjoining rooms in a circular fashion, clopping along as fast as he could and laughing. I loved to hear him laugh. And, I loved to have him sit and talk to me. Being semi-captive, he had time to do this, which was lucky for me.

After healing, though, John went back to his old life, and I to mine.

One bright spot on the farm was the day my brother Jim (no longer Jimmy) bought a pony for me at a local auction. I don't really know what prompted him to do so, but it was a wonderful gift. I was able to saddle him up and take short rides. The joy did not last long, however, because my brother Charley decided that he would teach my pony to buck. I could no longer control it, and that meant the end of my pony riding days.

It was then November 1963, and I was just shy of eleven. My brother Jim was to be married on Friday, the 22nd. Thing is, on that day all of the United States and the world would be alerted to the news that President Kennedy had been assassinated. Of course, this surely cut into the feelings of festivity, but I was still very happy that day to welcome my sister-in-law Sharon into the family.

Sharon's family lived a mile or so from us, so we were all acquainted. And since our family, Jane's, and now Sharon's all shared a rural upbringing, we all seemed to understand each other fairly well.

The small family wedding at Zion Lutheran Church went nicely, and then we were all off to the Clearview Restaurant for a family style chicken dinner. The Clearview, a few miles west of Marengo, sat conveniently close to the house with an upstairs apartment where Jim and Sharon lived for the first few years of their married life.

The wedding meal was enjoyable from what I remember, but I am sure that our happiness was subdued in light of President Kennedy's death that day. I know that our eyes were glued to the television that weekend and on until his funeral had taken place.

The relationship between my father and my now-married brother Jim seemed to improve significantly. It wasn't long before Jim bought the 1-1/4 acre corner of our farm that held the old one-room Poyer Schoolhouse. Jim had become a carpenter like our father, and he had plans to renovate the neglected school into their home.

I enjoyed being able to tromp across the corn field to visit with him while he worked on his house. Jim was a tremendously hard worker, and he finished the home within the year. That, in addition to working his regular union job. We were all very proud of him.

Our family living on the Marengo farm had shrunk back to its low of four after Jim was married. It was inevitable that my father would focus in more and more on Charley. It was also predictable that the more my dad pushed him, the more outrageous Charley's behavior would likely become.

The following summer when I was 11 and Charley 15, my parents decided it was time to take our every-other-year (usually) jaunt to Minnesota to visit all of my mother's family. My brother Charley decided to stay home that year, declaring that he could take care of chores while we were gone. I was very excited about the trip because I loved getting together with my cousins who were close to my own age and to see my grandfather and aunts and uncles who I adored. At that time, it was a large family, and it was so much fun getting together at each of their homes for food and card games. My Aunt Elsie made the best homemade bread ever.

We had a great time on our trip as always, but when we got home, we found out that in our absence, Charley had chosen to take a spin in my father's pickup. While doing so, he ended up flipping and totaling it. My father's anger was quick to spin out of control. He immediately kicked Charley out of the house, as if that would rectify anything. I was horrified. It was down to just me.

Charley was now expected to take care of himself, and I must say that he made a valiant attempt. He got a job, and he tried at first to stay in school even while working nights. He rented a room in town. Since his job was at the Clearview bussing tables, I am guessing he was able to tap into free food that kept him going. It wasn't long before he had to drop out of school because he just couldn't keep up.

The rift between my parents kept growing wider and wider. If I was appalled at seeing three of my brothers booted out of the house within several years of each other, I cannot imagine how my mother felt. She had gone deeper within again, and I know she was seriously contemplating what to do.

I think it was about this time when she called me upstairs into her bedroom. "Mary Lee, I want you to see what your father did to me. This is not the first time." She pulled up her dress and showed me a huge black and blue bruise on her thigh.

"Ma, how could he do this to you? I hate him!"

"I'm not going to let him do this again. I'll figure things out, I promise you."

My mother did get busy trying to make things better for herself. First of all, she learned to drive. I don't remember who taught her, but I'm guessing it might have been John or Jim. By the time I was 12, my mother was driving herself to work at the Admiral television manufacturing plan in Harvard, a nearby town. I was very proud of her. An added plus for me was that she was then able to pay me to keep up the house and get meals started each day.

And, in the evenings, we watched TV together. Peyton Place was our big favorite. In retrospect, I can only imagine the horror of my grade school teachers and pastor if they knew we were watching Peyton Place, of all shows.

There was one final "incident" in this time period that almost literally made my heart stop. In addition to the bruise that my mother had shown me a year or so prior, she now shared another abusive event perpetrated by our father. He had the night before threatened to cut out her tongue. I had seen the man in action, and I was terrified that some day or night he might actually follow through with such a threat. I was only 12, but I begged her to leave, frightened for her safety, but she wasn't ready and she still felt that the man was mainly bluster. I, on the other hand, would have been happy to leave on any day, at any time.

Chapter 7

John's friend Warren filled me in years later on what John's "old life" was about, between those years of working for my brother Derald and the time he would come back home. If anyone, John included, had shared any of these things with me, I did not remember any of it. In his friend Warren Wahl's own words:

"Here is my recollection of those few years between the winter of 1962/63 and 1967 when John and I were the best of friends. None of his family may ever have had the opportunity to experience John the way I did. These may have been the happiest years and days of his life.

"At that time, I was 19 years old and working at Little Les's Pizza in Arlington Heights to pay for school. Mrs. Vaughan operated Little Les's. She had a young daughter about 10 or so; her name was Garnet.

"I believe it was a time when there was a break in the winter weather of 1962/63 that I first met John. When Mrs. Vaughan introduced me to him, my first thought was, 'Is she going to get rid of me?' That did not happen. John and I worked quietly together every day for a long time before we began to talk about more things than pizzas and deliveries. Mostly we talked about cars. He loved big fast cars, especially Pontiacs, which is what he had then.

"I learned that John worked days at the Century Auto Parts store and then he started around 4:00 p.m. at the pizza place. His typical day was from 7:00 a.m. to 11:30 p.m. To me, he seemed a bit young to be working two jobs. To this day, I do not know for sure exactly how old John was at the time. He must have been at least 17 because he had a car and was making deliveries for the auto parts store and the pizza place.

"One time, he asked me to take him to his home because he needed a clean shirt to wear at work. I took him to a small white house, just west of downtown Arlington Heights on Wing Street, right next to the railroad tracks. When he came out, I asked him how long he had lived there. I expected him to say something like a couple of years. To my surprise, he told me it was only a couple of weeks, and he just rented a room there for sleeping. He told me that he had left home after dropping out of high school. He gave no reasons; I never asked.

"My school was out for the summer, and John and I became friends, good friends. There was nothing that we did not share. We went places together, ate together, and if one of us had the evening off from the pizza place, we went in anyway. Mrs. Vaughan and Garnet also became like family to him because we were always together.

"We became experts at throwing darts in the back room. We could change the thermostat in a car in ten minutes and a tire in five. Saturdays we would show up for work a few hours early to throw darts and just talk.

"After the pizza place closed for the evening at 11:30 p.m., we would go out for coffee. We went to either a small restaurant in downtown Palatine or a little hash joint at the corner of Northwest Highway and Palatine Road named Dutch Garden, but locally known as the Glass House. Most often we were there until closing, around 2:00 or 3:00 a.m. We kept the juke box rocking all night. He loved Johnny Rivers' records. I'll bet we each had a minimum of ten cups of coffee each time. This was our routine for months. We talked and talked and talked. We shared our dreams for the future. We talked about where we wanted to live and what we wanted to do. We had good dreams, exciting dreams, and nothing was going to stop us.

"One of our wildest plans was to open a dance palace where there would be live rock bands with people coming from miles away to dance to the music. We actually found two sites and talked to the owners of the property about leasing or buying the property. One was an unused Buick dealership in downtown Arlington Heights, and the other was a barn on Route 62 near Algonquin. I had worked for the farmer who owned the barn property when I was 15 and 16, shoveling horse manure from sunrise to sunset. He wanted $25,000 for the barn with 5 acres of road frontage. There was no way we could raise that kind of money, so we moved on.

"Oh boy, did we have dreams. It never occurred to me until right now that John and I never had a disagreement. There was never name calling or arguing. We never fought over things. If anything, it was more like one of us offering something to the other or sharing whatever we had. So many times it was, 'Here, I got this for you.'

"I saw him upset and angry a couple of times, but on each occasion the anger was for good reason. Most often it was for self protection or for the people we were with. He would not be intimidated by anyone, and he was not afraid to let them know it. This was in sharp contrast to his normal behavior. He was always the most polite person I had ever met. It was as if he had memorized Emily Post's Book of Etiquette.

"Summer and then fall rolled by, and I was back in school while John was working the two jobs. I must admit there were a few occasions when I left school early, and he took a sick day, and we would just go out to a beach or some swimming hole he had found.

"Our friendship grew as another winter took us into 1964. The financial demands of school tuition meant that that summer I had to make more money. John was in a similar situation; he needed to find another place to live. We started our search to make BIG money. Anything would be more than relying on what we were making at the pizza place. We finally located a company that would hire both of us. That was a condition we set: If they wanted us, it was both or nothing.

"John moved into our house for awhile during the summer, and he became part of my family now. He was welcomed with open arms by my parents.

"In the spring of 1964, we began working for Winston-Muss Builders, where we were hired as laborers. We had to join the International AFL of CIO Hod Carriers and Laborers Union. We thought the same thing, 'What is a hod?' We became laborers for carpenters building homes in a subdivision called Winston Park in Palatine. John and I must have positioned pre-made wall, flooring, and ceiling joists for hundreds of houses. We became true specimens of fitness - if there was any fat, it was on our sandwich!

"There were a couple of times when I had a bit of stomach flu. John covered for me by doing both our jobs on those days while I basically hid in an unfurnished house, involuntarily turning myself inside out. He would warn me when he saw the foreman coming so I could make myself visible and later return to my place of refuge.

"The scariest task we were assigned was to place the pre-assembled roof rafters at certain increments so the carpenters just had to put them upright and nail them tight. The roof rafter sections were large triangles about 25 to 30 feet wide (width of the house) x 7 feet tall at the apex. Some of houses were two stories tall with basements, so the maximum fall would be about 30 feet inside and 20 feet on the outside if you were not careful. I most often got the point in the middle of the house where I had to walk on top of the interior walls. To me that seemed safer. John nearly always took the top of the outside walls to walk on. I guess we had great self assurance of our balancing skills; we had no fear, or we did not know any better. I can still close my eyes and see us walking on the 3-1/2 inch wide walls, 20 feet up from the ground, hurrying to spread 40 or 50 of these 100+ pound sections as fast as we could because the carpenters were close behind.

"When our day was done, we would be completely exhausted. We were young, though, and we recovered rapidly because we had things to do and places to go. Sometimes I think we were more tired going to work than leaving work. And then construction work tapered off, and we both were laid off because we had the lowest seniority. Out of a job. Now what?

"John moved out of our house around August of 1964. I know he needed to regain the privacy to which he had become accustomed and get back to a room of his own. He moved in with a married couple he knew who were living north of Palatine.

"Construction work again tapered off, and again we both were laid off because we had the lowest seniority. So, John and I went to the Union

Hall in Chicago, where we signed up for another job as laborers. Again, as our fortune would have it, we were both told to report for work at an Inland Construction Company site where they were building a large two-story addition to Montgomery Ward at Old Orchard Shopping Center in Skokie. It was the most popular shopping center in the Chicagoland area at that time, and Montgomery Ward had just bought all 'The Fair' stores and were expanding big time.

"John lived in Palatine and drove to my home in Arlington Heights; from there, I drove the rest of the way to work. When we took turns driving, the other would sleep because of our being out late the night before. My mother continued packing lunches for both of us, probably out of pity and protection from starvation.

"On most days, working for the carpenters was the easiest job assignment. Because the entire store was being remodeled, there were large portions open for shoppers. One of the rules that John and I thought unusual was that any object over 6 feet long had to have a person on the front and another person on the back. That made sense for drywall (and there were mountains of that to be moved), but it amazed us when a carpenter would send us down to the outside yard from the second floor to get a piece of trim limber. There we were, with all the building activity going on around us, John on the front and me on the back of a 10 foot long piece of ½" quarter round. Then we had to use the service elevator because we were not allowed to use the stairwells or escalators. That got us glares from the other workers, but we just smiled and kept going.

"It was truly an amazing thing that we were always assigned to work together. I feel that we made it obvious that somehow the two of us, as friends, were better workers than if they had assigned three workers who were not friends to do the same task. There were times when we would be carrying four sheets of drywall at one time, and the foreman would come over and tell us we only needed to carry two. I really think they liked us.

"Sometime toward the end of summer, John hurt his right arm, I think while working on his car. He did not have money to go to a doctor or clinic. He was also afraid if anybody at work found out, he would lose his job. This time, it was my turn to cover as best I could for him. As bad luck would have it, we were assigned to move all the crates of metal shelving for the shoe department storage area to the second floor up a narrow stairway. The 100 or so wooden cases filled with steel shelving were at least 120 pounds each. There was no place to hide. John would take the lead, grabbing the crate handle with his left hand, and I followed, supporting the weight from the bottom as we went up the stairs. Time and time again, John was not able to use the hand rail to support himself. All he could do was bend over and grab the crate. He was in constant pain the entire time. We lost it a bunch of times, and a crate would drop. It was so loud, and others would always come running into the store room to see if we were alright. It took us two days, but we made it.

"John also could not drive during this time, so I became his chauffeur. Gratefully, we were reassigned to working with the carpenters, and John had time to heal. No one at work other than me ever knew what had happened to John. Many times we were so tired after work, we just drove in silence, knowing that we would recover and get our second wind and tomorrow would come. Sometimes there was comfort in our silence; sometimes it was enough.

"As of that Labor Day weekend, I had about a week left on the job before I had to return to school. We both had our 40 hours in for the week, and we were asked to come in on that holiday Saturday to sweep floors. It seems that the builder's contract stipulated that the store could not occupy or use the areas completed until the construction company first swept the floors. We were in heaven. They paid us double time to sweep floors. What made it even better was that the Union steward came around and told us not to sweep so fast or we would take away all the work. It was easy for us to slow down for once; we had earned every bit of the rest.

"During the construction months in 1964, John and I continued to work at Little Les's Pizza Place. There was no time for anything but work that summer. No parties. Just work and sleep and work and sleep, day after day.

"In the fall, I returned to my school schedule of commuting to Chicago and working at the pizza place. John stayed with the construction job until it was finished and worked at the pizza place on the weekends. I lived at home, and my money went for school, but he was on his own, and the expense of living on your own was just as difficult then as it is now. He was proud that he had become so independent and self-sufficient."

Warren's memories helped flesh out much of John's life on his way to early adulthood – the years between when he left home at 15 and moved back in at 19. I believe it was Warren's influence (his story about John through 1967 continues below) that gave John a push toward completing his high school education. I believe it was also his influence that later drew John into his artwork. To go back to school, though, meant moving back to the family home in Marengo for a time.

John did not return to high school until 1964 when he was nearing 19 years old, now with a drive to get that diploma. He attended Marengo High School for the fall 1964 semester and the spring 1965 semester. Overall, he buckled down and did a pretty good job of finishing that year. He earned predominantly B's and C's, with some A's but with a few D's (Latin - it was understandable). I can still see him at our dining room table, typing away on his portable blue Smith Corona, which was still in his house in Missouri when I cleaned it out in 2003.

"On many occasions," Warrren said, "we talked about him finishing high school. I do not know for sure that I can take credit for it, but John went 'home' to Marengo and started back to school. I think it was always in his mind to go back and finish, so maybe talking about it kept his hope alive. Distance became a problem for me, but I made a trip to see him almost every week. Sometimes I skipped classes and would meet John for lunch at the Yum Yum, a little burger place across the street from the high school in Marengo. We would have the biggest hamburger and fries and coffee. We always consumed lots and lots of coffee.

"He once asked me if I would drive out early and meet him by the school. I had done that before a number of times, but this time he had a surprise for me, something special. And what a surprise it was. He had gotten permission for me to attend all his classes with him that day. He introduced me to all his classmates and teachers as his friend. That was a thrill for me that he would even think of asking me to do something like that. He was so very proud of what he was doing. After that, he took me into the local farm goods store. We used to kid about that store, and I had never seen one. It wasn't much, but it was one of the kinds of things we did. He was so happy.

"I would stay at the farm house with him sometimes overnight. [I really never saw Warren on these occasions as they would come in so late at night.] No matter where or when, we would pick up our conversations where they left off from the previous times. He taught me to play the card games Over/Under and Rummy on the screened-in porch one night. The big hit that year was "A Hard Day's Night" by the Beatles. I do not remember ever meeting his parents. [Again, they'd come in late and leave early the next morning.]

"My trips became less frequent as winter approached, but I tried as best I could to visit at least on Saturday nights. He took me to places he knew in the area that he wanted to show me. We went to Woodstock, Harvard, Huntley, Crystal Lake, Union and Belvidere. Places I had never been; I was in his old territory now. We would find a place and drink coffee and talk until we were exhausted, leaving me just enough travel time to get home before sunrise.

"One evening we were driving around with nothing to do but talk and have coffee, when all of a sudden he told me he had to show me something. To this day, I do not know where he took me, other than it was a very small cemetery on a lonely country road. [Our brother Ronnie is buried in a cemetery a ways out of East Dundee just off a highway, but it may have seemed deserted at night in the dark.] We climbed over a fence, and I would swear he said he was going to show me something. He knew where he was going, but it was very dark, and I wasn't sure what I should be looking for. I think he said it was the grave of his brother; I only thought he had a sister. [Strange that John never told his best friend that he not only had a sister, but *four* brothers.]

"We drove away in silence. I went home. We never discussed that again. It must have been something he needed to share with someone. I am proud it was me.

"I am not sure when, but I think John earned his diploma from high school. I knew he stopped attending school, however, because he became very uncomfortable being in classes with 'kids.' My trips became less frequent, though I was still trying to make a weekly visit. School and work made demands on my time that could not be ignored. I had also become engaged to be married in August of 1965.

"I asked John to be Best Man at our wedding. Nobody else would do, and he said he would be honored."

Chapter 8

When I was in my freshman year at Marengo High School, I was elated when Charley was allowed to move back home - with the criteria that he go back to school. Even though he was three years older than me, he had dropped out and was behind, so he ended up as a sophomore. This meant that we were at the same end of the building. We didn't actually have any classes together, but it seemed strange to know he was there and that there was the possibility of seeing him in the halls or in study hall. I needn't have worried because he didn't stay all that long. His new classmates were not his friends, and he felt awkward with them.

John also decided to move back home since he was now running Coachlight Inn Pizza in Woodstock, which was only 15 miles from the farm. It was wonderful for me to have him back with us. Unlike the rest of us, he had become more sophisticated and more gregarious. He had plenty of friends both male and female. It surely livened up our relatively secluded lives when his friends would come and visit.

I recall that on one particular night I had fallen asleep on the living room floor, as was fairly common for me after watching TV late into the night. I wasn't expecting, though, that John would come home and bring someone with him. I didn't like lying there like that in my pajamas while he brought a male stranger into the room. I pretended to be asleep. John walked over to me, peered down, and said to his friend, "That's my little sister."

His friend said, "She's beautiful."

Hopefully, I didn't make that up just to make myself feel good, and I've always attributed it to his best friend, Warren.

John tried his best to open my eyes (in fact, the whole family's eyes) to the world beyond the farm while he was living there, but this was countered with him wanting me to be his personal assistant. He paid me for some of the work - his ironing, cleaning his room – but it wasn't much for thework performed. He knew quite well that I would just be happy to do it for him, and he didn't hesitate to take advantage of it.

While I was just a freshman, John also decided to go back to school and earn his diploma. He had to drop out when he was 15, just like Charley, because he had been kicked out of the house by our father.

"I'm going to take Latin this semester, Mary. Do you believe it? Me, taking Latin?" He laughed at the thought, and I laughed with him. In subsequent months, I saw him struggling with that Latin, and I believe that he finally dropped it. Because he was putting in so many late hours at the Coachlight, he struggled to keep up in all of his classes. I do not think he ever got his actual high school diploma, but he did pass his equivalency exam.

I know that John had also been uncomfortable with the "kids" in high school. He was already 19 years old. And later he would ask me if I had been uncomfortable having him at school with me. Not a chance. And anyway, our classes were in totally different wings of the school.

"Mary, I've got a proposition for you. How would you like to earn some money working at the Coachlight? You could help me in the kitchen and you could take orders and maybe waitress a bit."

"You really think I could do that? I don't know if I could handle being a waitress."

"Okay, maybe you won't have to waitress, just help in the kitchen and at the counter."

"I'll try it, but I'm not sure how much help I'll be."

John took me to work with him the next night. It had to have been a week night or the place would have been terribly swamped, and I wouldn't have been able to handle anything. Everything was fascinating to me since I had never been in a pizza place in my life. I can't really remember what I actually did to help him. I know I took pizzas over to the counters – the one in front off the dining area and the one in back between the kitchen and the pool room – and I think I might have cleared a few tables.

I do, however, remember distinctly being introduced to some of his friends as they came in, and I remember specifically that I didn't wear my glasses that night because they were so horribly old-fashioned. (Since my eye sight is so bad, that had to have been a huge detriment to my doing any kind of work correctly.) Meeting his friends, though younger than him but still older than me, made me feel very grown up, and I developed secret crushes on a few of them.

Not so very long after, John invited several of his friends to our house for a spontaneous party. His one friend played his guitar and sang Bob Dylan songs, and, of course, I thought he was fantastic. His other friend spent a lot of time flirting with me though I was all of 14 years old. My parents were there, though I doubt our father ever joined us in the room. John had brought malt liquor for the occasion, and he talked my mother into letting me have some. That was the first time, and it wasn't long before I was a bit tipsy. My mother was not exactly pleased, but I know that John was only mildly reprimanded the next day.

Since Charley was home again, too, he also had friends come by now and again, plus he had a steady girlfriend. "Hey Mary," he called to me one day, "Do you want to go to the beach with us tomorrow? Her brother and his friend are going, too."

I had to spend some time thinking about his offer. First of all, I did not swim. I had always been afraid to learn after my brother Ronnie had drowned. Secondly, I had never been to the beach – not ever. Thirdly, my skinny self would have to wear my two-piece suit in front of boys that I had never met. I did not want them making fun of me in the same manner as my brothers always did. And, fourthly, I still had those awful eyeglasses. But, the intrigue of the offer overpowered me, along with Charley's cajoling about how much fun it would be, and I decided I would go.

I did not wear my glasses that day either, and when the two boys laughingly threatened to throw me in the water, they thankfully backed off after my very vehement protests. First of all, I couldn't swim, and secondly, I panicked with the thought I would have drowned without even being able to see anything.

While cleaning John's room, I was able to play his stereo, and I loved listening to Buddy Holly, Gene Pitney, Johnny Rivers, and The Supremes. John wasn't around too much as he was either working or with his steady girl. And, when there, I did not appreciate the few times he compared me to other females he knew or sometimes to his idea of a "perfect" woman. He said several things that colored the opinion of myself to this day. I don't think he ever really understood how much I looked up to him and took his words to heart. Or how much his offhand comments might hurt me.

Even at that, I relished the days that John and Charley still lived with us. I did not feel so alone. But those days of having them there with us were quickly coming to an end. Charley started to take off with friends for weeks and months at a time, and John's draft notice arrived. It was the end of 1966.

Chapter 9

John was 21 years old when his draft notice arrived, and it came just as things had been going very well for him. He loved his job running the Coachlight Inn, and he loved his steady girlfriend. He had plenty of friends, and plenty of plans for the future. He had even thought about asking his girlfriend to marry him. Being forced to go into the Army would change each and every one of his plans and destroy his dreams.

At the time, I don't recall hearing him speak about his stance regarding the Vietnam War. We all knew of the dangers the soldiers faced when being sent to the jungles of Vietnam; we heard about it and saw footage of it on the news each and every night. When I thought about John most likely being sent there, it was hard to even fathom.

John had several months before he had to report for duty, and those months passed by very quickly. I wanted to spend time with him, my brothers wanted to spend time with him, and my mother wanted to spend time with him. Most of his time, however, was spent with his girlfriend and with his friends. Of course, this was natural, but it was hard for his family. It was hard for me.

I remember tearfully hugging my brother John goodbye, but I'm not sure if it was the night before or the morning of.

"Aw, Mary. I'm only going to basic right now. I'll be back before you know it."

I would have had to catch the bus at 7:00 a.m., and I'm not sure what time my mother (parents?) drove him to the reception station. What he said about "just going into basic" really didn't make me feel any better. I would still miss him terribly.

I was elated when a letter finally arrived, addressed to me, in May 1967. John wrote that he didn't want me to feel left out so he decided to write to me personally. I have been ever thankful that he made that decision.

In that first letter John shared, "Remember how I used to talk about how much I would hate the army and its way of life? Now, I'm here, and it's worse than I thought it would be. Every minute of the day, you have to do a certain thing exactly and precisely what they want you to do. I hardly have time to think for myself. Boy do I wish I were home again."

He went on to say that he hated KP duty and he hated not getting enough sleep. He hadn't much liked getting his head shaved, but he didn't think it looked half bad, though I might laugh at it when I saw him when he had leave.

He ended his letter with: "And, write back."

A separate sheet was enclosed with his letter, along with a copy of a life insurance document. The note read, "Should anything happen to me while I'm in here, you will receive the amount shown on the receipt [$10,000, which was a big deal in the late 60s]. Save this receipt and keep it in a safe spot and make sure if anything does happen, you claim the money. I trust it will be used for your education. It better be."

In the letter he sent to my parents that same week, he wrote: "I never realized a person, any person, could live with such bare necessities. All we have is our shaving toiletries and a bunch of army clothes that look ridiculous."

I am certain that not having access to his own clothing made him extremely uncomfortable. Although he didn't have a huge wardrobe, John bought the best, and everything was clean and pressed, every day. He was always the best groomed and best dressed in our family.

John wrote further to my parents: "They started the brainwashing routine right away. It's hard to keep from believing everything they say … . Today we were told it was our duty to die for our country, but they don't say whether it's right or wrong as far as what our country is doing over there."

He told my parents in their next letter on June 4 that he had completely dislocated his shoulder and ended up in the hospital. He was told to wear an arm sling for two weeks, and the doctor said further that he might need an operation. He said he was frightened about such an operation, and he asked them to write back to tell him what they thought.

Instead of writing back, our mother went to Fort Leonardwood to visit him. A follow-up letter highlighted how much he had appreciated her visit, how he was sorry that my father hadn't been able to make the trip as well, and how he was sorry to see her leave. He added that he had been released from the hospital and was on light duty. The operation must not have occurred.

"Well, I ended up Wednesday where I was expecting to go for the past week, in the hospital," John wrote to me on June 16. "After my shoulder mishap, I lost a lot of sleep and my appetite, which brought my resistance down to nil. They admitted me here for pneumonia after some kind of breakdown."

"I was in the first sergeant's office trying to tell him what was wrong with me when my head starched aching so, I started shaking all over, getting hot and cold, then breathing real deeply and hard and sort of blacked out. Not exactly blacked out, but sort of collapsed. Well, anyhow, I was rushed to the hospital."

He wrote further that he was very nervous about the impending visit of my mom and his girlfriend. He thought they might not even recognize him since he had no hair and was so skinny and sickly looking. He mentioned that his knees had started bothering him on 10 mile marches prior to his hospitalization, and he ended his letter with, "Suffering in your defense."

Thus, things had not gone well for John in those early weeks of his service, and he was concerned that he would be "recycled," that he would have to start basic all over again. While things were not going well for John, things were also not going well for Charley.

Charley had bought himself a sharp little Malibu. The thing is, he had a tough time making the payments since he didn't always make it to work, and this meant that my mother was on the hook since she had cosigned for the loan. Additionally, Charley managed to rack up quite a number of traffic tickets, which he always said was because the County Sheriff's deputies had it in for him. He racked up so many for which he never made a court appearance that they issued a warrant for his arrest. He was 18.

Because my father was always angry at Charley anyway, he latched onto the arrest warrant as his opportunity to apparently pay Charley back for wrecking his truck. When Charley came home one day, my father called the Sheriff's office to let them know where they could pick him up. And, pick him up, they did. Charley had raced out into the corn field trying to hide, but they eventually found him and hauled him off.

This was the first time my fury at my father ever came spewing out. "I hope you are proud of yourself!" I spit out at him with the most deprecating look I could muster.

He actually stood there smiling and said, "Yes, I am."

I stormed out of the house and walked over to my brother's. No one was home, but I sat on their front porch, crying and crying.

Chapter 10

John wrote to me again on June 26 in response to my laments of how things were going in my life. "It doesn't sound like things are going so well," he wrote. "I'll tell you something, they never do. All through your life you keep getting knocked down just because someone wants to see if you can get back up again. If you don't get up, they win and you lose. If you get up, you're all the stronger, and the same thing won't knock you down again. Unless you're a fool."

And, in response to my teen angst about boys and the issues I was then experiencing, he offered further advice. "... Keep yourself straight, don't give them [boyfriends] something just to keep them. If they want things you don't, tell them. There are more guys than one. And, you've got brains and looks enough to be choosy."

"I'll tell you what a guy hates more than anything in a girl and that's her own unconfidence in herself. You're no dummy. So don't let anyone think you are. And, Mary, if there is something you want to know about that you're afraid to ask anyone else, ask me. And don't worry about me telling anyone else."

But, just how would a 14 year old girl really ask her brother those very private female teen questions? It's not as if I had older sisters who would share or a mother who would talk to me about such things. I had no clear guidance, other than being told, mainly by the church, that much of what I was questioning was a sin and that I would go to hell.

"Just do what you know is right and you'll be happy for it. Look at me, I didn't and I'm suffering for it all the time. Constantly feeling guilty." I might add here that our Lutheran School upbringing is what contributed to our lifelong feelings of guilt. As if we could control the dysfunctional family dynamics we were born into.

John wrote me again on July 30. Because he was done with basic, he wrote that he was actually starting to like being in the army. "Sounds funny probably, but now we don't have all the harassment we had in basic."

"I hope I can pass all the tests to get into warrant officer school. I really want to fly. If I get in and make it through school, I may stay in the army 20 years.

"Mary, I'm really sorry about not giving you much attention when I was home. I gave it all to [my girlfriend] and now it looks like things are just about to end anyhow. Don't say anything to her if you see her." (I don't know how he thought I would be seeing her; she didn't come and visit or call us.)

In letters to my parents, he mostly shared about the confusion he faced concerning where he would be placed for training after completing basic. Initially he had been offered a school teaching him how to land, route and see off aircraft, which was basically air traffic control. That would have been in Mississippi, and it intrigued him greatly.

He didn't write again for a full month, and John said that was because he still didn't know to what school he would be assigned. He was waiting to get a physical that would clear him for the air traffic control school, but he wrote, "Seems like they don't like the idea of me being unconscious in 1963," and they were waiting to get his medical records from Illinois.

My mother had shared at least parts of that August 10 letter, and I learned something that I did not like at all. He made mention of coming home and getting married, and it would probably be that Christmas when he would have a week's leave. I did not care for his girlfriend, and I certainly was not happy about the thought of him marrying her. And, hadn't he written that "it looks like things are just about to end" a few weeks prior?

In an August 14 letter to me, he wrote that he wanted to get home for a few hours over Labor Day. "I'm going to get my car I think, unless [my girlfriend] wants it." What??

John wrote a letter to me again on August 26 that contained news/advice on diverse topics. "Sounds like you're coming out of your depression. That's all part of growing up. For awhile you're in good spirits then for awhile you're not. Keep your chin up, Babes, you'll make it."

"Well, they flunked me on my physical. So, I won't be going to Mississippi. Damn it. I really wanted that school.

"I thought you might like the picture. You can show it to all your boyfriends. Tell them you used to go out with the guy whose car it is. It'll make them think you're great. It might.

"You asked when I was getting married. I couldn't tell you because I don't know myself. Maybe at Christmas. If things are looking good by then." Reading that bit of news again made me very unhappy.

Late in August, my parents received another letter. He shared his disappointment with them about not passing his physical for air traffic control school. Instead of that, he was to be sent to aircraft maintenance school.

"I don't really want to be a mechanic, but then the army doesn't really give you much of a choice. Most of the guys from these schools after completing school go to Vietnam. So ... . I was really looking forward to going to Mississippi, maybe that's why they decided not to send me. They make sure you get what you don't want."

He wrote further about perhaps hitchhiking home, figuring he could make it in about 24 hours. But, he would stand the chance of getting caught and in trouble. Yet, he wrote, "Lots of guys do it all the time. I don't blame them. This gets to be too much after awhile."

Even though John didn't get into the school he wanted, he wrote on September 10, " ... at least I'm not in the infantry." His mechanic school kept him super busy. It began at 7:00 a.m. and ended at 4:00 p.m. each day. And apparently, he had hitchhiked home because he wrote of not getting back until 10:00 p.m. and of not having been missed at all " ... so I'm safe there."

"So anyhow, I'll go to school now for five weeks. Then, I kind of think I'll be shipped over to Paradise."

That's what we were all afraid of.

School started again that fall, and I entered my sophomore year. John wrote asking me, "What kind of subjects do you have? And how many recesses or nap times do you have?" Of course I had to laugh at his wit, and I'd be sure to get back at him when I wrote him next.

He told me how he didn't have any spending money, but he was devising schemes in which to get some. His army buddies would pay him certain amounts to take them places on their time off since he apparently was the only one who had his car with him. This particular trip would be from Fort Rucker, Alabama, (where he went after basic) to New Orleans, but only if they paid him enough.

My brother Charley had come back home after his stint in the county jail, which had afforded me my first visit to anyone behind bars. John asked in his September 11 letter if my father had asked anything about his taking Charley with him when he left to go back to Fort Rucker after his last leave, and further, "if things have cooled off at home again or not?" I am sure that my mother had finally put her foot down in allowing Charley back in the house, and our father would have been furious during the time John had been home. But, I'm fairly certain that our father had held his tongue in front of John knowing that John would back my mother.

I must have commented to him when he had been home that he hadn't been writing to me because he wrote in this letter not to think that he forgets about me when he doesn't write, it's just that he doesn't have much to write about. At least not to a 14-year-old sister, I would guess.

In late September, he wrote to me again. He responded to my previous letter, which had obviously yet again been full of teenage girl troubles, that it sounded like I was typical and "confused."

"Just take it as it comes and don't worry about it." Easy for him to say.

He mentioned that now that he had his car with him and he was able to get out and about, he didn't like Alabama. Most counties were dry and "the streets are deserted at 9:00."

"Girls you don't see. They all hide out somewhere. Unless there just aren't any."

He told me that he found a new hangout just outside the fort. He likened it to the Ace Cafe where he would take me for coffee not far from the Coachlight Inn. "A restaurant that sort of reminds me of the Ace Lounge a Go Go in Woodstock." I laughed out loud when I read that, and I could envision him sitting in there, drinking coffee, and laughing about his memories of being at the Ace. The memory of that makes me laugh still.

It broke my heart to read the following, though, even if he did write about it satirically.

"Finish school in five more days. If I don't get a second school, I'll get leave before going on my Southeast Asian tour. Which incidentally is expense paid by the firm I'm with."

John wrote to me again on November 5, and he apparently did get into another school, one that he said he would now be finishing in six days. After that, he still had some further training, after which he would be allowed to come back home.

In a letter sent to my brother Derald, John wrote in much greater depth about the training he was in, information he had not shared with me. He had completed his introductory course to aviation mechanics and was then attending a 67N20 course for crew chief, UH-1 helicopters. The UH-1's main purpose, John wrote, was for use in Viet Nam.

"The crew chief is the one person in charge of a certain one craft's maintenance and repair. Maybe I'll never get my own ship, but I sure hope I do. That's what this school is for."

Also, he wrote, "I pointed out M60 machine guns (on the picture I enclosed). I get a week of M60 training and combat training before I graduate. The crew chief is usually the machine gunner. I think this answers your questions as to how I know I'm going to Vietnam. Well, at least I'll be riding and not walking. About 99% of the graduates from this school go to Nam. OK! I'm ready for that party."

I eagerly anticipated the days when John would be home with us before being taken away to Viet Nam and the hell that would accompany that. I know that he tried to spend time with all of us, but our family was large, and he had his girlfriend and his friends as well. There was no wedding, however.

It would be the last time we would all be together for Christmas in the Marengo farmhouse. I know that my mother spent as much time as she could making it as special as possible. Since she now earned her own money, she had been able to buy sets of nice china, silverware and glassware, and the set table that year looked especially beautiful. There would have been 14 of us: our parents; Derald and Jane and their four kids; Jim and Sharon and their baby girl; John, Charley, and me. John, I'm sure, had brought a fine bottle of wine for us to share. Overall, it was a great Christmas.

Unfortunately, Christmas was quickly gone, and then New Year's as well, and it was almost time for John to leave.

"John," my mother said, "Derald and Jane and Jim and Sharon are coming over on Saturday night. They want to have a small gathering in your honor before you leave on Monday. Would that work for you?"

"Sure, Ma. I do have some plans, but I can be here for awhile first and then go out later."

When Saturday came, John had left in the morning. Later, the whole family gathered at the set time but had now been waiting for several hours for him to return. Most of them were not happy that he hadn't appeared.

We finally heard John's car drive up and the entry room door opening and closing. I know that things got said that night about his not having time for his family, and I know that feelings got hurt and that relationships had been bruised. Because of the things that got said, John did not stay for long, and I was very sad indeed.

Chapter 11

1968 thus began with a bang for us. John left on a crisp January day at the beginning of the new year for his hopefully-one-year stint in Viet Nam. Our parents drove him to the airport to catch his flight to San Diego, while I had to give him a giant hug, run outside, get on the bus, and ride off to school with my heart breaking. There would be none of his sporadic jaunts home during that year, and there was the great possibility that he would never come home at all. It was pretty tough concentrating on school that day is what I do remember. And, it would remain that way for much of the time John was overseas.

On January 17, John's first letter from Vietnam arrived, though we couldn't tell from the envelope that it had actually come from overseas. All of his mail ran through Company "B," 709th Maintenance Battalion, APO 96370.

John wrote to my mother, "Don't be concerned with my safety. I'm safe here at Bearcat. Work on the compound here. The place is heavily guarded and we have artillery and all."

What was really going on is that in 1968 the war was escalating. According to the US Department of Veterans Affairs, "Between 1965 and 1969, US troop strength rose from 60,000 to over 543,000 in country. Despite the US's superior firepower against the guerilla forces of the enemy, the two sides fought to a highly destructive draw."

John wrote to me on January 23. His tune differed from what he had written to my mother a week earlier.

"Last night I was scared, I'll tell you. The ground was shaking and the noise sounded like it was just outside. Immediately after, the warning siren went off. I thought for sure we were being attacked. I never dressed so fast in my life. Actually all I did was slip my pants on, my boots no socks, my shirt, grabbed my rifle and helmet and headed for shelter. I guess the VC killed a few guys not more than a mile from my tent just off the fort."

He wrote further about being disappointed that he wouldn't get to fly. "I'd like to crew or be door gunner on a Huey," he wrote. Of course, my mother and I were plenty relieved that he wasn't allowed to do either of those.

In this letter, he asked me what had been going on the last night he was home. He felt that we had all had a "good chat" about him and suggested that if we had a problem with him that we should have said it to his face. He mentioned that he had written our oldest brother Derald and told him off.

After other "small talk," he wrote that he had been very disappointed in opening an envelope of records (must have been some kind of documentation) that had been sent to him that there had been no note. "I don't know, maybe none around there is speaking to me anymore." As if any of us would stop writing him or worrying about him while he was overseas.

What John didn't know when he wrote me that January 23 letter but would soon find out is that my mother and I had packed up and moved out to a local motel. I cannot remember if a particular incident occurred that spurred a hasty departure or whether she had just reached her limit of what she could tolerate from our father. I do know she had been thinking about doing so for quite some time, and I was actually relieved that we were now released from that house of unhappiness. That didn't mean, however, that all of those bad memories would not continue to haunt me, to haunt all of us.

After a few days, my mother found us an apartment that was just several blocks from downtown Marengo. I felt like I was in heaven. I could now walk to see friends. I could even walk to school when weather was good. My mother only had to walk four blocks to her new job. It seemed perfect. Charley even moved in (for a time, anyway).

John's January 27 letter to my mother indicated that she had broken the news of my parents' separation to him, and though he said he was disappointed, he understood that she had to do what was right for herself and her happiness. He mentioned having received the records from our father, "I wondered why there had been no letter or note. I see now."

He also wrote to her about having told Derald off, and that he felt he was in the right. John felt that his brothers had always been jealous of him, and that outsiders had corroborated that feeling. So, his attitude towards them had not been started by he himself, but by them and how they treated him.

It seems that there was always family enmity in one form or another. As I look back I can see that there was never any strong structure of support other than all of us being within the same elemental structure of "family." I think we all loved each other, but we had never really been taught how to express that and how to really care for one another. A Lutheran school upbringing cannot take the place of being in an actually "loving" and caring family.

John expressed concern within that letter of "the new trouble in Korea," and he was concerned that his deployment would be extended. Additionally, "I see now why we can't go anywhere. Last week three guys were killed just outside the camp gates. It's not safe anywhere here. But really I'm not worried. I don't believe I've done my life's duty as yet and I will return."

According to Wikipedia:

On January 28: General Westmoreland in his annual report said "In many areas the enemy has been driven away from the population centers; in others he has been compelled to disperse and evade contact thus nullifying much of his potential. The year ended with the enemy increasingly resorting to desperation tactics in attempting to achieve military/psychological victory; and he has experienced only failure in those attempts."

On January 29:   At half-past midnight on Wednesday morning the North Vietnamese launch the Tet Offensive at

Nha Trang. At 2:45 that morning the US Embassy in Saigon is attacked.

On February 5, John wrote my mother stating, "Man, things have really been getting bad over here, Saigon and all. All with no exception the camps around here have been hit except us. We feel the shock waves from artillery rounds here, so they aren't landing too far away.

To change the subject, he wrote, "I'm waiting to start cashing in on the mail. I even wrote and apologized to a few girls so they'd write to me. If they're smart, they won't even bother." John was a very good looking guy, and he had never had problems having girls interested in him. On the contrary, there were many times he would have preferred them to become disinterested.

John wrote a long letter to my mother on February 14 in which he thanks her for writing so often. "It really helps, believe me. It's been two days now that I haven't gotten mail. Just two days and already I start to feel that everyone forgot about me."

He wrote that maybe things would seem better once he got to know the other guys better, but then he stated, "Everyone seems to be wary of making close friends. The reason probably is that you just watch them go right away anyhow."

"I was put on a team for the recovery of downed aircraft. Last night we went out to get one. Took machine guns with and all. Viet Cong like to keep aircraft down once they are there. Fortunately this one wasn't but ¾ to 1 mile outside the gates, but then it still isn't safe there. With a wrecker we lift the ship on to a big flatbed and hope we get it on and back to camp before anything happens. It's a little excitement anyhow."

Further in the letter he wrote that he was thinking of voluntarily extending for six months because in that time span, he would get one month of leave. He thought perhaps he could tour Europe since his transportation would be paid. Additionally, he would get "salary and ½ for extended time."

"As bad as it is here, I can't really say I'm any more dissatisfied than

I was before I came in the Army. I want something and can't find it. Maybe I never will."

On February 18, per Wikipedia, "During the week of February 11–17, 1968 the record for the highest US casualty toll during one week was set. The record coming off after the Tet Offensive was 543 Americans killed in action, and 2547 wounded."

John's next letter to me was dated February 25. He said that he had been having trouble breathing and that he had finally gone to the doctor. "As I suspected, I was advised to quit smoking." He told me that he had quit for three days so far, but admitted he would probably smoke again. Believe me, he did go back to smoking, and in a big way.

He corrected me on what I thought he had written to me in a prior letter. And, it was some of the first of his brotherly/fatherly advice to me.

"No, I didn't say you want what 'you can't get.' I say what you don't have you want. I say one can get what he wants. It sometimes takes a whole lot of planning ahead and a lot of going out of the way, but eventually the goal can be obtained. Either you're tough enough to stand through the tearing down or you're weak enough to fall to the feet of those that stand."

"Life is a struggle to get to the top. It's a rotten road up, but what else is life for. We're all trying to better ourselves. Here is where this truth comes in that the other guy wants to beat you out of the top position. So you have to maneuver and manipulate him. That's the way it is. Take your choice. Your road is still open. Either you'll stand or you'll fall. You can't do both."

In my last letter to him, I must have written about me seemingly having a lot of boyfriends at that time. Now that we had moved into town where I actually could socialize with friends, yes, I did have many friends who were male, and not all were "boyfriends." Then again, hadn't I grown up with all brothers?

John told me, "Use them to your advantage. They'd use you if they could, right? Think about it. I'll bet you can get your kicks by outsmarting all your boyfriends. Use the fact that a guy wants what he can't have and you'll have no problem handling the guys."

Many, many times have I wished I had been mature enough to take John's advice. My life would have been so very much easier.

It's ironic that in his February 27 letter to our mother, he mentions that he was getting so much mail that he couldn't keep up with it. Along with other friends and family, he was hearing now from some of the friends he made while in basic, one of which would be deployed to Vietnam in March.

"There are two company of VC suspected in the area," John wrote. "We're on 'gray alert,' which means very possible attack. I have berm guard tomorrow." He didn't get the letter sent that day, so added the following on the 28th.

"Our suspicions came to pass. We were hit lightly with seven 122mm rockets about 2:00 a.m. Slept the rest of the night in the bunker. Had to sit and sleep. Crowded, you know.

"I'm even less anxious now to go on guard duty in an hour. The very first time this place has been hit in a year. No one was hurt that I heard. I get the M-60 machine gun for guard. So I'm well prepared, or should I say equipped.

"Bien Hoa where I landed was hit real bad last night. That's about 10 miles from here. The VC are trying to take this area."

He ended the letter with, "So anyhow take care of yourself. Keep Mary out of trouble. Charles I guess is on his way out of school? Send my best to anyone who asks about me. Tell them I'm fine. Having a good time."

Chapter 12

Unlike the propaganda the American people heard on the 5:00, 6:00 or 10:00 news every night, the U.S. was not winning the war. According to Wikiipedia's account of the Vietnam War:

> Walter Cronkite, reporting after his recent trip to Vietnam for his television special "Who, What, When, Where, Why?" gives a highly critical editorial and urges America to leave Vietnam " ...not as victors, but as an honorable people who lived up to their pledge to defend democracy, and did the best they could."

On March 1 and on March 11, John wrote my mother lamenting the fact that he had not gotten any mail from her. "Apparently you find yourself very busy or else I would have heard from you sooner. Sooner than what? I haven't heard lately."

He wrote that he was trying to make things as "homey" as possible for himself under the circumstances. Making a "canopy like thing out of my mosquito net to obtain a more private sense." He bought a small table, a coffee pot, new pottery coffee cup and ash tray. "Just like downtown," he wrote.

As in many letters, John asked that certain things be sent to him. "Maybe this, too, you could send me. Get ready for the shock. A Bible. Now that you've recovered, I'd like mine but don't try digging it up. Buy one and I'll pay you back." He even ended the letter with, "Write soon and God be with you."

John next wrote me on March 15. "No big news here. You probably hear or view more on TV of the war than I hear about. I try to keep up on the war and politics in the U.S. and Vietnam. I've got to get things straight because I can and will vote in the election."

In most every letter to me or my mother, he always asked about Charley. I finally had written that Charley had left again. "He got tired of all work and no play, I guess, huh?" John wrote. "I really didn't think he'd give up so fast. After this time, there's no turning back for him I don't believe. He's what you say 'lost face.'" He went on further to say that he himself had lost face with the girlfriend he had proposed to marry not so long ago.

John thought that perhaps Charley having been in school and now gone again had impacted me negatively. However, I can't say that it did. I really don't remember anyone ever saying anything about it to me one way or the other.

He mentioned that for a time he had been the barber in camp, but now he was working as a carpenter. He wrote that they were building a "saloon." "So what? I didn't really enjoy working on helicopters anyhow."

John asked if I had heard him on the radio. If not, he thought perhaps he had said the wrong thing and they didn't broadcast it. I'm not sure what station I would have heard anything on anyway, particularly since we weren't alerted in advance.

They were awaiting the monsoon season in Viet Nam, and he wrote that it was extremely hot, "like a hundred or some in the shade. I'm getting a good tan out of it though."

On March 21, John wrote to my mother that he was just appointed "permanent barber." This precipitated a list of barbering tools that he asked her to buy immediately and send to him. "With good equipment, I can cut good hair and in turn make more money."

He included some good advice and supportive words for my mother while she was deciding what best to do with the settlement from the sale of our farm after my parents' divorce was finalized. "I do believe that like you said of buying an apartment house would be your best bet. You can't work in a factory forever. It would give you an income and a place to live both. Sort of self sufficiency." Those words never rang truer because that is exactly what she did, and the rental income kept her afloat for the rest of her life.

More requests followed, specifically to please send ink pens because he couldn't buy any at camp and to send "educational enlightening literature to read to stimulate my mind a bit. The mind can grow stagnant in the army very easily. I've experienced this already and don't like it. There are no challenges, no situations to encounter. Just be led around like an imbecile. That's how the men are treated in here. It's disgusting to say the least."

He ended this letter by writing, "You said to me what I've been telling myself and other people for a couple of years. There is something God wants me to do, but I don't know what it is. Maybe I'm just using that as an excuse for not doing anything yet, but I don't think so."

John's March 27 letter to me came with more brotherly advice. Apparently I had written him about one thing or another, and he sent me a comic having to do with moodiness. "People take defense and draw away from a moody person. Like it says, envy is a result of association with one who keeps a cool head and cheerful attitude." I'm not quite sure why envy should be what I wanted to inspire in my "associates," but I "got" what he was trying to tell me. I can't say that my moodiness disappeared, however.

"All is fine here," John wrote. "Just having a good old time." Sarcasm always did run strong in our family.

"Would you believe I'm now writing 10 girls regular? They write too. Plus all the family. That's a lot of writing and probably why your letters don't come so often."

And, as usual, he added, "What about Chas. [Charley]?"

March 30 was his next letter to our mother, starting out with, "All is well here."

"We've (the guy next to me and a couple others) started now playing cards at night. Hearts, 500 (which I'm teaching) [a big family game with all of us Wolffs] and rummy. Mix up tea or lemonade, usually someone has cookies from home, then we have coffee later on. Lessens the loneliness. For a time we just enjoy ourselves. It's good.

"I'll write again soon. I've got some of my fans pressing me for answers so I've got to create masterful writings to send off. Perhaps this evening I will be inspired to write the right thing for a change. The wrong thing seems to be the truth. Were I a liar, I'd make out fine."

A Wikipedia entry for March 31 reads, "President Lyndon Johnson delivers his Address to the Nation announcing steps to limit the war in Vietnam and reporting his decision not to seek reelection. The speech announces the first in a series of limitations on US bombing, promising to halt these activities above the 20th parallel."

By April 4, John was no longer a carpenter and no longer a barber, though he did still cut hair at night. "So anyhow, my new job is alright. I inspect aircraft after the mechanics finish and more or less supervise the test flight of each ship that comes out of the hangar. I don't get dirty. I don't have to do much of anything, but see to it the log books are correct, make minor adjustments to make more efficient the aircraft's operation."

"The job itself is a position to be held by an E-6. I am anticipating from this knowledge a promotion to E-5. Like I said I'd make. Anyone can do whatever they want to within reason. I'm impressing as much as I can the people that can make me E-5. At the same time praying it would mean no more KP or shitty details."

I had written to John about my teenage going steady experiences, which apparently had not been going so well for me. "Mary, do you find the need for a guy already? [I was only 15.] He wrote about the ideals that I might have for the "perfect" guy and what he might have for the "perfect" woman, but that no one could meet all of our expectations. He himself was looking for someone with "brains, looks, money, and first of all a 'real' person who can love and want to be loved. Haven't found her yet, but I will. I know that."

Further advice followed, and I truly wish that at my young age I could have understood, taken it to heart, and implemented it in my life. But, I'm not sure if any 15-year-old would have been mature enough.

"Mary, honestly what do you want to do with your life? Don't say I don't know because you do. [Sadly, I didn't.] Perhaps you have to concentrate and dig deep for the answer to what you really want, but you do know. [Again, sadly I didn't.]

"Now visualize (really) yourself as what you want to do. Keeping this always in mind, you can't help but find it. It worked for me. I'm not there yet, but compare me to what I was four years ago. Mary, I'm going to get there, I know it. After putting an honest effort and gaining by it, you don't ever give up. You can't."

As far as some kind of awkward situation I was experiencing with a girlfriend, John surmised that she was simply jealous of me for some reason. "When I find myself jealous of what someone else is or has, I just change myself or go and get something better than what they have. Sets my mind at ease."

On April 9, it was my mother's turn to receive John's words of understanding and wisdom. He wondered about how she was "really getting along." He figured that she was writing him about the good stuff, but not about the bad.

"Chas. [Charley] being the reason for your step. [Not sure what the "step" was.] Took off and left you disappointed again as usual. When will he learn there are other people and that people don't owe him a thing. Or, do you think they do? And Mary out every night but you know it would make it worse to say anything; all the time wanting to."

Yes, I can confess that I was pretty out of control at 15. Although, I was not doing anything "wrong" at that point, I wanted only to be with my friends – male and female.

"Boy, the things I hear of the riots and stuff back home, I'm safer here. ... I registered to vote. That will be a tough decision."

"Yes, I changed the insurance. 50/50 you and Pa." Obviously, it was no longer available for my education should something happen to him, but he had never written that to me.

I must have written back to John that I did not really appreciate the comic he had sent me about moodiness. He wrote back on April 11 that from what I was writing to him, he had the impression that I was always moody.

"I can't cover my true feelings myself, but it's not so bad a habit to pursue. Lots of times I wish I <u>could</u> conceal my true feelings."

"If you're like me in some of my ways, it's bad. Like my seeking the what most people consider to be the false things in life: money, fame, honor, respect. Good if you have my ambition, awareness, the desire to pull yourself up and out of pit we [we siblings] were forced into. My good looks, charm, really I don't know whether my pride is good or bad. Do you? It keeps me striving so how can it be all bad?"

About my questioning whether going steady with someone was a good or bad thing, he didn't want to steer me one way or the other. He cautioned that I needed to figure it out for myself. "Weigh both sides, choose the brighter and best as far as you're concerned. Don't <u>pity</u> the other side. They too make of life what they desire. Whether misery or happiness."

Again, he had given me some great advice that I wish I had been mature enough to put into play in my life. As he had alluded to previously, because of my background, he was right. I already had a "need" for a guy.

On April 19, he wrote to my mother that he was in a fairly good mood, but wondered what things would be like "when the time comes to leave this all behind." He told her that he had gotten his hands on a Bible [not sure if she just hadn't sent him one, or that this one presented itself first].

"The first night of possession I read the book of Revelations. I find the unknown fascinating. The obscureness of the obvious and inevitable."

He included a – in my opinion profound - poem that he had just completed and asked my mother to comment.

Confusion
If life would unmolested be,
by hopes and dreams and tyranny.
What would be hopes conformity?
Or toy with dreams reality.
What comfort without tyranny?
Let life be thus.
For death is.

"I've got to go on PX guard tonight. This will be a new experience, though even so, I'm not enthused.

"I still haven't found a camera so I had my picture taken. ... Do I look any different? I tried to look sweet and innocent. Actually my facial expression has aged considerably since I've been here. But then that's my problem.

"I won't forget ever and have to tell you. Three days ago they served for lunch a fabulously good roast beef meal. The first good meal. I hope not the last. I've got to go eat now."

Chapter 13

The U.S. Department of Veterans Affairs reported the following:

> In the U.S., increased casualties and higher taxes to support the war lead to great public dissatisfaction and a growing anti-war movement. In January 1968, the Tet Offensive began a new phase with savage attacks on the cities of South Vietnam. In May of 1968, the U.S. began peace negotiations, which eventually broke down. However, a change in U.S. policy led to the greater emphasis on training and supplying South Vietnamese troops and U.S. withdrawal began in July 1968. TV coverage brought the war directly into America's living rooms in a way never before experienced. Anti-war demonstrations intensified as did concern over war crimes and the environmental impact of Agent Orange.

In early May, John wrote that he was still taking on others' KP duties to earn some extra money, as well as cutting hair in the evening. His goal was to buy an expensive stereo system to bring home with him. He ended his May 2 letter with, "All's fine here except I think we're moving to a place that gets mortared every night. Let you know."

On May 8, John spent time responding to questions I had posed in several previous letters. I had asked him why he tended to set himself apart from everyone else. He replied that earlier in his life, some people had called him conceited, and that then he would feel bad, but at the same time knowing he had done nothing wrong. He felt they had tried to make him into a "detestful conceited nothing."

This went on for years, he wrote, but "I do believe it was that fatefully beneficial conk on the head in my car accident that woke me up.

You can laugh at that but I see things now and have since that crash. Two different worlds of reality they are in making comparison. I realized since then it was not me being conceited nor me trying to be different. I am. And can be no other."

(Again I must note the Danish study showing a link between concussions and schizophrenia. If John were seeing things differently, perhaps this was the earliest manifestation of his mental illness.)

On May 11, he wrote my mother wishing her a happy Mother's Day, though it was late and he hadn't sent a card. "To tell the truth, it wasn't till yesterday that I realized that mother's day was the next day. So here is a belated Mother's Day wish." This was followed by several blank lines on the page, followed by: "If you knew what it was it wouldn't come true."

"The days go by slower and slower it seems. I wonder if I'd be on my way home already if I didn't really want to go home. Probably."

"Seems to me also that I've come to a point when what and where I am here have more or less lost relativity with what and where I was back there. Makes writing quite difficult. Me and the people that I write just don't seem to relate in my mind as they did before. I'm reality here. They are reality there. Two different worlds of reality aren't about to coincide merely by the thought of my once being a part of the other. That seems so long ago. And so far away. And an even longer way off."

He ended her letter by saying he was "studying up on ESP" and soon he would start practicing it. He thought perhaps he could profit by the existence of "these extra powers of the mind." "I do believe they are there and need only be released."

Derald, our oldest brother, received a letter from John dated May 14. He wrote that on Easter he was very irritated that not only had he had KP and "watched the sun rise over the immediate horizon of greasy pots and pans," but worse was that none of the guys had Easter Sunday off.

"You know I wrote to a few people that these peace talks were put off by the North because with the ceasefire called, they with time could infiltrate the South again. As over Tet. By the news, you can see that's exactly what they were doing while they stalled. Seems to me we help them fight us more than we don't."

According to Wikipedia, on May 13, "The first US and North Vietnamese delegations meet at the Paris peace talks to discuss American withdrawal." They ended quite quickly.

He wrote to our mother on May 16 that, "No, we weren't hit here at Bearcat. They know better than to come here. With the artillery units here (although most have moved) and all the gunships (armed helicopters), the VC I don't think would accomplish very much here. Unless they got a few rocket and mortar sites set up before they are found."

"Not too long ago, there was a site located and destroyed about two miles from here. They (VC) had already dug a complete tunnel system and had a food and ammo cache. It's suspected that that's where the rocket came from if you remember me saying we were rocketed one night."

On June 3, he wrote a letter to me and said he was sorry that he hadn't been writing much. "I get in moods where I don't want to write. Moods where nothing really is worthwhile. Surely it must be the atmosphere, as I don't remember ever feeling so downcast before in my life."

"Seems to be a constant struggle to hold on to reality if that makes sense to you. It's all quite difficult to explain. Perhaps what makes it so difficult for me personally is that I cannot constitute in my mind a necessity or a worthy cause of my presence here in Vietnam. Surely someone somewhere has a need or cause, but I can't apply it personally."

I can't find evidence of when the actual break up came between John and his former girlfriend, but in this letter he wrote – in response to asking him if he had felt trapped when going steady - "Yes, being as you ask, I did feel trapped going steady. That's probably why I'm against getting married. After that, I'd really be trapped." He wrote that another woman, and this one I actually liked very much, was "hinting around about marriage." He said that he did let her know that he "liked his freedom" even though he thought a lot of her.

John wrote another letter to our mother on June 3. She had written him that she had taken his poem to an English instructor at the high school, and that this teacher (one that I had had and didn't like at all) had inferred that John had plagiarized it.

"Thank Tom for all the faith in what I say! Yes, I wrote it and for very sure didn't read it anywhere. I was writing a letter and wrote a paragraph out of nowhere that was just that thought and made it more condensed and in poet's form. I surprised myself, I'll tell you."

He asked my mother to try submitting it to perhaps a magazine or two or perhaps even to a publishing house to see what they thought. I am not sure if she ever followed up on that.

I'm not sure what happened to any other letters my mother might have received between June and July, but I received several. He wrote on June 6 that he had a chest cold he couldn't get rid of. I'm guessing that that might have had a lot to do with how much he was smoking.

His depressive funk must have passed because this letter was full of information about the things he was interested in that would take a lifetime to "fit them all in." The bottom line: "I find myself wanting to learn all I can about everything."

He included a small drawing of his "quarters" so that I could see how he was living. "You can see that living is crude, but it's not the worst. I do have a canopy made that adds a little class."

On June 29, he wrote me that he had "seven months left, Mar. SHORT! Be home before you know it."

Apparently I had written him while in one of my own funks and must have mentioned that I didn't see a reason for my being. "When I get home, Mary, I'll show you a reason for living. Promise. It's hard to put on paper. It's a feeling that is transmitted from one to another."

He went on to mention that he would find me some earrings when he went to Hong Kong. (I do remember getting a charm from Hong Kong, but I do not remember earrings.) The most ironic thing he wrote in that letter was that he wanted me to teach him to dance when he got home. I myself had never been taught to dance having had no sisters and no girlfriends who were into dancing in particular. I bumbled my way on the dance floor, so there's surely not much I could ever show him.

On July 3, he mainly wrote me about the stereo tape deck he had bought. "Tapes are the thing now, as you know, records are on the way out I'd say. So, I've got this $200 tape deck I can't play because I have no amplifier or speakers. One of the prices I must pay for getting the best. I'll have to wait till after Hong Kong to buy more or I won't have enough money for Hong Kong."

"Our fireworks were a day late here," he wrote to our brother Derald. "We were mortared and rocketed. Not bad. I think 9 or 10 landed inside Bearcat, and I know 2 fell short. Those short ones were pretty close to me, though. I was on berm guard. The one fell about 100 yards from me. Sure are pretty when they go off."

"I may be dreaming too freely, but there is now a deal that if one has less than 5 months left in service, upon return from Vietnam, he gets out. Used to be 3 months. Then, too, there is supposed to be a Christmas drop where those whose time is up here before January 15, they leave in December so they're home for Christmas. So, I may be out of the army in 150 more days. SHORT!"

On July 11, he wrote, "Well, it's a night. How are ya, Mary? Hope you're enjoying life more than I."

He said that I had devoted my last letter to religion, but he didn't like to write down his beliefs and that we would talk about them when he got back. "I have a weird religion. I call it 'Wolffianism.' Check that. Just kidding, it's my beliefs, but I really didn't name it that. Could though, I guess."

"We were rocketed on the 5th, 6th and 7th. No big thing. The excitement's gone or else I'd write about it. Sorry."

John wrote the same thing to me as to Derald about releasing Vietnam vets upon their return instead of making them finish up their last few months. That sure sounded good to me.

"Now I've decided that shortly after I get back home, I'm going to England and Europe. Maybe when Mother cashes in [from the sale of the farm], she'd lend or give you the money and we could go together. I want to find someone to go with and probably will be a girl, but I'd just as soon go with you." Unfortunately, that trip never materialized upon his return, which could have been just as much my fault as his.

In my last July letter written on the 26th, John wrote he was getting excited about his Hong Kong trip that was scheduled eight days from then. He had been able to get some travel literature so that he'd know what to expect, and he planned to take lots of pictures to share when he got back home. (I don't remember ever seeing them upon his return.)

"Had berm guard again last night. This time, we saw cigarette smoking back in the jungle tree line. The jungle is cleared about 100 yards out from the berm. They are pretty close, aren't they? Someone started shooting from the berm last night, too. I don't know at what. I wish I'd make SP/5 so I wouldn't have to go out there anymore."

In this letter, John reneged on letting me wear any of his clothes. "That may sound greedy and all, but that is how I feel about it. So now if I come home and find you've been wearing the stuff, I get to slug you. HA HA. My clothes are a lot of my life, and I think you know that."

"How's the summer going? Pretty fast I'll bet. Next summer we can do a few things together. I've got a summer to make up for."

"My best buddy here leaves tomorrow. I'll be sort of lost without him. Though I've been a loner more or less too long to let it bother me too much."

"My hair is grown out pretty long now again. I've decided I don't want to play this army game at all."

He and his buddies had been hitchhiking into Saigon against orders that all places "are off limits to 9th infantry." On this particular day, "We were in an accident on the highway going in. We narrowly escaped as we told the johnnie-on-the-spot MP that the driver is over there. As soon as he turned his back, we hitched another ride and made it. At any rate, we got back to Bearcat without incident after a good day in Saigon."

He wrote me that he was called a "Cheap Charlie" because he didn't pay for prostitutes. "I don't really like the idea of buying it," and he didn't "throw money away like most stupid guys do."

Chapter 14

Our mother received a letter dated September 4 that contained John's apologies for not writing for so long. "I've more or less given up writing. I'm only fooling myself by trying to write. I don't want to write anymore and I don't."

"All is going against what I previously had anticipated. I've been attached to D troop 3/5 Cavalry here at Bearcat. I can't under this 'test,' as it is called, be promoted. By the time the test is over, I'll be about ready to leave Vietnam. I now have nothing whatever to inspire my working.

"Here at D troop, I was made a clerk. Work day and night with no time off whatever. Sorry, I'm allowed 9 hours a day to eat, sleep, shower, etc. The days are as weeks, and weeks months.

"Here at D troop, I've also come in contact with the war itself. Guys I talk to one night I never see again. Killed in aircraft crashes or in battle. These are infantry men in the barracks I live in. We lost 3 helicopters that crashed and burned last week alone. Before I worked in a support maintenance unit. Here the ships on the airfield are the ones that go out day and night to do the fighting. And like I said, some don't come back.

"We were rocketed last week again for a few days straight. When the rockets started landing one morning at 8:00 a.m., I thought for sure that was the day. Always before it was nighttime.

"Oh yes, and I doubt that I'll be home for Christmas. Like I said, things just aren't going as planned.

"There has been a lot of fighting in our close vicinity. The nearest village about 3 or 4 miles away is no longer. And except for real necessity, no one leaves Bearcat.

"Sounds as all is well back in the world. Hope you're taking good care of it."

On September 23, John wrote to me, "I can't understand one thing. I quit writing and everyone quits writing to me. Why is that?"

He shared the same information as he did to my mother about his new assignment at Bearcat. And, he added the following story.

"The night before last there was a pretty bad thunder storm. … Right next to B Company where I used to live and work, etc., is a heliport. There lightning hit a helicopter and set off seven rockets in the one pad. These rockets (I don't know how many) hit another helicopter that was taking off and blew the front end (nose) off it. Killed the pilot as the rocket went right through his chest and sent 4 others to the hospital. The rest of the rockets landed in an army post about 6 miles from here and sort of went off there. I don't know if anyone was hurt there or not.

"Last night, there was fighting in and around the closest village to Bearcat. Long Than, which incidentally is only half there now. Oh, the ravages of war.

"The way things are going around here lately, I don't know if I'll get home or not. I'm planning on it regardless. 105 days by the way. Short!"

A letter written on September 27 to Derald and family was a bit more upbeat. John responded to Derald's and Jane's questions about what he would "like to have" in the following manner.

"I'll tell you. If you could get a beautiful <u>American</u> blonde into a box and mail her. Other than that, there's not too much my little heart desires that I would use over here. You could even send her COD. Probably would be cheaper than what it costs me now the few occasions I get anywhere.

"Since I've been in this unit, we've lost about 7 ships total. That's about $2 million of <u>your</u> tax money in not even two months just out of this company. I don't pay taxes here you know. Of course, I don't make enough to afford paying them. These pilots here are carzy. That's why there's so many ships get shot down.

"Yep, the longer I'm over here the more I think to myself that what I should have is a little kid of my own. I haven't talked myself into wanting a wife though."

Our mother heard from John again in an October 16 letter, and he told her he was happy about the peanuts and candy that she had sent him. "Shared them with the guys and we all enjoyed them."

"Glad to hear that both you and Dad are investing your shares of the money instead of just renting and wasting the money away."

Our mother had bought the apartment building that she had moved us into in Marengo. It had three units, and they were generally all occupied. Our father bought what I think was a three or four unit apartment building in Palatine. I don't remember ever going to visit him in that apartment building since I wasn't yet driving. And, I believe he got married again and moved into his new wife's home not all that long after I got my license.

What John wrote indicated he had gotten a new job, and was feeling better about things. And he was happy that my mother was still sending him packages. "I just opened the package. Thought it was a book, but it's edible. Good! For we've been living on C rations as the mess hall is closed."

"We're in the process of moving to Dong Tam. I expect I'll go down tomorrow after staying up all tonight loading the trucks."

"Also, in case you didn't notice my address, NOTICE IT! And, it's just about time I got the promotion!

"Sevens days now till I leave for Singapore or wherever I might end up for my seven day leave. 80 days left to go now. Their termination will come none too soon either."

On October 31, 1968, according to Wikipedia, "President Johnson announces a total halt to US bombing in North Vietnam."

And, on November 1, Alan Rohn's Vietnam Time Line reports:

Operation Rolling Thunder was halted after 3 and a half years. Altogether, the U.S lost more than 900 aircrafts; 818 pilots were killed or missing while hundreds were captured. On the other side, an estimated 182,000 and 20,000 North

Vietnamese civilians and Chinese supporting personnel were killed respectively while nearly 120 planes were destroyed.

He wrote to our mother again on November 7 about being called down to the Red Cross to get the news that our grandmother had died. "I experienced what people call mental telepathy while in Taipei, Taiwan, and felt what was going on, but didn't know till I got back what I was feeling it for. The day I got back, the 3rd is when I was informed, and I'll say I was more relieved than anything else because I was worried and scared from my experience. Strange things do happen."

"Like I told you before I moved down here, this place gets rocketed all the time. It does. I just got back from the bunker. I don't even get worried any more when they hit. I think I know what's in store for me [he surely didn't] and it is not dying over here.

"54 days left, by the way. I got my orders for January 1."

The next day, the 8th, he wrote a letter to me. "I found it humorous, but at the same time felt badly, about your statement 'write back when you're finally ready to.' Cute, very cute."

"I'll say that I'm not sorry now that I got drafted and came to Vietnam and got to see parts of the Far East like Hong Kong and Taipei, Taiwan. Fascinating and educational.

"The one thing I was thinking on my way back was a hope that D troop would have a shower built by the time I got back. Gone 11 days and then yet I came back to take a hose shower next to the old water truck.

"You know I'm in the middle of the Mekong Delta now, right? Well, I am and it's awful. Check the map. Dong Tam, insignificant as this map drawer might think, it is now base camp for the 9th Division.

"Check out Da Nang up north. That's where they dumped me off when I came back from Taipei. So, I had a good tour of Vietnam getting back to Dong Tam. Saw most of Vietnam as I flew, rode, and walked back the some 500 miles between Da Nang and Dong Tam.

"Don't use such large figures in calculating my return date. Try 53, love. SHORT! Be back before you know it."

In my previous letter I must have written him about my steady and I talking about getting married after high school. Heck, I wouldn't even have been 16 yet. What a fool.

"Now check out your little brother John. Here I am almost 23, and I'll tell you I'm now just learning to enjoy life and really understand and get along with people. The more experiences a person has in or to his or her favor, the better the chances of really being able to get along with another. Maybe I'm slow, but I just can't believe that." (Again, sure wish I could have really taken in the wisdom he was trying to impart to me.)

"About college – yes, I'd be happy and proud to help you through, Mary. I don't have to say any more on that." (And yet again, too bad I didn't follow up with attending college immediately upon graduation instead of getting married as soon as I turned 18.)

John added a P.S. to this particular letter. "SP/5 J.C. now so don't degrade my rank in the future. Thank you." So, he finally and actually got the promotion he was seeking, even though it was right before he was to return.

To Derald, he wrote on November 16 about his promotion and his leave to Taipei. "I finally got my promotion. 3 cheers! No big thing, but it's the best I could have done according to regulations for the short time I'll be in the Army. Sp/5 is about the same rank as a buck sergeant. The pay is the same. The job differs somewhat sometimes, that's the difference."

"My 7 day leave to Taipei, Taiwan (Formosa) was expensive, enjoyable and strange.

"Only 44 days left unless some good luck comes my way which will get me home for Christmas. I doubt it. Bought a suitcase tonight. Getting anxious.

"Next day I'm going into Saigon again for a day or two. I make up excuses to go and seem to get away with it. Saves me from going mental to get away once in awhile."

A final Wikipedia entry for the year 1968 reads:

December 1968 to May 11, 1969:   Operation Speedy
Express was a controversial United States military operation
conducted in the Mekong Delta provinces Kien Hoa and
Vinh Binh. The operation was launched to prevent Viet Cong
units from interfering with pacification efforts and to
interdict lines of Viet Cong communication and deny them
the use of base areas.

My final letter from Vietnam was dated December 3. "Listen Mar,"
John wrote, "the last letter you wrote was a full one, there's no doubt. Hope
you have enough patience to wait till I get home so I can talk to you about it
all."

"I've got the feeling someone is checking my mail. I may be wrong,
but I've been getting a lot of letters that obviously have been opened. Perhaps
my outgoing is being checked, too. Pretty rotten, huh?

"Maybe you'd want to write one more time. That is how short I am.
By the time you get this, I'll have 20 days left at the most.

"So, Chas. left again? I had a feeling he'd leave before I got home.

"Take care, Mary, and don't do anything rash until you talk to your
big brother."

In a January 16, 2018 wrap up of 1968 by the New York
Times:

From January to December, people demonstrated against
racial injustice and economic inequality. Abroad, the United
States military slogged through a seemingly interminable
war."

"It was the year between the Summer of Love and the
summer of Woodstock, and some men grew their hair long
while others were drafted to fight in Vietnam. "The country
was bitterly divided: hawks and doves," said Marc Leepson,
an author, historian and Vietnam veteran.

It was also the year of the Tet offensive, an enormous attack by North Vietnamese forces, and of more than 16,000 American deaths in the Vietnam War, more than in any other year. Domestic support for the war effort faltered as antiwar protests exploded, most notably the riots at the Democratic National Convention in Chicago, to which the police responded with tear gas. Demonstrators, journalists and even some delegates were beaten and arrested.

December 14, 1968 – John received The Army Commendation Medal for meritorious service in connection with military operations against a hostile force in the Republic of Vietnam during the period January 1968 to December 1968. Signed: Julian J. Ewell, Major General, USA Commanding, 9th Infantry Division.

And, so, John came home to a very different world. Our family was further split apart. His friends had moved on without him. The United States itself seemed to be a battle ground. And the war in Vietnam continued.

Chapter 15

From this point on in his story, I have no letters upon which to rely for John's personal viewpoint, and I only have vague recollections of conversations. What I do have are bits and pieces of much documentation, some of the cards and notes I had sent to John after his return, letters from our mother to John, and his brief notes back to her.

The brother portrayed through his foregoing letters is the brother that I had hoped to have around for the next 30, 40, 50, even 60 years of my life. But, that is not how things would work out for us. In some ways, it was extremely painful reading all of the letters again because it brought home with a vengeance what a terrible loss it was when John became no longer John, but someone who could no longer communicate successfully with any of us. In other ways, I felt extremely close to him once again, as if in this moment in time I could actually make contact with him again. As if I could still get in touch with him to clarify things that had been written about in his letters.

John's outprocessing order was dated December 22, 1968, which directed him to "report to the 9th Replacement Battalion in Long Binh, Vietnam, for transportation aboard flight G2B4 at 1030 hours on January 5, 1969, departing and arriving at SUU Line #101". I also found shipping documentation for all of the electronics he had purchased in the Far East and some of the items that he had us mail to him from home. Additional documentation indicated all of the army paraphernalia he had to turn in, including, of course, any weapons.

John caught an American Airlines flight out of San Francisco to Chicago O'Hare on January 6, 1969. I do not know who was at the airport to greet John that day, but I do know that he would have made his way to our apartment in Marengo shortly thereafter.

When John arrived back home, he still looked like the handsome – albeit a bit skinnier – old John. And, yet, somehow the eyes within his smiling face had a different look to them. Something I couldn't put my finger on at the time. He may have thought the same thing of me. I had just turned 17 and was totally absorbed in my own growing up experience. I was much too absorbed with my boyfriend, my senior year at school, my part-time secretarial job, and partying on the weekends. I was so immature in comparison to John's state of maturity at the age of 17.

I do remember that I was so very happy when John came back safe and sound. Initially, I thought that I would be able to spend a lot of time with him and make up for the "missing" past two years he had been in service. That didn't really happen, however. As mentioned, I was in my own little co-dependent world with my soon-to-be-first-husband. My boyfriend knew that I idolized my big brother, that he was good looking, and he was jealous of him and our relationship even before John returned from Vietnam. He did not want me spending my time with him; I knew that unequivocally. And, mixed up 17-year-old that I was at that time, I complied with his wishes. Thus, I surely was not "there" for John.

I do recall vividly, though, one occasion when the three of us were together. My fiance was in the hospital, having just had hernia surgery, and John took me to visit him. We stopped at the hospital gift shop and bought a cute little green stuffed Pomeranian (which I still have). I remember John and I bouncing the little stuffed dog around the bed and making funny little statements to make my fiance laugh. I remember it so clearly because it hurt him to laugh, and that made it all the funnier.

We didn't have room for John to stay permanently in our Marengo apartment as there were only two bedrooms, but after first coming home, he slept on the couch at times. I also think he spent some time out at the farmhouse with our father.

My mother remarried in March of 1969. I stood up for her, but I do not remember John being at the wedding. I did find a picture of John at a reception with his then-girlfriend, one that I had liked from before he went to Vietnam, and it must have been taken at our mother's wedding. Our Grandpa Rinne wrote in a November 7, 1969, letter that "I enjoyed it very much when your dad and John Jr. were here." I have no recollection of John and my dad traveling together, but perhaps this was when my father was first considering a move back to St. James, Minnesota, where he had grown up.

John stayed at my brother Jim's for a time, in the renovated school house in the corner of what had been our old family farm in Marengo. I do know that that situation ended badly because John began thinking that they were trying to poison him. Later I learned that John had made threats of bodily harm against them because of his fear.

From there, John stayed with our brother Charley and his wife for a few months in an old farmhouse outside of Woodstock. I would be sure that John and Charley spent a lot of their time going out for coffee somewhere.

In 1970, John went to live with our dad at his apartment building in Palatine. It was so sad to hear that John had taken to sleeping in a closet under the staircase, which, of course, all of the family thought was pretty strange. I believe now that he was mentally back in his Vietnam days and that the closet may have felt like a bunker.

Derald hired John as a storekeeper and cashier from July to September 1970 at his news agency in Arlington Heights. Sadly, that was short-lived because he was "not minding the store," according to my sister-in-law. I found some documentation that indicated that he had lived on his own around this time.

I, having just turned 18 in December, got married in January 1971 to my first husband. I do not remember John attending my wedding. He had been increasingly drawing away from all of his personal relationships with family and friends.

Tax documents, along with John's record of all of his jobs throughout the years, show that he worked from February to March 1971 at a restaurant in Des Plaines doing food prep. From March through June 1971, John recorded that he did food prep and was a server at a nursing home in Arlington Heights where our father worked. Thereafter, he went to work at a Marengo restaurant, the Yum Yum, just across from the high school which we had both attended. This was the joint that John would take his friend Warren to when they were out and about in our area. John noted in his log that he worked at the Yum Yum from February through May 1971. Thus, he must have been working in both the Des Plaines and the Marengo restaurants for part of the same time. The story I heard later was that he lost his job at the Yum Yum because he had gotten involved with the owner's wife.

From June 1971 to October 1971, John worked for our stepdad, who was a painting contractor. It would have made sense that he lived with them during this time.

John's last valid Illinois drivers license was dated 09/21/71. The license data shows him to be 5'8," 145 lbs., with blond hair and blue eyes. Other paperwork indicated that on September 23, 1971, John bought a 1965 Ford Thunderbird.

John again noted working for Spencer Decorating (our stepdad) from April until July 1972. There is no notation about where he had been between October 1971 and April 1972.

Things go downhill for John from here. It's seems very odd, but I do not recollect these events, but it's possible my mother tried to keep them all a secret at that time. What I found through investigating John's paperwork is that in June of 1972, he had received a Criminal Complaint for theft of gas from a local gas station. He had just purchased a 22 caliber Anschutz Savage rifle, and that was impounded by the Sheriff's office. There was another criminal complaint for resisting or obstructing a police officer. Then, there was a receipt for a local attorney.

On September 13, 1972, John bought a 1961 4-door hardtop Chevy. John was off to San Diego, which I'm presuming he was familiar with having flown into that city's airport when going and coming from Vietnam. He had driven the Chevy there, but then had to relinquish it in payment of a storage facility.

He had written to a woman he had met in Taipei, and he must have asked her to come to San Diego to visit him. She wrote back that although she was happy to hear from him and would like to see him again, she was unable to fly to the U.S.

I found a short note I had written to John in November 1972. It appeared I was immediately writing notes and sending cards after his move, so I can only guess that I really did try to have conversations with him while he had been at my mother's. I surely wish that I could remember some of them. My notes and letters to him are short and rather cryptic because they were essentially one-way monologues. He never wrote anything back to me.

> John,
> Got the card in the mail. Thought I best send it to you right away. How is everything going for you? Do you have a job and an apartment, etc.? I hope you're doing all right; I really worry about you. Everything is so different from what it used to be, I hardly believe it. Are you going to come home for Christmas or don't you have the money? Take care of yourself and have a happy Thanksgiving.
> Love,
> Mary
> P.S. I put the two dollars in for your Thanksgiving dinner.

Thereafter I sent him a birthday card, his birthday having been December 20.

> Dear John,
> Hope everything is going all right for you. Wish you'd let us know once where you're living and what you're doing.
> We're in the midst of a storm again it looks like. We had more snow last night and this morning it's been sleeting. A few nights ago, it was like 10 degrees below zero.
> Take care and hope you have a nice birthday.
> Love,
> Mary

I found another letter from the woman in Taipei dated December 11, 1972. Her response to what he had sent her after her last letter indicated that John was having a very tough time already dealing with his worsening mental state. Mona wrote, thanking him for a charcoal drawing of her and "another a real big animal, and of course contain a great sense of humor and meaningful for something, and you know that I do not know much English and besides you have to write proper then I will be able to understand." She goes on, " ... Also the last part of your letter you have been writing so much and hard for me to understand and even I asked many friends to explain to me and still can not understand. Of course I would not blame you perhaps this way you intended to show some sense of humor and I wish that you could teach me gradually and let me understand step by step."

John listed three different addresses during his 1973 stay in San Diego. Because of his condition, which made it impossible for him to stay at any one job, I am sure that he had to move around because he could not pay the rent.

He was employed as a storekeeper and cashier at the Art Center in San Diego from January through April of 1973. In January, he sent a Free Zone Shopping in Tijuana, Old Mexico postcard to my mother. He wrote, "Exciting wait for med. Operation in S.D. [San Diego] understand demands to trade. John"

Unfortunately, that's about as clear thinking as any future communications would be from John - to our mother, to me, to anyone.

A February 2, 1973 letter from the Veterans Administration in Los Angeles addressed to John in San Diego states, "Your recent VA hospital report shows you were admitted for hernia. Since service-connection for this condition has previously been denied, Paragraph 30 benefits do not apply. Pneumonia was not found on your last examination. Our prior decision is confirmed and continued." This is the first of many battles that John would undertake in an effort to obtain benefits for himself. However, only some claims were justified while some seemed non-justified and even preposterous.

I subsequently found a January 23, 1974, statement from Maricopa County General Hospital in Phoenix, Arizona. The total charges of $365.25 seem quite expensive, and I could not discover what they were for. I also found a May 1974 statement from the Phoenix Ambulance Service requesting payment of $46.92, which was overdue.

John received a replacement Firearm Owners Identification Division (FOID) card from Springfield, Illinois, on April 5, 1974.

By December 9, 1974, my brother John was in Hines Hospital, Clinic #51D. I do believe that this is when our mother helped get him signed into the psychiatric unit there. Our father subsequently got him signed out because he just couldn't seem to acknowledge that John was truly mentally ill. Then again, John may have called and played on his emotions (Yes, at times, though seldom, my father actually did express emotions to us other than anger). I wrote to John on that date, as follows. (At this time, my son had just been born on October 30, and my divorce from my first husband was pending.)

> Dear John,
> Your package is still in the attic – don't worry about it.
> I'm enclosing a picture of the baby – he's healthy and really growing. He changes all the time – so different from when he was first born.
> You certainly didn't say much in your letter. [Unfortunately, I did not keep that letter, which he must have written while on meds at Hines.] How are you doing? Hope you're eating well and everything.
> I'd send you a few bucks, John, if I had it. I'm broke – flat broke.
> Love, Mary

Later in the month I sent another note to him at Hines, along with his birthday card.

Thanks for the Christmas card – sorry I didn't get yours off sooner. I needed to get the money for the stamps first.

Have to start baking Christmas cookies tomorrow. Next week I'll be back to work and I certainly won't have time then. Anyway, I'll send you some when I get them made.

Take care and write sometime when you feel like it.

Love,

Mary

P.S. You should be hearing from Pa – he called about you last week.

As mentioned, our father helped John get out of Hines Hospital. I know that our mother was livid, knowing that John was mentally ill and needed treatment. The rest of our family, aside from me and my mother, seemed to agree with my dad, that John was not really mentally ill, but "acting."

A few months after he was checked out of Hines, John moved into a small motel on the outskirts of Hebron and began working at Kenosha Packing in that town. I found an April 1975 Packing House Membership Card that was issued to John through Local 189 of the United Food & Commercial Workers International Union. The "old" John, the extremely meticulous handsome man with multiple girlfriends would certainly not have chosen to work in a meat packing plant and live at that dismal motel like this "new" John.

I visited John a time or two while he was staying at the Hi-De-Ho motel, but never in his room, only at the restaurant next door. John, while living there, spent hours and hours and hours drawing and painting. Because the original artwork from this period is gone, I'm thankful to have found photos that he took of his earliest work. I remember him calling his first life size figures the Goy people, and he claimed he knew about them from when he had been abducted on a space ship that had landed in the field beyond our family farm.

When going through John's belongings, I came across a cashiers check copy made out from John to me on April 10, 1975 for $17.20. The only thing I can think of is that was payment to me for a colored pencil picture I had drawn of a bantam rooster; I was taking an art class at that time. I remember him asking me if he could buy it, and I sold it to him. (I have my rooster back now.)

I moved down to Houston, Texas, during May 1975, where I spent six months with our brother Charley and his wife. I wrote to John that October.

> Dear John,
> How's your ankle doing? Hope you're getting along all right. Have you had a place to stay and everything? I sure hope so. And I suppose you've been doing a lot of drawing. Thanks for the picture you sent – it was really good. You seem to be getting better – I suppose because you do a lot of practicing. That was my problem, I didn't practice enough.
>
> Have you been going out at all lately? Kind of hard when money is so tight. It's not really tight here in general, just in my case. I just make it each month – hopefully I'll get a raise soon.
>
> So take care, John, and I hope everything is going okay.
> Love,
> Mary

John had suffered an ankle injury in the spring of 1975 at the meat packing plant and that injury would become a major issue as it precipitated a workers comp claim that took years to settle, plus legal battles for disability claims. When it all began, however, Kenosha Packing demanded that John be examined by a psychiatrist. I found an October 1975 statement from Family

Service and Mental Health Clinic for McHenry County, noting John was
working at Kenosha Packing, and listing the following:

> Diagnostic Evaluation on April 5, 1975
> Psychotherapy on September 11, 1975
> Appt. cancelled by patient for September 18, 1975
> Psychotherapy on September 25
> Psychotherapy on on October 9
> Psychotherapy on on October 16
> Did not keep appt. on October 23
> End of entries

Chapter 16

It became more and more painful to see what was happening to my brother as the years went by. Gone were any ideas of he and I even having an intelligent conversation about where we were going in life, relationships, religion or ESP, let alone taking a trip abroad together. I had given up going to college, but even if I had decided to go, he would have been unable to help me do so as he had once promised.

Not only did I find evidence that John got into stamp collecting in 1975 and 1976, I also discovered that he had begun collecting real estate, both within and outside of the United States. The properties he purchased would later cause me hours and hours of research and frustration when executing his estate. I found it fascinating that even though he was quite mentally ill by that time, he was able to follow through making payments on most of these properties, even while he very nearly lost many of them later due to late payments to lenders or to taxing bodies.

It was especially fascinating because by this time John was no longer at the motel but living in a tent just outside of Hebron. Somehow the authorities simply left him alone to live in this manner and go about his eccentricities.

On July 24, 1976, John bought 133.67 acres in the County of Rogers, Parish of Mackie, Australia. He had signed a contract to a couple from Victoria, B.C., Canada, in early July. When settling the estate, I found that taxes had been current through 1990. After I submitted an inquiry to the Australian government in 2004, however, I found out that John's name no longer appeared as the owner.

A few months later, in September 1976, John bought a lot from Sangre de Cristo Ranches in Colorado. He paid this property off in 1981, making sure that taxes were paid each year. This property I would have to sell.

Apparently, John had also become enamored with astrology, and I found a questionnaire-generated report dated September 1976. Some of it seemed profound considering the things John had written from Vietnam about his interests and experiences, and his proclivity for many love interests. I would have no idea, however, how much personal information John gave this company before they produced their "Research Project 7 Output."

In January 1977, John signed a contract for 20 acres of land in Sweetwater County, Wyoming. He only made payments through 1980, however.

Also in January 1977, John bought 5.1 acres midway between Pensacola and Tallahassee, Florida. He kept up payments on this piece of land, and the value of the property actually escalated significantly by the time of sale.

Sadly, though, John's life was becoming increasingly disjointed. He became embroiled in quite a number of legal proceedings that were difficult to follow and seemingly unwarranted. Time and time again he was rebuffed by attorneys and/or sent elsewhere to plead his case.

In April 1977, he was apparently trying to sue the City of Phoenix, Arizona, for the injuries he sustained on his way back from San Diego back in 1974.

During 1977, John also started buying and selling stock. From what I can determine, he invariably ended up on the losing end of the transaction.

It became clear when I ran across a July 1977 bill of sale that John had actually held onto the 1965 Ford Thunderbird he had bought years earlier. I wondered why he drove his Chevy to San Diego and not the Thunderbird, which he had bought first.

In July of 1977 he sought help from an attorney for an incident in 1974 (possibly in Phoenix) where John had stated that he had been beaten and robbed and suffered injuries. The attorney wrote him that "in Illinois, any suit for an injury to the person must be commenced within two years from the date when the injury occurred."

Art-N-Attic, Inc. in Memphis, Tennessee, sent an undated note in reference to John's trellis paintings, which I know were done while he was at the Hi-De-Ho in Hebron. His paintings, unfortunately, had not been on stretch frames and they had been damaged in shipping.

Subsequently, John had copies of one trellis painting made in various colors. I do not know what he had planned to do with all of the copies, but he kept them for the balance of his life. When he first painted the trellises, he gave me a signed original that I still have in my possession.

I found a prescription for Mellaril 25 mg dated July 16, 1977, which he was to have filled at a pharmacy in Lake Geneva, Wisconsin. I know that John had finally been diagnosed with paranoid schizophrenia, perhaps at Hines, yet I have been unable to find any solid substantiation of that diagnosis within any of his hospitalization documents, nor from any of the psychiatrists that he visited. However, research on Mellaril would substantiate it.

Mellaril is used in the treatment of schizophrenia and belongs to the drug class phenothiazine antipsychotics.

MELLARIL® (THIORIDAZINE HCl) HAS BEEN SHOWN TO PROLONG THE QTc INTERVAL IN A DOSE RELATED MANNER, AND DRUGS WITH THIS POTENTIAL, INCLUDING MELLARIL, HAVE BEEN ASSOCIATED WITH TORSADE DE POINTES-TYPE ARRHYTHMIAS AND SUDDEN DEATH. DUE TO ITS POTENTIAL FOR SIGNIFICANT, POSSIBLY LIFE-THREATENING, PROARRHYTHMIC EFFECTS, MELLARIL SHOULD BE RESERVED FOR USE IN THE TREATMENT OF SCHIZOPHRENIC PATIENTS WHO FAIL TO SHOW AN ACCEPTABLE RESPONSE TO ADEQUATE COURSES OF TREATMENT WITH OTHER

ANTIPSYCHOTIC DRUGS, EITHER BECAUSE OF
INSUFFICIENT EFFECTIVENESS OR THE INABILITY
TO ACHIEVE AN EFFECTIVE DOSE DUE TO
INTOLERABLE ADVERSE EFFECTS FROM THOSE
DRUGS. (SEE WARNINGS, CONTRAINDICATIONS,
AND INDICATIONS).   (http://www.rxlist.com/mellaril-
drug.htm)

On July 26, 1977, John had reached out to an attorney just over the
border in Wisconsin for a leg injury sustained at work. His letter to the
attorney must have been cryptic because he got one back saying he needed to
make an appointment to clarify.

On August 11 of 1977, John bought the first of two properties in
Sunshine Valley Ranchettes, Luna County, New Mexico.

The Wisconsin lawyer wrote to John again on August 17 advising
that, though he had received John's packet of information, he would need a
$1,000 retainer. John replied that "because of no correspondence necessary
to my feelings I'd like to cancel the offer of service and request my papers to
be returned to me at address P.O. Box 207, Hebron, IL 60034. Excuse please
the late deposit for service, I'll have payment within 4 weeks. I didn't expect
problems with making payment." (John kept copies of most all
correspondence that he sent out to anyone.)

I found an original packet dated November 1, 1977, that had been
sent Special Delivery by John to the United States Department of Commerce
Patent and Trademark Office. It contained the second mailing of application
and testimony dated October 29, 1977. John wrote:

In pretense of misleading presentation; the above named
inventor [John's name and address had been printed at top of
handwritten letter] requests for a patent to be registered in
United States of unit named 'gadget #2077.'

Gadget #2077 were originated intended for purpose of

clearing myself of police radio the month of November 1975.

Gadget #2077 with DC power can be engaged to function by pushing button or multiple of buttons.

Working gadget #2077 functions to disassociate place of police radio from immediate designation, multiply engaged in respect of transfer of theators self.
Inventors signature,
[John signed it]

In November 1977, I found an order for jewelry from Bangkok, Thailand – bracelets, rings, pendants, tie tacks. Much of this I found in his personal effects.

I'm sure John was disappointed when he received a letter that November from the United States Department of Commerce Patent and Trademark Office indicating he had not applied properly. They enclosed his payment for patent, along with a book on how to apply.

John received a letter from our father (now in Minnesota) to John (in Hebron) dated January 28, 1978:

Dear Son John,
Hoped to find out your address from Harry Rinne [our great uncle]. Tried to find you when I was still in Illinois, but nobody would tell me. How have you been?

I am sick and been in the hospital 3 times. You know, you got $1,300 from me when you went to California. If you sent me some money, I would like it.

God bless you. Hope to hear from you.
Your Dad
[adding his address, presumably for payment purposes]

The following is from an undated letter from John to First Interstate Bank of Albuquerque, Trust Division, NM. Since he was threatening to sue the City of Phoenix, I presume he intended that his potential award should go into this account:

> I left my will with my attorney in Lake Geneva. Please dispatch to bank in cash (receipts of collection). I'll arrange for payments to myself, John C. Wolff, Jr., on record of account. Please negotiate all legal transfer with [my Wisconsin attorney].

I suppose the following letter should not have taken me by surprise. And, it shouldn't automatically be presumed that John was just "crazy" by claiming such a thing. He really had been good looking and well dressed enough to have had his photo in such a magazine. I think, though, that at the time he had the attorney write this – 10 years after he was in Vietnam – he possibly still envisioned himself this way.

On February 28, 1978, his attorney sent a letter to the New Yorker Magazine in New York stating that he represented John Wolff of Hebron, Illinois, and that: "In your most recent edition of your magazine, a picture appeared on page 63 of a young man. Mr. Wolff is certain that picture is one taken of him some years ago." Further, he said that John had not authorized its use.

Although the Wisconsin attorney had written that letter on John's behalf, he obviously knew that John needed psychiatric help. John received a March 30 letter. I have to respect this attorney for clearly trying to help John even though John would not completely comply with his requests. In this letter he told John that he had spoken to a counselor at the McHenry County (Illinois) Mental Health Center and that the counselor wanted to set up a "more comprehensive program ... meaning that you would be going for appointments there much more often than once every three months."

On April 27, 1978, the Wisconsin attorney wrote John that he had received his recent letter which said he was having difficulties with the psychiatrist he had seen through the McHenry County Mental Health Center. His attorney asked that John let him know specifically what difficulties those were. The attorney also stated that if the McHenry group wasn't working that he had another avenue for John to try. John noted in red and blue pencil on a piece of brown paper bag put within this letter: "mental abuse: personal mental schedule were hindered; suffering: cannot control only personable drift(?); distress to not complete schedule as two years done."

In May of 1978 he tried to employ yet another attorney to file claims for his injuries in Arizona and one against his employer for injuries. John had actually given this new firm a retainer of $4,000 of which they returned $3,720, keeping $280 for the services they said they had "performed for you over a period of several months. My statement of fees and a release of all claims for your signature is attached." At least this attorney also seemed to be ethical.

Sometime in 1978 – as determined through a letter with a student number designation of 78-187003 and addressed to John in Hebron – John had decided to take a course on money investment. I can only guess that it had to do with losses that he had suffered when buying and selling stock through Paine Webber.

The Wisconsin attorney consistently wrote (remember that John had no phone) to encourage John to get the psychiatric treatment that he so obviously needed. John, however, did not think that he needed to do so. I am not sure if the attorney ever had conversations with my mother about John's condition, and I would imagine that client confidentiality wouldn't have allowed him to do so.

A May 25, 1978, letter to John from his attorney stated that an appointment had been set up (and he mentioned having discussed this with John in advance) with a psychiatrist in Lake Geneva. His attorney wrote, "I think he will be able to help us and I wish to stress how important that it is that you cooperate fully with him." He also told John that he would need a check sent to him in payment of the new doctor's deposit of $500.00. "If it turns out not that much is expended in visits, he will return the unused portion to you." He ended by saying that he would meet John to discuss things after his first visit to the Lake Geneva doctor.

On June 19, 1978, John signed an Agreement for Deed for his second piece of property in Sunshine Valley Ranchettes in Luna County, New Mexico. After probate in the State of New Mexico, he essentially broke even for the two Luna County properties.

Apparently John told his attorney that he had no need to see the new doctor because he was taking aspirins for his medical conditions, probably for the pain in his leg. A July 5, 1978 letter from the attorney said, "Again I cannot emphasize strongly enough how important I think it is that you keep all your appointments and also follow any medical prescriptions that he prescribes. I also cannot help but feel the taking of too many aspirins can have anything but a harmful affect upon you."

John bought his first piece of property in Missouri on November 11, 1978. For $2,333, he purchased "All of Block Forty-six (46) in Price and Gist's Addition to the City of Breckenridge, Missouri."

A letter from our mother dated March 24, 1978, had been sent inside an Easter card to a post office box in Hebron. She wrote, "Hope you got your ham eaten up before the warm weather comes, if you had to depend on your 'outdoor refrigerator.'" At that time, John was living in his tent outside Hebron and was obviously not socially interacting with any of us on the holidays (or any day for that matter, though I do recall meeting up with him at the "downtown" Hebron restaurant on one occasion).

December 9, 1978, marks the date John bought the property he was to live on and die on in Ethel, Missouri. John's house sat up the hill from Rt. 149, one of the main roads into town, at 111 Commercial, overlooking the post office.

December 20 (John's birthday) brings yet another letter from his attorney that spoke of yet more problems. The attorney did not understand the issues John was experiencing with the Hebron State Bank. He told John that he would have to come into the office to explain it and to call his secretary for an appointment.

Chapter 17

John's attorney continues to push him to get himself in for psychiatric treatment and to complete whatever program they prescribe for him. A February 1, 1979, letter stated that he was not pleased that John had not followed up with his psychiatric appointments and that the doctor said "that you would not take the prescribed medication that he wanted you to take and also that he felt it was necessary that you rent a room or apartment to live in." His attorney ended by stating that if he were to be of help to John at all it would be essential that he follow his doctor's orders.

On February 12, his attorney gave John his legal title opinion regarding the new Missouri property and deed. But on February 28, he is back to his advice regarding psychiatric treatment. He told John that he had spoken with the psychiatrist, who felt that John needed to resume treatments. He again asked John for a $500.00 deposit check and stated he would set up an appointment for John with the psychiatrist and would let him know the date.

In March of 1979, John hired yet another legal firm to try and get payment for the car he had sold back in January 1977. The contract stated that $900 be paid on or before January 1979. There's no further indication that John ever got paid. Or probably, he had already been paid and forgot that he had been paid.

John signed a contract for 10 acres of property in Van Horn, Texas, on April 4, 1979. It appeared that John made payments through the end of 1979, but no deed was found, so apparently he decided he did not want it badly enough to continue paying for it.

John continued to live in his tent in Hebron. His accommodations were a bit more elaborate than would normally be imagined for such a living environment. He actually had several tents because he had kept quite a few belongings – belongings that he did not entrust any of us to house for him.

John traveled by foot around McHenry County since he no longer had his drivers license. His hair was long, but not unkempt. His clothes never appeared to be too dirty. He must have figured out a way to keep himself relatively clean within his camp. But then, he had learned to get by with so little while in Vietnam.

John showed up at our Hampshire home sometime during late 1979 or early 1980. I have a vague memory of him having dinner with us during this visit. I was remarried and part of a blended family with three very young children. I recall that John would not sleep in an upstairs bedroom on a bed. He insisted on sleeping in one of the downstairs rooms on the floor. It also seems that he was gone by the time we got up the next morning. So long ago, and so hard to remember.

His Wisconsin attorney continues pleading with John to seek treatment in January of 1980. He wrote that it was absolutely necessary for John to get in to see the psychiatrist and follow recommendations. He stated that the doctor he had recommended had now left the area, but he would help John get in touch with a different psychiatrist if he chose to seek treatment.

Because of the way John lived and his mannerisms, there were many people who shied away from him. And then there were those who knew no better than to make fun of the mentally ill.

Our father visited me during the summer of 1980, and he requested that I take him to see John as he had not seen him for quite a long while. I told him that I did not know where John's camp was actually located, but that we could go inquire about him at the little restaurant in Hebron that John frequented. I surmised that there would be people there who might be able to send us in the right direction. After I had asked the person working at the counter about John, I heard several people sitting further down talking and snickering about John. I simply said loudly, "He's my brother!" They shut up. Unfortunately for our father, and for me as well, we did not find John that day.

I found a contract dated September 3, 1980, for ten acres of the "subdivided Old Wolf Creek Ranch" in Texas. It was unsigned.

Possibly the contract remained unsigned because John had admitted himself into St. Joseph Hospital's psychiatric ward in Elgin on September 4, 1980. On the admission form, he lists his emergency contacts as his Wisconsin attorney and another attorney from Woodstock. He signed off on the following goals for September 9 to 11: "Determine readiness for hospital testing schedule." His plan: "active to reasonable dispatch of and to testing procedures." I believe that he admitted himself for testing in order to comply with his attorney's demands that he get treatment if he wanted any of his legal actions pursued, including his Workmen's Comp suit.

During his St. Joseph's stay, he was treated by a doctor from Crystal Lake; he was billed for three sessions. A statement from St. Joseph Hospital indicates that John was kept as an inpatient from September 4-18.

During his two week's stay, I went with my mother to visit him. I distinctly remember how uncomfortable I was when they locked the door behind us as we entered the psychiatric unit's common area. When we sat and chatted with John at a small table, though, I remember being so very happy to see such an improvement in his behavior. He was actually able to carry on a "normal" conversation. He shared a goofy little art project he had made in an art therapy session. We were able to talk and laugh. It was undoubtedly the last time we could really do so because he most certainly did not stay on any medications once he checked himself out and went back to his world of living in his tent and working at the meat packing plant. (I still cannot even imagine him working there and doing such a job. Even though he had put in a full year of at-times very menial KP duty in Vietnam, he still had to be a total misfit.)

A bill from Memorial Hospital in Woodstock from October 7, 1980, indicates "healing laceration right index finger." Obviously, he had again hurt himself at work.

Additionally, it appeared he wanted to file a grievance about the Wisconsin attorney for not moving forward with any legal actions on his behalf. Another Illinois attorney sent him a pamphlet with Wisconsin grievance information. An October 14 letter from that firm stated that they had received a letter from John's former attorney which said he had contacted "St. Joseph's Hospital to obtain records of your treatment and was advised that no such records exist. To help your case, I would suggest that you contact St. Joseph's Hospital directly [to get release of your records]."

John was directed to see a doctor in Rockford in order to comply with Workmen's Comp provisions. He made visits to this doctor between and including the dates of October 23, 1980, and January 12, 1981. I have no idea how he found transportation for those visits.

Early in 1981, documents began to arrive for John at his Ethel, Missouri, address. It seems that between 1981 and 1983, he resided there part of the time, while traveling to and from many states.

On February 17, 1981, John's Wisconsin attorney formally ended his services to John. "Due to your lack of repeatedly ignoring my instructions and because of your repeated lack of giving me information that I need, it will no longer be possible for me to act as your attorney." He completed his letter by stating if John hired a new attorney he would forward John's information as requested.

Within a month, John attempts to retaliate against the attorney's decision through the Supreme Court of Wisconsin. They responded to him on March 31 asking that more information be submitted within 30 days. No other correspondence was found from the Supreme Court of Wisconsin.

In the summer of 1981, John purchased yet another piece of property. This newest purchase was in Grand Bahama, Bahamas; the cover from Conveyance from the Commonwealth of the Bahamas dated July 1, 1981.

The property must have been purchased site unseen because he did not travel to the Bahamas until December 21, 1982, returning on December 27. At that time, he gave his return address as that of our mother's in Marengo. It would be interesting to know whether he went there in 1982 expecting to find a place where he could live and finding instead that it was virtually uninhabitable.

I found out when settling his estate that it would cost me more to pay fines for late taxes and for legal fees in the Bahamas than the property would probably be worth. So, I let it go.

My own family had to move out of our farm place in Hampshire in early 1980 during the dead of winter when the owner decided to sell the property. Sometime during the following summer of 1981, John came walking up to our new home in Woodstock. He had walked from Hebron, which is about a 15 mile distance. I do not know whether he was lucky enough to still hitch rides at that time.

John brought me some iris rhizomes, which I planted immediately. I have to say that they were my favorite of all the irises I have ever grown – dark purple with the most magnificent sweet grape smell. When we moved yet again, after our house burned, I dug some and took them with me. Sadly, they didn't make it over the years, and I still miss that wonderful grapey fragrance and the deep purple color. I do not know where John got the irises, but I thought it a beautiful gesture that he brought them to me. When we cleaned out his house in Missouri, I made sure to dig some clumps of the irises that were there. I had hoped they were of the same variety, but they were not. Nonetheless, I still have a clump from Ethel as a remembrance of him and of those earlier wonderfully fragrant irises.

On July 7, 1981, for Workmen's Comp, an Emergency Medical Record for Memorial Hospital for McHenry County in Woodstock had been generated. It noted John's ankle injury.

John sent a postcard to our mother in November 1981 from San Diego. He wrote, "Realized holiday, cleared doctors at VA. I enjoyed dinner for Thanksgiving – busy here in San Diego with futures, medicals & reference jobs."

Amongst John's belongings, I discovered a very strange memo dated November 30, 1981, on a form that came from Watkins-Johnson Company in Gaithersburg, MD. He had signed it: John C. Yarbrough Jr., and he had stapled this to a notice of a Coolfont Camping Weekend in Berkley Springs, West Virginia.

Another postcard from John to our mother was sent from San Diego in December 1981.

> Costing me a fortune waiting for VA – should find a job as payment comp is waited proofs at hotel and eat out, tour 10 paintings in room.
> John

And yet another postcard was sent on December 20, 1981 (his birthday) to our mother, postmarked in San Diego simply saying, "Merry Christmas & Happy New Year."

I could not identify the name of the hospital that generated the diagnosis sheet dated January 4, 1982, documenting the following information. It would seem logical to presume that it was from the Veterans Hospital in San Diego, since John had remarked about it on that earlier postcard.

> "5 years ago R. foot and ankle 'broken apart' when work platform (on which he was working) cable broke and fell. No surgery. Cast x4 mos. Intermittent pain since. Hospitalized on January 1980. Rt. Foot pain at St. Joseph's Hospital Elgin, Ill. Told his foot was 'ruined. They wouldn't do anything for me.' Has also seen a psychiatrist for the pain."

> Their medical certificate states that he told them:
> "Nov., 1980 called VAH San Diego re his pain and was told they would help him. States he was there 4 weeks, had x-rays, but did not see a doctor. Has a return appointment to ortho clinic there April 2, 1982. Unable to afford to stay in Calif. Moved to his home at Ethel, MO. States the pain 'fatigues and exhausts me' when on his feet 'things get darker.' Foot swells at times. Meds – 0 (Psychiatrist told him not to take any meds)."

After all this time – since he first contacted the Supreme Court in Wisconsin on March 31, 1981 – he received a letter dated January 14, 1982, from an Illinois attorney. It would indicate to me, since another letter was not found dated between those two dates, that the following information had been conveyed to him via phone.

> Dear Mr. Wolff:
> Thank you for your letter dated January 2, 1982. As I stated to you earlier, I am not able to take any action against [your former attorney] because he is located in the State of Wisconsin, and I have a license to practice law only in the State of Illinois. Accordingly, I cannot help you any further on this matter. A copy of my statement for services previously rendered is enclosed.
> (Bill was for $90.00 for one conference, 2 phone calls, 4 letters.)

It would appear that from San Diego, John either headed home and then on to Florida, or that he went directly from San Diego to Florida. Since he was not driving at that time, I can only guess that he hitchhiked or maybe caught a bus.

On January 23, 1982, he sent a postcard to our mother from Marianna, Florida. He cryptically wrote:

> Warm here – my feet demands arranged finance off empl. Costs are higher in tax level and devise to visit dad & to Bahamas. John

Then, an undated postcard was sent to our mother from Birmingham, Alabama. Even though it has no date, it would make sense that it was sent during his return trip from Florida and the Bahamas. John simply said:

Delayed in journey my feet froze in cold snap. I telephoned
no report for returning yet. John

John apparently contributed to the Republican party since he had
received a Republican National Committee 1982 Sustaining Member card.
Additionally, I found a receipt from the Amalgamated Meat Cutters and
Butcher Workmen of N.A., affiliated with AFL-CIO. This was for his
February 1982 United Food & Commercial Workers International Union
card.

A portion of the letter our mother wrote to John in Ethel on February
19, 1982, follows. After he received this letter, my mother received various
postcards, which John perhaps collected as he traveled, since some of the
dates postmarked do not coincide with him being in those particular places
on those particular dates. Our mother wrote:

Dear John,
John, would you do something for me? Would you send a
postcard once a week to let me know you're okay? Better
yet, couldn't you have a phone put in, so I could call you
now and then? You're really cut off from everyone out there
[Ethel is in very rural Missouri]. Another thing I wonder
about is whether you have a card in your wallet that states
who to call in case of emergency, if something should
happen to you, especially when you are hitchhiking. It's just
a good idea. Hope you think so, too.

[Our stepdad had helped John move there, so he and my
mother knew the remoteness of John's house and that there
was really nothing available to him locally.]

Hope that you can find something [work] around there,
somewhere. If you can't, maybe you'll have to take your old
job back in Hebron. Couldn't you get a driver's license in
Missouri and get a car so you could get around? Illinois

couldn't hold anything against you after all these years. If
you applied for a license there, and they knew you haven't
driven for 8 years, or how many, I don't think they'd have
many questions, do you think they would?
[I think they would have had many questions.]
With Love, Mother

A March 9, 1982, letter from a Woodstock attorney was sent to John
at his Ethel address. John's move had complicated matters in trying to work
out possible legal angles through any of his former Illinois attorneys.

Dear Mr. Wolff:
This will respond to the letter which you mailed me from
Ethel, Missouri on February 16, 1982, regarding your bank
account in Birmingham.

I am interested to hear from you, and I am surprised to learn
that you are in Missouri. Have you left Hebron, Illinois,
permanently?

Even if I were to act as your attorney in such a matter, I
could not represent you by closing out a bank account in
Birmingham, Alabama, since I do not have the pass-book
which constitutes the necessary authority in dealing with the
bank in addition to some authorization from you
communicated to the bank.

On March 12, 1982, a Voters Registration card for Ethel Precinct,
White Township, Macon County, Missouri, indicates that John had registered
to vote in an upcoming election. It would be interesting to know if he had
actually voted after obtaining his registration card.
    Our mother wrote to John on March 13, 1982, in part, as follows:

Ralph [our step-dad] talked to [your attorney] and he told

Ralph that the money you paid had been used up in the process of buying your properties in Missouri and trying to do something for you in the suit in Arizona for your injuries. Better send your money, it seems useless to try to get any compensation for that injury. It was a long time ago [1974], too, and that makes it more difficult.

I'm not sure yet, just why you moved away from Hebron. Did anyone really ask or demand that you move? If that is the case, the chief of police in Hebron knows nothing about it. [The Chief]... told Ralph that you could come back anytime and live in your tent. If there was a problem where you were located, maybe he could tell you of another location. Wouldn't be as handy to work as the one you had, probably, but maybe not too far away. You did say, I think, that you could go back to work for Kenosha Beef if you came back here.

Thanks for keeping in touch, John. I feel better when I hear from you.
With Love, Mother

The following postcard was not date stamped, but I can only surmise that it was sent when John was fairly new to his Ethel residence. The postcard itself declares, "Greetings from Missouri." John wrote as follows:

Spencer's Decorating
Trade & Jobs are on indifference with my position – the checks are worn & dirty – write a new one as I thanked you for the gift. I'm starving & can't find my money – I've no payment!

A letter arrived, dated March 23, 1982, from First Interstate Bank, Albuquerque, New Mexico, to John in Ethel:

Dear Mr. Wolff:

This letter is being written to inform you that our Trust Department did receive the letter which you sent (copy enclosed) relating to the disposition of the proceeds of some collections items. The Trust Department turned over the documents to the audit Department as we are unable to ascertain exactly what your intent of mailing the documents to us was. Please be advised that we did receive the information request about trust, the shipping receipts, and a savings deposit slip, however no currency nor other financial instruments were received. If you should have any questions regarding this matter, please feel free to contact me.

Sincerely,

General Auditor

John must have initially had plans to fix up the house on the Breckenridge, Missouri, property he had purchased back in 1978. On March 26, 1982, a letter to John from the City of Breckenridge let him know that there are "no special building codes in our little town so you would not need a permit." They referenced that John had written them for a "permit to reconstruct [his] house in Breckenridge." Tax records indicate that that property was 2-1/2 acres, consisting of 6 lots.

In July 1982, John sent the City of Breckenridge Tax Collector a check for $25.00 for 1981 taxes, explaining taxes were late because, "I've been months in the hospital since Nov. 1981 and am – disabled. My moving displaced papers and tax statements." They responded they were sending his check back because taxes were $3.52, with a penalty of $0.28. (None of John's medical records would put him in the hospital immediately after November 1981; I am not sure if he was staying with our mother at that time, or if he was still living in Hebron.)

John tried to sell the Breckenridge property; a listing agreement was signed on June 11, 1985. However, John did not sell this property until much, much later. There is a copy of a General Warranty Deed dated June 17, 1999 detailing sale from John to "Teddy Joe Gardner and Ruth Ann Gardner, husband and wife, of the County of Caldwell in the:

> Party of the First Part, in consideration of the sum of Ten Dollars and other good and valuable considerations to him paid by the said Parties of the Second Part, the receipt of which is hereby acknowledged, does by these presents, Grant, Bargain and Sell, Convey and Confirm unto the Parties of the Second Part, their heirs and assigns, the following described Lots, Tracts or Parcels of Land, lying, being and situate in the County of Caldwell and State of Missouri, to-wit: All of Block Forty-six (46) in Price and Gist's Addition to the City of Breckenridge, Missouri, Caldwell County, Missouri.

Now, why in the world would John sell his property for $10.00 when he paid $2,333.00? And, what in the world was the "other good and valuable considerations to him paid by the Said Parties of the Second Part?" My brother had no friends, so I can't imagine a bartering deal taking place. That was my first reaction. Subsequently, I learned that the use of "sum of Ten Dollars and other good and valuable considerations" is standard language on many if not most deeds.

Yet another postcard to our mother was postmarked in Knoxville, Tennessee. It had a date stamp from 1982 in which the month and day could not be read. The postcard touted the 1982 World's Fair, held from May 1 through October 31, 1982, in Knoxville. John wrote:

> "Slow travel to woods from metro Florida – fair site 3-1/2 block area west of river. Card late Atlanta the stamps weren't available & I was busy."

Our father sent John a "Happy Easter Son" card on April 5, 1982 (our dad was remarried and living in Florida at that time). All he wrote on this card to John was, "Hope you are well as we are. Theresa, John" Odd that he did not sign the card as "Dad," although, as I recall, he signed some of his cards to me with "John" as well.

Apparently John had ultimately decided to fix up the property in Ethel, Missouri, instead of the property in Breckenridge, Missouri. An April 14, 1982, letter from the City of Ethel follows.

> Dear Mr. Wolff:
> The City of Ethel does not have any building codes to abide by when renovating or constructing buildings. The only thing we do have on record is an ordinance that when a building becomes hazardous to the public, we request the owner to correct the situation. Feel free to repair your home in any fashion you feel necessary.
> Thank you, City Clerk

John filed a Small Claim Complaint in McHenry County against the Wisconsin attorney for failure to provide representation for fees paid to him by John. The Complaint was dated April 16, 1982. The attorney apparently filed a motion on the same date to dismiss the case because he was in Wisconsin, while John was in Missouri, thus no jurisdiction in Illinois. This information appeared within a copy of a Notice to People Acting as Their Own Attorneys from McHenry County, Illinois. Afterwards, the attorney sent this curt, final statement to John.

> Dear Mr. Wolff:
> I am herewith returning all of your documents. As I stated many times, I am no longer willing to represent you in any matters. Any documents, etc. you send me in the future will be thrown away.

I discovered the following information found within a document dated April 29, 1982, from the Harry S. Truman Memorial Veterans Hospital in Columbia, Missouri:

- John had requested all previous VA medical records.
- On December 22, 1981, John was seen for pain in foot and ankle "and told he would be scheduled for corrective foot surgery. Received appt. for ortho clinic 4/2/82 and 'states he cannot wait that long.' App agitated and angry."
- Notes Lx fx R. foot/ankle 1974. "Pt. states he is in constant
- pain and needs surgery. Able to walk from bus stop into hospital without difficulty. 'Disabled now.'"

The photos taken of my brother John at our Grandpa Rinne's 95th birthday party on September 14, 1982, are not flattering. They clearly portray the inexorable decline inherent in untreated schizophrenia, the flat effect that so often accompanies it. According to Dr. Mark Moronell on the Sharecare web site:

Flat affect, which is also called blunted affect, is one of the negative symptoms of schizophrenia. A person with negative symptoms lacks a normal range of feelings and behaviors. The word 'affect' means one's emotional state. To have a flat, or blunt affect means that a person appears to lack any emotion at all. People with schizophrenia often show flat affect, and they do not smile, frown, grimace, or make any emotional expressions with their face. Even when others are laughing, or very upset, a person with schizophrenia may maintain a flat appearance. In addition to a flat affect, people with schizophrenia might speak in a flat tone of voice as well. Their voices do not show the normal emotional range that most people display. Rather, they speak in a monotone.

I did not attend this party, so I have no first-hand knowledge of John's behavior or whether he was able to – or did – communicate with anyone. I don't recall our mother commenting on any particular issues. It's clear from a group photo at this event that he made sure to keep a certain distance from everyone else in the picture, standing way off to the right of all relatives.

I am guessing that he had spent some time with our mother in Marengo, Illinois, before returning to Ethel. A November 18 postcard arrived, which said,

> Mr. & Mrs. Spencer [apparently, she was no longer "Mother"],
> My bus trip was as traveling directly to trauma. I may walk back. Frost already stopped my fall transplant of trees. I should demise leaving destruction.
> John

The following card, on which there is no postmark at all, would seem to follow the one above:

> Ralph and Marie Spencer
> Merry Christmas. Please deliver package.
> [Was that a "funny remark" or a "demand?" No one would ever know.]

Chapter 18

A Western Union Mailgram from John (in Marengo) to the IRS in St. Joseph, Missouri, was dated January 24, 1983. The mailgram concerned John's taxes filed for the year 1981.

> Contact by telephone was impossible number 815-xxx-xxxx [our mother's phone number] John C. Wolff Jr. re December 28th 1982 appointment to Internal Revenue Service 120 West Missouri Kirksville MO stop Mail was received late and I'm disabled at temporary address 312 West Prairie Marengo IL 60152.

Apparently, the IRS had disallowed a number of deductions John was claiming, and he wrote back to them much later, on December 17.

> All of my forms for deductions were OK for a refund in 1981. The IRS computed my taxes. I want the chief taxpayer to adjudicate billing taxes to me for 1981 year and any other previous years. I've not worked since 1980 because doctors advised me disabled to not work. John C. Wolff, Jr.

No date, but obviously tied into the dispute above, John wrote the following letter to the Republican National Committee in Washington, DC.

> I paid 6000 by money order check this week to your office.

> [I certainly hope that John did not actually give the Republican National Committee $6000!]

I want the Republican principle to advise me concerning unauthorized (billing taxes on and interest) taxes checking IRS vouched and computed credit as copy enclosed with this mailing proves <u>no other taxes due for 1981</u>. John C. Wolff Jr.

Another brief document, I don't know to whom it was meant, found along with this "mess" reads:

I have a crime again.

Mother Marie Spencer suggested several times that I should contact you. I did pay my Federal income tax, but have a problem with the check paid to IRS and H&R Block noted that I need attorney for a reclaim which the H&R Block representative agreed to prepare.

A letter about John's Workmen's Comp (now Workers Comp) dated March 10, 1983, from the State of Illinois Supreme Court Clerk arrived. As his friend Warren had stated about a younger John, he surely didn't back down from fights. He went all the way to the Supreme Court with his complaints and allegations.

Dear Mr. Wolff:
Our office has received your letter of February 22, 1983, concerning your Workmen's Compensation claim. As you may know, your claim is not pending in the Supreme Court. If you are having difficulty claiming compensation, perhaps you should bring the matter to the attention of your lawyer or to the attention of the Circuit Clerk.
Very truly yours,
Clerk of the Supreme Court

On August 9, 1983, he finally received a response to a February inquiry regarding disability from the Department of Health and Human Services in Baltimore, Maryland.

Dear Mr. Wolff:

This is in response to your inquiry of February 9, 1983.It has been established that you became disabled as of November 17, 1981, and your date of entitlement to disability benefits is May 1982. At the present time, we have no claims for any incorrect payments made to you.

Any questions concerning income taxes should be referred to the Internal Revenue Service.

Sincerely yours,

Director

Office of Disability Operations

I am sure that John was elated on September 16, 1983, to finally receive a settlement from his Workmen's Comp claim from the meat packing plant in Hebron, Illinois:

"Approved" Settlement Contract from the State of Illinois Industrial Commission

John C. Wolff Jr. vs. Kenosha Beef International in Hebron

Lump sum of $5,425.00 for 35% loss of use of the right foot

Disabled August 22, 1975 to February 22, 1976; 26 and 4/7 weeks

Petitioner fell 5 ft. from wash stand

John's path of injuries continued with burning his eyes on November 11 at his home in Ethel. An Emergency Room bill from Samaritan Memorial in Macon, Missouri, included charges for eye pads and documentation indicated burning in both eyes. "Pt. states he was stoking his wood furnace earlier today and now he cannot open his eyes due to pain. Pt. states he is legally blind in Lt. Eye."

> Our mother wrote to John on November 26.
> Dear John,
> How come you don't let us know whether or not everything is okay? Have been wondering if your eyes healed up all right.
>
> Were you able to get to a restaurant for dinner on Thanksgiving Day? Probably hard to find one open. Wish you were closer, so we could invite you. Are you going to be in your home at Christmas time, or will you be gone somewhere else?
>
> Did you get your mail from the Post Office? I wrote a letter right after you got out of the hospital and was expecting a response.
>
> Are you keeping warm? Hope you've been able to get some coal or wood. There has to be wood for sale around there, somewhere, I would think.
>
> Anyway, I hope you are okay. That your eyes healed, and you have food and are warm.
> God bless you, John!
> With Love,
> Mother

On November 29, 1983, I wrote to John, with a plea that he try to get some help through a new grassroots organization called VietNow. At that particular time, I was convinced that John's psychological problems, at least in part, had developed because of exposure to Agent Orange.

Dear John,

Please read the booklet I'm enclosing and see if it makes sense to you. I know all of your problems started after you came home from Vietnam. I've been doing a lot of reading on just what Agent Orange did to all of you guys over there, and I think that could be what happened to you.

At any rate, I'm looking into if the government is going to compensate the guys that were over there and were sprayed with all that stuff and who now have health and psychological problems. I went to a meeting last night of an organization called VietNow in Woodstock. They had some of our wonderful government people there to see if they could get much information out of them.

There is a giant court case pending that should come up in May – the Vietnam veterans suing Dow chemical who manufactured Agent Orange. If you want to get in on that, I guess the charge for the legal fees is only $350 and you don't have to pay that all at once.

This VietNow group also has regular meetings and what they call rap sessions of all the veterans in the area. The guys that I talked to there have been helped tremendously by it. They had all become pretty much loners, too, and felt like no one cared or understood them or what they felt like. They also have psychologists that help them (they are also veterans). This is all done for no charge. There is a $15 yearly membership fee, but they'll even forget about that if someone doesn't have the money.

If you're interested in any of this, I can send you more information, or give me a call collect. Maybe you should come back for a visit again. I'm sure Mother would like to see you again – and so would we.

Love,

Mary

P.S. The envelope is from where I work.

I found the envelope noted in my postscript above, along with the Agent Orange booklet, among John's things. He had never gotten back to me about any of it.

In December, John had sent a Christmas card to our dad in Florida, which was returned to him for insufficient address. The card itself he had signed, "John C. Wolff Jr.;" the card contained a postcard from Wallace State Park in Cameron, Missouri, on which John had written:

Haven't accomplished much building yet being disabled. I'm not slept out though after 2 years rest – Have nice holiday season. Veterans Administration afforded me finance: disabled.

John

John received a December 16, 1983, letter from a Phoenix, Arizona, attorney.

Dear Mr. Wolff:

This letter is in response to your December 8, 1983, letter to my office and your request for a determination of whether or not a lawsuit has been filed in the name of John C. Wolff, Jr.

against either the State of Arizona or the City of Phoenix. When you contacted the Maricopa County Lawyer Referral Service, the $15 fee charged by them was for the purpose of your obtaining a consultation from my office at no additional charge. This fee did not include drafting of documents or research outside of the office.

I have, however, as a courtesy to an out-of-state resident, determined that the records of the Maricopa County Superior Court clerk do not contain the name of any lawsuit by John C. Wolff, Jr., against either the State of Arizona or the City of Phoenix during the period of January 1, 1979, through December 2, 1983.

I hope that this answers your questions.

A postcard arrived at our mother's dated January 5, 1984. It was from John and was postmarked in Los Angeles, California. There was no message, though the postcard was printed with a story about early Southern Pacific trains, with no clue as to why he was again in California.

On January 21, 1984, at exactly 5:53 p.m. EST, our stepdad sent a Western Union Mailgram for John, as follows. I am sure the recipient must have thought it was some kind of a joke, and one might wonder why our stepdad agreed to send it.

Law Offices
1005 North 2 Street
Phoenix, AZ 85004

Actually the attitude to the subject reported and pending case of John C. Wolff Jr. vs State of Arizona, City of Phoenix, do not correspond the object that have determined.

My paid attorney worked again for two weeks in Phoenix Arizona for prescription of case suit and prompt payment of settlement for $8,000,000 United States currency.

Determined for the trust of John C. Wolff Jr. So no other contact with your office by myself will be necessary.

John C. Wolff Jr.

John completed an Application for Hearing, Worker's Compensation Act Form, plus letter to an office in Kenosha, Wisconsin, and dated it January 23, 1984. Once again, I am sure the recipient had an extremely difficult time knowing what to make of it.

Because my mail is disrupted, I'm not certain of my rights of appeals for more compensation although I telephoned again Industrial Commission office in Chicago and replied appeal; the fifteen day notice has not occurred for me.

The contract of GLUG master policy Mutual of Omaha.
X insurance permanently disabled income
X continual insured coverage
X fulfillment of consignments

Therefore subscripting Industrial Dept. of Labor State of Wisconsin have been contacted by myself for assurance that my permanent disability claims accords settlement.

[And further …]
Case suit for weekly benefits and continued insurance, insured subject accidental injuries now determined permanent disablements.

- petitioner seeks all other compensations for claims accorded GLUG master Mutual of Omaha policy and settlements for accrued sums previously requested for order of subscription affording John C. Wolff Jr. plaintiff John C. Wolff Jr. vs. Kenosha Packing Company now Kenosha Beef International for respondance order also/entered by [his Wisconsin attorney] for five million dollars United States currency to devise settlement and prompt payment inasmuch for the plaintiff John C. Wolff Jr. now permanently disabled.

I have mailed four petitions to Workers Compensation Division P.O. Box 7901 Madison, Wisconsin 53707 since December 18, 1983 – two of the petition copies you have received.

1 copy of DISHRWC7R 12/79 application for hearing.
3 copies proof of doctors opinions
1 copy referral service notice for rights to cancel
3 copies confirming respondance for hearing
1 copy letter to reference

Our mother wrote to John once again on February 21, 1984. A few paragraphs appear below. This must have been in response to a note from John in which he was angry at all of his family, or she may have gotten one of his sporadic phone calls expressing his anger. Or else she wrote it because he was withholding any kind of information about his well-being or whereabouts. Sadly, our fervent pleas for information were always disregarded.

Dear John,
We have been waiting to hear from you to let us know when you got there. Hope you had a good trip back.

I am sorry, John, that you didn't wake me before you left. Never know when we see each other again, and I am sorry that you have been so angry with us. John, we certainly are not using you for any financial gain. It probably won't do any good to write it, but we do <u>care about you</u>.

I was going to tell you when you left to "go with God, because He is the only one who can help you." He uses other people to help us, but I guess sometimes it's up to us to find those people. Mary [me, John's sister] said the VA Hospital in Milwaukee is better than most, so maybe that's where you should go. You need to get your health back. You can't go on the way you are.

Do let us hear from you, John. We <u>do care about you</u>!
With Love,
Mother

The Office of Disability Operations in Baltimore, Maryland, sent a letter to John on March 12, 1984: "It has been determined that the lump sum award of $5,425.00 paid to you as a result of the injury to your foot will not cause any adjustment in your disability benefits." The letter goes on to say if there is any other kind of award or settlement, it very well could affect disability benefits.

Once again I reached out to John in a very short letter dated April 6, 1984.

Dear John,
Are you staying warm? It got mighty cold again!

I was going to tell you before you left that I found out that the VA hospital in Milwaukee is supposed to be really good

at working with Vietnam vets. So, if you get sick and have to
go in again, it might be a good thing to look at.
Love,
Mary

On April 6, 1984, my mother wrote to John from The Oasis in Tilly,
Arkansas. While there trying to discover just exactly what her illness was
(she had been experiencing decline for at least two years prior), she found the
horrible diagnosis to be amyotrophic lateral sclerosis (ALS, or Lou Gehrig's
Disease). She wondered in the letter whether Ralph (our stepdad) when
returning to Illinois "went around your way. He said he might, but we had
talked of doing that when I am ready to go home, if I'm able to, which I
certainly hope to be."

John received a Health Insurance card – Social Security Act,
Medicare Health Insurance, Health Care Financing Administration, Hospital
Part A, Medical Part B, dated May 1, 1984. I was very thankful that he was
able to get these services established. Under the circumstances of his illness,
I am amazed that he managed to do so.

My mother wrote to John on May 13, 1985, to let him know about
our Uncle Bill's death (one of our very favorite uncles). More than that, she
wanted to let him know about her own illness and the fact that it was
incurable.

Dear John,
This will be short, but I want you to know that your Uncle
Bill died last Friday, May 10th. Klarice [our cousin] found
him lying dead, in the barn. The funeral is tomorrow and I
am unable to be there. My condition is much worse than
when you were here. It is really a terrible feeling not to be
able to be with my father and brothers and sisters at this
time.

John, I hope you will be able to come and see me sometime, yet. Except for a miracle, there isn't much hope for me to get better. Went to a neurologist in Iowa and he said I don't have multiple sclerosis, but that it's Lou Gehrig's disease, which is worse than MS. It would be good to see you.

Write sometime, John. We care a lot about you, and know that God loves you.
With Love, Mother

Very surprisingly, I found a Warrant for Arrest – Macon County, MO, dated May 14, 1985, for Trespass in the Second Degree. Note the luckily minimal punishment for said act.

In violation of Section 569.150, RSMO, committed the infraction of trespass in the second degree, punishable upon conviction under Section S60.016, RSMO, in that on May 5, 1985, in the County of Macon, State of Missouri, the defendant entered unlawfully upon real property owned by Bill St. Clair and located south of Elm Street in Ethel, Missouri.
Signed by the Honorable William E. Neff

Court charges of $95.45
Received 1 year Unsupervised Probation
Imposition of sentence suspended for two years on condition of good behavior, no trespassing on other people's property.

John FINALLY called our mother, and I know she was elated. Her June 3, 1985 letter indicated so, and she very much desired that he visit her again.

Dear John,

We were so glad you called, and hope that everything turned out alright for you concerning the trees. Perhaps it would be a good idea to find someone who can tell you where your lot lines are, so you don't have any further problems.

I hope you will be able to come for a visit. Would be nice to see you again. If you can't then do call again. If you don't have money, call collect, but call like you did last time, when rates are cheapest.

Will end this for now, hoping that everything has turned out well for you. Was the Social Security reinstated? Let us know how you are doing.

With Love,

Mother

I would believe that the following contact was initiated in order to maintain his disability status. John received this letter in June 1985.

Psychiatric Services in Columbia, MO

Dear Mr. Wolff:

Enclosed please find an appointment card from Dr. Tom R. Anderson.

I have set your appointment for Tuesday, June 18th at 1:00 p.m.

If this is not satisfactory, please let me know.

Also, I am returning the $2.00 which was enclosed with your letter. There is no charge for setting appointments.

Thank you,

Services Secretary

I know that I had written to John asking if I could visit him in Ethel because I wanted to talk to him about our mother's condition and hopefully talk him into coming back with me to visit. I knew that my mother desperately wanted to see John again before she died. I included these paragraphs within the following letter of July 1, 1985, after no response to my previous request to visit him in Missouri:

> Dear John,
> I couldn't tell from your last note whether you wanted me to visit or not. I took it that you didn't.
>
> I'm wondering whether you're going to come and visit Mother this summer. Next summer she may not even be able to talk to you. The disease she has ends up where she's totally paralyzed and can't even speak. So, if you can make it, it would be nice because she'd surely like to see you.
>
> Hope you're doing OK. You must be keeping yourself busy working on your house.
> Take care.
> Love, Mary

I found a receipt from Reed's Furniture in Macon, Missouri, dated October 3, 1985, for the purchase of "6 pc. Wood group" (this must have been the sofa and chairs that we found in John's living room after his murder) and "Mirror, Table with 4 chairs" (which ding set I used for a number of years following our rescue of his belongings).

I was happy to find artwork that John had produced in Ethel in 1986. The bulk of what I found, though, were architectural drawings of house construction/repairs. These were pencil sketches of masonry/foundation, an electrical plan, a plumbing plan for bathroom, along with materials lists showing dimensions.

I additionally have several large, 22" x 28" poster size, pencil sketches dated 1986 that I think are quite good. (The investigators pointed them out to me because they had carefully laid them out when discovered in John's home.) These drawings are in the same style of some I found at the the Intuit Show of Folk & Outsider Art exhibit in Chicago in November 2010. Those were drawn by Charles Steffen, a Chicago native, who I found out had also suffered from schizophrenia.

I added these drawings to a large collection that my son discovered in a strangely configured "room" off the Ethel house, which John had obviously built. The investigators had not even gone through that room since it appeared to not have been entered during the night of John's murder. Indeed, it would have been very strange for the two men to have gone into an area so dark and uninviting, one that literally looked like a full-blown booby trap. The drawings my son found there encompassed John's work from back in Hebron in the 1970s to a year or so before his death.

One of the more astounding things that I found in John's house was a musical composition – dated 1986 and entitled "Star Wars Four" – which he had carefully stored in a plastic bag inside a suitcase packed with his best clothes. Some "notes" are written on music composition sheets, with others "composed" on regular graph paper. Some are originals; some are carbon copies. Separate sheets are marked: Pipe, string, drum. One is marked "thesis," and the markings are not even note-like. One is marked "voice," and, again, markings are not note-like. I know that we had relatives several generations back who were musically oriented, but to my knowledge, John had no musical training whatsoever. I'm guessing that it was the form of the musical notes themselves that appealed to his schizophrenic mind.

Our mother wrote to John again on January 11, 1986, inquiring most of all about when she might hear from him.

Dear John,
Time for a short letter again. I keep waiting to hear from you. We do wonder if you are okay or not, you know.

Did you enjoy your little Christmas tree? I was going to get you some lights that operate by battery, but didn't get the order off and didn't find any in the store. [We found this Christmas tree sitting on a table when we cleared his house out.]

]She goes on to talk about dividing and disbursing her things in preparation for her death, which came about a year later.] She ends with:

Don't have much to write about, just want you to know I think of you. Hope you are doing alright. Please do write, or call. God bless you, John!
With Love,
Mother

Our mother pleads again the following month for John to once again use postcards to keep in touch.

Dear John,
Happy Valentine's Day!
We are still waiting to hear from you. Why don't you at least send a postcard? They have them at the post office [maybe not in Ethel?]. Sure would be good to know if you're alright or not.

Do hope you are getting along okay and are keeping warm.
With Love, Mother

I found a letter from our mother to John dated August 18, 1986. This would be the last letter that she wrote to him, I'm guessing, because it became extremely difficult for her to use her arm and finger muscles to write.

Or, perhaps this was just the last letter from her that he kept.

> Dear John,
> Just a short letter to let you know I am thinking of you, like I do about every day at some time or other. And as always, hoping you are doing okay.
>
> How did you manage to keep cool on those hot, humid days? I thought of you, without electricity to run even a small fan. Have you ever thought about getting a generator to use for a few hours when needed? [We found that he had one.] I know you've got good light with your Coleman lantern.
>
> Sharon [our brother Jim's wife] and Mary [me, his sister] keep me supplied with nice fresh vegetables.
>
> I decided not to save the encyclopedia, unless you let me know that you want the set. If I don't hear from you by Oct. 1st, I'll get rid of them. If none of the other kids want them, I'll sell them.
>
> Sure do hope to hear from you soon, and do hope you're getting along alright.
>
> God bless you and keep you in His care every day.
> With Love,
> Mother

My stepdad left a message at the Ethel Post Office when our mother died. The original message was in with John's belongings I sorted through. "John Wolff, Jr. You had a call at the Ethel Post Office Saturday. Your mother died 01-31 at 1 AM. Funeral Tuesday 02-03-87. You may call [000-000-0000] Collect.

There was no response to that message. John's letters from Vietnam to my mother were always full of concern for her and appreciation of all she did for him. There was no falling out, except just before he left her home for Ethel (and that seemed to be in his own mind). By the time she died, he must have more or less closed her out of his thoughts. To me, at that time, it seemed inconceivable that John would not acknowledge his mother's death in any way whatsoever.

In the midst of all John's legal wheelings and dealings, it was interesting to find small, more trivial things. For instance, I found a February 2, 1988, USPS Customer Receipt for money paid to Weekend Chef Apron. I now have this apron hanging in my utility room, and I feel good in thinking that there were some little mundane things that might have made him feel somewhat happy at times.

I also came upon a small journal that John had kept that was dated December 15, 1988. Within it are six pages containing streams of numbers for which there are no references. Later pages contain shopping lists, such as this one: Candle, oil, screen, shovel, butt hinge, stove, doors, brushes, #10 pan, cat toy, glasses, poncho, 30-35 curtain rod, Bic, AAA batteries, 2A batteries. And another, including: Rag, scarf rag, cap goat, glove fur, boot, nails 8-12 finish, Theraflu hot liquid, owl pair, 3 PL screen 26w 31 h, screws, prime, Dap putty, block, yard, 3/8 3 PC, paint, wall retaining, then just a string of numbers, for whatever reason.

There is one page dedicated to an attorney's name and number in Jepson, plus Circuit Clerk's office and County clerk's office. And then several pages of obscure phone numbers and notes.

In the back appeared grocery lists.

Additionally, I found several very small phone/address "books," which predominantly contained local business numbers. There were NO phone numbers or addresses found for any of us back in Illinois. No mention anywhere amongst his belongings that we even existed, except for some of the letters we had sent him many years prior. (The very last of the cards and letters I sent to him over the years had been returned to me unopened.)

I found check #4170 made payable to John from our mother's attorney in Marengo, Illinois, dated August 12, 1988. It was his inheritance from our mother's estate. This check, however, had been unsigned by the law office, but then signed by John and endorsed by John. He had dated the Receipt for Full Distribution as Sept. 1988, signed it, and added: "authorize federal trust receive [x amount of money], 10 years stock."

When I looked into this check after John's death, the attorney's office told me that a stop payment had been placed on the original check, and another check had been reissued to John on September 16.

The inheritance check(s) sat around for awhile because it wasn't until January 25, 1989, that the Community Federal Savings & Loan in Macon sent John a letter, and apparently he had tried to deposit the "bad" check instead of the reissued one. It did make me happy to see, however, that he was trying to make a donation to the Disabled Veterans.

Dear Mr. Wolff:

We received your letter today requesting a new account, however there is some confusion concerning your request. Listed below are areas in your correspondence we need answered before we can proceed with your request.

1. The enclosed check is not signed.
2. You mention a trust certificate, do you have a formal trust set up? If you do have a formal trust, we need a copy of the trust papers for our file.
3. Do you want a testamentary trust? If you would like a testamentary trust, whom would you like to name as your beneficiary or beneficiaries?
4. The amount of $83.35, we would prefer to make the check payable to you, then you can endorse the

check and send it to the Disabled American
Veterans.

5. We would need to know the term you would like to
open your certificate for. I am enclosing a rate sheet
dated 1/15/89 for your information. However, the
rate for your new account will be the rate in effect
when we receive the signed check back in our office.

Enclosed is your letter; Receipt for Full Distribution from
the Circuit Court of McHenry County, Illinois; check from
Pollock, Meyers, & Eicksteadt, LTD. ... dated 8/12/88; and
envelopes for the Disabled American Veterans.

We will be happy to help you with this transaction when
some of the confusion is cleared. Please let us know if you
need further information.
Sincerely,
Branch Manager

On February 2, 1989, another letter was mailed to John from
Community Federal pointing out the error with his attempted deposit.

Dear Mr. Wolff:
After following procedures required by Community Federal
Savings & Loan Association, [Marengo attorneys] have
informed us that there is a stop payment on check #4170 and
cannot be cashed.
I am returning the check to you along with the $2.00 cash by
registered mail. [Marengo attorneys] are aware that you have
the check #4170 and you can expect correspondence from
them.
Sincerely, Branch Manager

As the letter above indicates, the Marengo attorneys were well aware of the unsigned check and wrote to John on February 3, 1989.

Dear Mr. Wolff:
I have been advised that you are in possession of our check No. 4170 which was sent to you unsigned.

Please tear your signature from the check and return it to my office. Any attempt to negotiate this check could lead to criminal penalties.

Thank you for your cooperation.

John obviously did not return this check since I had found it in his belongings.

Our mother with Johnnie
in 1946.

John in 3rd grade.

Family picture circa 1961:
John on far left, Mary in front of parents

Addison Youth
Seriously Hurt

An Addison youth is in serious condition in Northwest Community Hospital, Arlington H e i g h t s, as result of an automobile-truck collision early today.

He is John C. Wolff, 17, who resides on Highway 53, Addison Rt. 1. Wolff suffered a fractured right wrist and left leg, severe head and chest injuries. Full extent of his injuries has not been determined.

State troopers reported Wolff was driving north on Highway 53. Soon after crossing Highway 72, his car swerved out of control, hit the side of a trailer truck and then the rear tandem wheels of the trailer with force sufficient to tear apart trailer and tractor.

The t r u c k was southbound, driven by Fred J. Krause, 52, of 3616 Elliott Lane, Madison, Wis. It is owned by the Byrns Oil Co. Krause excaped injury.

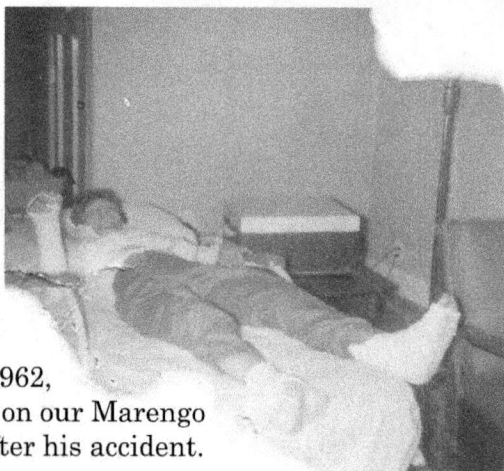

John, 1962,
laid up on our Marengo
farm after his accident.

John's senior picture
after returning to
school and earning
his diploma in 1967.

Mary's graduation
picture, 1970.

Best man at friend
Warren's wedding
1965.

Coachlight Inn, Woodstock, Illinois 1966.

John in a UH-1 helicopter
fitted with M-60 guns
for Vietnam.

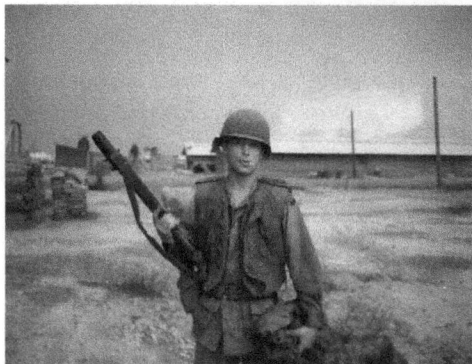

John at Bearcat
near Bien Hoa,
South Vietnam.

Left: One of John's
"outsider art"
paintings from 1973.

Below: John as artist in Hebron, IL.

Left: John in 1978.

Below: John's camp in
Hebron, IL.

John and our mother in 1982.

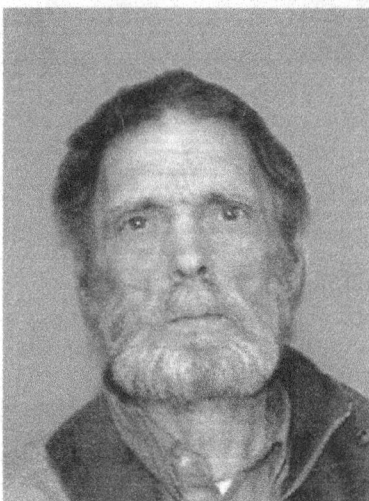

John's Missouri ID photo
provided to me after his
murder by Sgt. Hall in
December 2003.

Instead of a will, these
items were found in
John's bank safe
deposit box.

Chapter 19

As time goes by, discovered information about John's life dwindles leaving just dribs and drabs uncovered on small pieces of paper. No more land is being purchased. No more attorneys' services seem to be necessary. Only a glimpse into John's daily life was to be found.

I now have a beautiful cream and sugar service in my china cabinet, which John bought on December 2, 1990, from The Franklin Mint. It's called Birds & Flowers Oriental Cream & Sugar Service. The statement I found noted, "Your account balance is a credit. No payment is required."

Finding documentation for such "normal" items made it harder to keep in mind how disturbed John was. There was no date on this, but I could see it was from the approximate same time range, handwritten by John:

Dean Gordon subpoena fixed extension to account term
[then looks like] w Pres,
the asset presumes at less than 10 months duration
terms of contract
investment schedule describes
warrant sale then sell items
previous 1 year allowed to cash account

warrant sell 36M (looks like TMNB) the (date 5 DEC)
being the 5th month choice selling
dates as described in terms information (also gone w/receipts
cert 10M safe was thinned
(date) cert sold and reordered
Many deposits to reg savings six consumer certs were
purchased

Previously fixed rate sale of
1 year 5 month cert is paid
Request of transaction
World rule of 3rd cert. same amount (early maturity)

The bank agreed sell request (one cert 18M SOLD DEC) ten
day notice mailed
(20 days holiday rules of no securities trade)

Now sell 10M cert
Only short remainder of deposit credit.

Our Grandpa Rinne died on May 25, 1991, at the age of 103. I am fairly certain that I would have called the Ethel Post Office to let John know. As usual, there was no response.

I found another 1991 statement from Franklin Mint. This was for an Imperial Apple Tree Sculpture. I did not, however, find this on the Ethel premises.

The following USPS postal receipts, dated September through November 1991, indicate the catalog stores from which my brother ordered various items. Again, the names of the stores themselves, on various statements I found, lent some kind of "normalcy" to John's day-to-day Ethel life: Fingerhut, Bear in Mind Inc., Winterthur, Eddie Bauer, The Franklin Mint, and The San Francisco Music Box Company (no music boxes were found.)

I discovered combination instructions for one of his safes, dated December 1991. There were pamphlets for a Sisco Protector safe, several Sentry safes, and a Fire Fyter Safe. Only one document had a date stamp, so it is unknown when all of these were purchased. It was evident when going through his house that John was obsessed with keeping himself, his money, his papers, and other things he deemed valuable safe from harm and theft.

Several items let me see a very wee bit further into his world 1992.

- A January 7, 1992, USPS Customer Receipt for Fingerhut for a pair of shoes.
- A September 13, 1992, receipt from Ken's Country Store with grocery list attached. His needs that day were 16 D batteries; 1 case Busch beer; 2 case M Dew; 1 Box King size M&M peanut; 1 ctn. Merit cigarettes; 2 lighters; ½ gallon Red Johnnie Walker; ½ gallons Black Johnny Walker; 1 Medium size Red Wine & White Wine. (Hmmm ...)
- An October 20, 1992 statement from Pedigrees for various cat toys and paraphernalia.
- An October 21, 1992 letter from Mercantile Bank of North Central MO in Macon:

Dear John,

You have the original Certificate of Deposit in your possession. This is a single maturity investment and it will stop earning interest November 8th, 1992. You will need to mail the Certificate to us before that date if you plan to do this by mail. You will need to endorse the back and include your instructions as to the length of time you want to invest in, 182 days, 12 months, etc., up to 60 months. The rate of interest varies according to the term. Also you need to instruct us how you want your interest paid.

I could not update your Savings Book or enter your deposit of $10.00 that you sent. You did not include your Savings Book with your letter. You had included a proof of purchase for C&H sugar that I am sending back with your receipt for the Savings Deposit.

Sincerely, Personal Banking Officer

I did not discover even one document for anytime during 1993.

In 1994, there was a Dick Blick order for 12 oil pastels, Blendtel, sketch paper, a 1995 calendar, and one set of 6 oil paint tubes. Additionally, I found a Certificate of Authenticity from United States Commemorative Fine Art Gallery for a 24 x 15 (sofa size) Sierra Sunrise Lithograph, by D. John Massaroni. (Unfortunately, the lithograph we found hanging on John's wall was too damaged from wood smoke to be salvaged.)

Our father died on January 11, 1995. I know that I contacted John either by mail or through the Ethel Post Office, or possibly both, with no reply. I do know that he subsequently signed off on his very small inheritance, however. Again, even after no acknowledgement of our mother's death, his non-response to our father's death took me by surprise.

A November 30, 1995, postcard from Fingerhut was found. They were letting John know that the drapes he ordered (I saw these on his dining room windows) should arrive to him before Christmas.

The only item I found from the year 1996, was a June handwritten letter to the City of Ethel. John stated the following:

The retaining wall of the house on Commercial Ave. needs repair. The divided instance fell off the main wall, but were cleared from the bath area.

Several requests were made related with the repair.

I've resided here awhile: it seems like a complete retaining wall should be reinstalled.
(his name and address noted)

Also request a permit eligible repairs necessary.
(A sketch was enclosed with this handwritten letter, which bears no resemblance to his house, but almost looks like a church.)

Discoveries from 1997 reverted to medical and veterans issues. A statement dated April 29, 1997, from Samaritan Memorial Hospital, Macon, MO, noted "ambulance medical transport, plus an emergency room visit – diagnostic radiology service." Since my mother was no longer alive, I had no clue what was happening with John's health. The statement didn't lend much clarification. Radiology service for what? (His autopsy would show that he had emphysema.)

John received a letter dated May 14, 1997, from the Missouri Veterans Commission. I would be almost positive that he never responded.

> Dear John,
> As the service officer for the veterans in this area, I enjoy meeting with veterans and trying to help them with any problems they may be having with their VA benefits. Since I do not work for the VA, I can be on the side of the veteran.
>
> I remember meeting you at the courthouse many years ago, but I have not heard from you since. How have you been? Have you had any problems with your VA benefits? As a Vietnam combat veteran myself, I know it is hard at times just to survive. If we help each other, it makes it a little easier.
>
> Please feel free to contact me even if you want someone to talk to about things.
> Very truly yours,

From 1998, I found only one dated item. This consisted of: an entry label for a 1998 sweepstakes and a Strout Realty address ripped off an old envelope, stapled onto an October 1991 grocery list for Stoney's Grocery Store in New Cambria, requesting delivery on Friday. This was then affixed onto a May 30, 1985, handwritten note to the Social Security Administration regarding request of information about his medical condition; a sheet of paper with his own address label affixed on which he wrote "$124,000.00;" a recipe for pancakes cut off a box; and an End of Session Report for 1998 from State Representative Gary Wiggins.

No dated papers were found for the year 1999.

Much more information was discovered for the year 2000. A February 23, 2000, Sales Order from Sofas 'N Stuff in Brookfield, MO, let me know that John had ordered, to be delivered:

> One oak piece for $369, Holland House (not sure what)
> One oak finish computer desk
> One oak finish shelf
> One Spring Morning Set for $389 (not sure what the "set" was)
> To haul away: 3 pcs.

There was a March 24, 2000, Cash Sales Receipt from a lumber yard in Kirksville. The receipt notes the following, indicating John was once again busy with house repairs.

> 15 ea. Concrete 8.5 x 8.5-12" fluetile
> "Will pay driver"
> Receipt shows "paid"
>> This was stapled to:
> Handwritten receipt from April 8, 2000
> "Labor for hauling old shingles off $200, taking to landfill, my name _____, paid $200 in cash. JS John's name and address is printed below this.
>> Plus:
> Hand printed note on a paper bag saying: "Be back tomorrow to get the rest. Wouldn't all fit in truck today. Thanks."

I found a 2000 Calendar of Events for Ethel flyer, with names and phone numbers for all Ethel businesses on the back. I used this when handling John's estate (adding my brother Charley's phone number after he bought John's house in 2004 and was briefly staying there).

A handwritten document by John (from around this time period) stated:

No receipt of function

Legal advice

Am

Flipped

How could I make good money of the checks. Suspect they are not acceptable to Meck, Meck.

(too large increase; not correct to procedure)

Midwest absurd as they realized the portfolio my name meant close of Community Federal.

Customer not satisfied, redeposit to savings N Cambria.

Stranger still, an April 25, 2000, a handwritten "Warrant" by John had apparently actually been received by the Missouri Attorney General because it is date stamped May 1, 2000. It read as follows:

Warrant

We believe this guy John C. Wolff Jr., resident head of household at 111 Commercial Avenue at Ethel needs his money and a usual standard transaction of his certificate of deposit recorded at Macon Atlanta Bank, Macon, MO.

Another handwritten note by John:

Eldon Jones, Secretary

Past trial Securities trust purpose hold several days trust.

The document check and savings booklet is yet in #205 lock

box and the vault, Tuesday, May 30, 2000.

(stapled to this is a list of 5 numbers added together, maybe his combination?)

And, another handwritten letter from May 2000 (John kept copies of all of his handwritten letters, either copied on a photocopier or copied via carbon paper):

Firstar Bank

Marceline, MO

Please stop the process of the sign up form 1199 that was written early this week. Because the police of Lynn County were at Ethel some hours after my being at the bank and referred the form as not accepted.

Also the social security administration was mailed a stop process of the 1199 and I telephoned the office to stop the process.

Signed by John, with full address

And yet another May 2000 handwritten letter on the same topic:

Social Security Administration

Moberly, MO

The office at the plaza may have received a 1199 mailed from Marceline.

The police sheriff of the County Lynn was at Ethel some minutes after the form was reported as not accepted. So please do not process that transcients. Also J wrote and telephone stop the process at the Marceline banking unit.

Signed by John with full address.

A 2000 District Directory from Gary Wiggins was found. It had been opened to the   8th District Directory which included contact info for Medicare, Social Security, Lawyer Referral, and taxes.

John received a letter from Bank Midwest in Kirksville dated June 13, 2000. (Actual savings account information omitted.)

Dear John:

I received your letter today regarding a Savings Account #_____ Our records show that on July 28, 1997 you closed that account which held a balance of $_____ at Bank Midwest in Macon. On that date, you also opened another Savings Account # _____ , which you closed on July 22, 1998 for $_____. Our records indicate that you do not have any accounts open at Bank Midwest.

Regarding the check you mailed to me, I have enclosed it with this letter. There is no fee for transferring funds, however if you are wanting us to reopen your account with this check, we will need you to come by and sign new signature cards since it has been two years since you closed your Savings Account. …

Sincerely,

A December 26, 2000, handwritten note indicated: "1 truckload 16" split stove firewood," which was then attached to three separate newspaper ads from the December 6, 2000, Kirksville Crier.

There was only one dated find from 2001 - a May 2, 2001, Invoice from Cummins Industrial Tools in Spring Hill, Kansas, with a receipt showing Cummins Truckload Sales in Macon, MO.

John's order included: 250W light, AM/FM cassette stereo; 12 pc. Punch chisel, digital multi meter, 8 lb. splitting maul, 3 pc. Rubber mallet, 5" bench vise, Ryobi w/stand 10" table saw, bench grinder, Coleman Generator

Power Mate, ½" 5-speed bench drill press, and drill press vise, for a total of $1,465.96. These items were still in John's possession, and we took them when we cleared the house.

I discovered the receipt for John's better clothing amongst the clothes locked away in suitcases. This receipt was dated January 18, 2002, and it was from JP's Fine Clothing & Unique Gifts in Macon, MO. John had spent $565.14 on some fine quality clothing: a sweater, a jacket, 2 shirts, one suit, an all-weather coat, and a nautical coat. I believe I donated all of these items to Amvets because my relatives did not want them. Unfortunately, I was unable to use any of these items of clothing for John's viewing. I was not aware they existed at that time because the Sheriff's Department had taken the suitcases and did not release them to me until long after John had been cremated and buried.

A 2002 pocket calendar was found, which included notes throughout of what needed to be done and when: bank deposits, IRS payment, checks ordered, shopping, clean, cement, chimney, wood, build, repair. Some telephone numbers were noted, several legitimate for local businesses, several absurd.

John had devised a Shopping Schedule for September 2002 through May 2003:

Sept. – Heating – Fuel, Stove, Clothes
Oct. – Fencing, Vinyl, Chain, Gen. Woven, Barb
Nov. – Furniture
Dec. – Gutters
Jan. – Mattresses, Pillow, Frame
Feb. – Carpet, Laminate
March – Tile, Bath, Kitchen
Apr. – Clean, Window
May – Concrete, Floor, License, Insure, Plaster, Chimney

I came across the following three strange index-sized "cards" dated in 2003:

- June 2003: Tax credit, IRS, 16 trillion
- Aug. 9, 2003, 3:20 p.m., Denver Realty Trust, Iowa State Farm, 7 zillion, 600 trillion, 700 billion.
- August 10, 2003, AM 940, Sun Bank #1, Deposit 52 Hex-51, Interest Rate 10 percent, Bonus re 3Bil 016 Mil, Zoran.

Officially, my brother's date of death is shown on his death certificate as December 3, 2003. In actuality, he was murdered at the end of November and found in his Ethel home on December 3. His murder marks the second part of John's story. It took his life and changed mine definitively and forever.

Chapter 20

Anyone who has loved ones and awakens to pounding on the door in the middle of the night accompanied by the sight of flashing red lights in the driveway knows exactly the feelings that it invokes. A sense of panic is the automatic response, coupled with a wildly beating heart and sweaty palms. Your mind races to remember who is home and safe and sound and who may be out and about and subject to danger.

One son, who was living with us at the time, was safe and sleeping in his bedroom; car parked safely in the driveway. My husband had been lying next to me, and thus also safe and sound. It was close to midnight, and the possibility of something having happened to our daughter, who then worked nights as a nurse, was a possibility. Our other son might have been working late (or traveling) and something bad could have happened. What about my brother and his family who lived nearby? What about my brother who liked to drink and drive and who was God knows where? Strangely, I double-checked in my head a number of my family members who were already dead that did not in reality have to be worried about.

As my thoughts and emotions whirled, I woke my husband, who sleeps much harder than I do, and alerted him to our unwanted and fear-inducing visitors. I also woke our son on our way downstairs so that we could move down en masse to face the frightening unknown circumstance.

With all the different possibilities of tragedy that passed through my mind in those mere seconds prior to answering our door, I was totally unprepared for what I was about to hear. The officer at the door addressed me directly – being the only woman standing there – asking me if I had a brother named John Wolff. Because this was the one brother who had virtually been out of contact with me for over 20 years, I had to think a moment before I said, "Yes." The officer then told me that there had been a very unfortunate incident. My brother had been murdered in his home in Ethel, Missouri.

I can only share that until someone in your own family has been murdered do you understand the impact of those words. And, in my case, it certainly didn't matter that he and I had been out of touch for so long. This was my brother! My brother! This just doesn't happen to your very own brother! I immediately had to sit down for stability. My cat – who never, ever sat on my lap prior to that date – jumped up into my lap as I sat, stunned, at our kitchen table.

The officer said briefly that the Sheriff's department in McHenry County, where I resided, had just been contacted about the murder. He did not know the particulars, but would put me on the phone with the officer in charge at the scene of the crime. I don't know if all people in my situation immediately imprint on the officer in charge of funneling them the details, but I certainly became very dependent on this individual, initially via phone, during the ensuing weeks and months to come. He was my lifeline in knowing and trying to understand everything that happened and how in the world I would be able to handle this new circumstance in my life.

Thus, Sgt. David Hall of the Northeast Missouri Major Case Squad became my savior for a time. He explained that night that someone had somehow entered my brother's home, and in the course of apparently robbing him had killed him. It was explained that they had found the body during the afternoon of December 3, 2003, but he also shared that he knew that John had been killed several days earlier.

I was told that several people in the town of Ethel had noticed that John did not come into the post office that Monday for his mail nor did he come out to go to town that Monday or Tuesday when his usual friend/driver stopped by to pick him up. It was noted on Wednesday, December 3, that there was no smoke coming from his chimney. This final clue prompted them to contact the sheriff's department to have someone check to see if John was okay.

When the deputies came to check, it was quickly apparent that things were not okay. John did not respond to their pounding, and they found that the door was locked up tight so they could not enter. Because my brother was a paranoid schizophrenic, he had made it quite difficult for anyone to get inside his home through any doors or windows. At this point, the deputies and driver/friend who accompanied them to make the check still thought that perhaps he had had a heart attack or some other accident had befallen him while in his home alone. The deputies had to call the local fire department for assistance in entering John's house.

It was ultimately decided that they would need to enter the house through a small window near a porched entry. After breaking it out and knocking out the boards that had been nailed tight from the inside, they could see that John lay dead against the entry door. After gaining entry, they discovered that it would be very hard to investigate the circumstances of his death since John had no electricity. They called to have a generator brought in to illuminate the scene. Once they had light enough to look a bit further inside the house, it was easy to see that his whole home had been ransacked and that he was the victim of an attack. It would be unclear to me for months and months just how vicious that attack had been.

I hung on Sgt. Hall's every word, but yet still did not fully comprehend the enormity of what I was hearing. Now that this had happened to my brother – even though a 20-plus-year disconnect existed – I immediately knew that I had to go there to take care of whatever would need to be taken care of. I had no inkling that the "taking-care-of" responsibilities would consume the next two years of my life, as well as influence the direction my life has taken since that date.

I notified close family members about John's murder the next day. I must have contacted my cousin in Wauconda as well because it was she who alerted me to breaking news about John. The Macon Chronicle-Herald ran a photo of the crime scene that Wednesday night (the outside of John's home with yellow crime scene tape strung around it, frightening in and of itself) and a short paragraph with the headline: "Law Enforcement Investigating Ethel Man's Death." The only thing that may not have been shared with me earlier was that the coroner had ordered a "routine autopsy" of John's body.

KTVO-TV3, the Spirit of the Heartland, reported on December 4 that an investigation was underway into John's "suspicious death." The transcript states, "Authorities would not comment on the condition of the body or about any visible trauma to Wolff's body. Thursday evening, investigators were canvassing the area and interviewing Ethel residents, trying to determine what happened to Wolff." They found it necessary to mention that John had neither running water nor electricity, so investigators had to bring in generators. They described John as "a hermit-type who's lived in Ethel since the mid-1970s." A witness had shared that "Wolff was a Vietnam War veteran who apparently had never completely recovered from his experience in the war." A resident named Gail Allard added, "That's the sad part, he put his life on the line to serve this country and for someone to do this, this time of the year, it's really sad because he was harmless and everyone knew this."

Within the next few days, Sgt. Hall kept in touch frequently. At one point, he emailed me a photo of John.

The photos taken of my brother John at our Grandpa Rinne's 95th birthday party back in 1982 were not flattering. They clearly highlighted John's schizophrenic decline. And yet, they were far more flattering than the picture I held before me in 2003. It was difficult to believe that this was my brother. Anyone else would most likely believe that this was the picture of a derelict homeless man, maybe someone who had been abusing drugs to boot. This person in the State of Missouri ID photo looked – at least to me then – unkempt, with unwashed hair, a frazzled beard, bloodshot eyes, and dirty looking clothing.

When psychology book authors write about a schizophrenic person developing a "flat" affect, not only is that evidenced by their responses to various situational stimuli, it is also evident in their eyes and in the very structure of their face. The eyes appear to lose their luster and their ability to "light up" as the face tightens up and loses its ability to show spontaneous delight or sadness. There is no "depth" left to the person as they have withdrawn into themselves, hiding all of the reactions to their experiences. We are only left to guess at what is actually taking place in their minds. (Encyclopedia of Public Health: Schizophrenia, retrieved in 2006).

And so, that face in that ID photo was most certainly not the brother I had known when I was young. And, it was not even reminiscent of the brother who moved away when I was 30 years old with hardly a backward glance at me or his other family members. Twenty one years later, this was what was left of him – what looked to be his very shell.

Four days of wait-and-see followed my first notification. Because of the cold and the lack of light in the house at night, Sgt. Hall was unsure when the investigation would be complete. Each day, I would await his call to see what progress had been made. During this time, though, other concerns needed to be attended to. Mainly, how was I to handle arrangements for his body?

I had contacted all family members who I thought would want to know about the horrid news. Because of my brother's mental illness and his estrangement from us, I was unclear to what level some of those family members would care. I called several of my aunts and several of my cousins and asked that they let other family members know. I had hoped for some emotional support from my remaining two brothers during these trying events, but as had been the case in other family crises, I pretty much stood alone.

My own family, my husband and our live-in son in particular, were extremely supportive, for which I will be eternally grateful. My colleagues at work were tremendously empathetic, as only workers who socially serve others can be. Some of my nieces and my nephew showed much more concern than anticipated. My Wauconda cousin was to become my grounding element for the next several years, another person to whom I will always be grateful.

The day finally arrived – Sunday, Dec. 7 – when Sgt. Hall informed me that they would be finishing up their investigation, and that we would need to be there to "secure" the property. He had initially thought that they would be able to assign someone to watch over the property for a certain period of time after the investigation was complete, thereby giving us a better time frame in which to make our 7-hour trip to Ethel. However, it turned out that the Major Case Squad needed to vacate almost immediately once they were done.

I had been on-line in the preceding several days to check out where we would be able to pick up a rental truck in which to haul John's belongings. I also needed to arrange a place for us to spend the night. No matter when the day would fall, we would not be able to make it there, clean out the house, go to the funeral home, and then drive back home all in one day. I had also been in touch with the funeral director, Brian Hayes at Greening Eagen-Hayes Funeral Homes in Macon, who also happened to be the county coroner, about how to handle our visit.

Now that Sgt. Hall had called to say that we could pick up John's things on Monday, December 8 (which regrettably fell on my birthday), I called to solidify all arrangements. I found a U-Haul facility in Kirksville, 33 miles northeast of Ethel. We would pick up a 26-ft. truck first thing Monday morning, which we would be able to return at a location close to our home.

Our son was adamant that we not stay in any motel anywhere close to the town of Ethel. We knew John had been murdered, and he was afraid that since they did not have anyone in custody, that there could be fellow criminals looking for John's relatives as well. Not having ever experienced anything like this before, I wasn't sure whether his fears were legitimate or not.

In retrospect, I guess it was a blessing that John's murder occurred at the end of November and that it was fairly cold. Because they had not found John for three or four days after the murder was speculated to have occurred, the cold had helped preserve his body. I asked the funeral home if it would be possible to hold him there until we could get into the house to get John's things. Brian assured me that he would be able to hold him for approximately a week with no ill effects.

I can't say enough about Brian's reassurance and guidance through this whole ordeal. It was of the utmost importance to me that I get to view my brother, but it was also important to us that we only have to make one trip if at all possible. We didn't want to spend any more time there under the circumstances than we had to. So, to have Sgt. Hall and Brian work with us to keep us informed and to do whatever they could to help us was priceless.

During the drive to Missouri that December 7, we were all filled with trepidation of what was to come. Making arrangements for a trip of any kind can be stressful, but add to that the totally unknown element of a family member's murder and you can reach an almost borderline terror. We forced ourselves to act ordinary, as if that were at all possible.

We had decided to head out the afternoon of December 7 and spend the night en route so as to be at the U-Haul facility as soon as it opened on Monday. We ended up staying in Quincy, Illinois, which was a totally unremarkable event, except for trying to find someplace open at 5 a.m. the next morning to grab a bite to eat. Because we started out so early that Monday, we ended up arriving too early at the U-Haul facility. When it finally opened, we learned we were at the wrong U-Haul. If we had gone to the correct location, they would have been open when we arrived. It didn't really matter, though, because our vehicle was just at that moment being cleaned for us.

I gave Sgt. Hall a call to let him know we were on our way but were running a bit later than anticipated. As it turned out, it would take us even longer than expected because of the geography of the area. When we hit Highway 149 going south, I could clearly see that we were in the middle of nowhere. Not only that, it was a hellish ride through that middle of nowhere.

I had never been on such tortuous roads as these, not even in remote Wisconsin terrain. Up and down hills and around curves – all at the same time. Coming up a hill, you couldn't be sure where the drop off would be. These were roads that whittled down to one lane in order to cross a bridge, which had a road sign posted that informed you that the bridge might be flooded out depending on the season of the year. Couple these roads, the abandoned little shacks, and the circumstances of my brother's demise, and all I could think was that we were in the middle of the movie "Deliverance."

We finally arrived in the town of Ethel and followed Sgt. Hall's directions to John's house. It would have been hard to miss it. There was the post office, just as described, to the right of us. There was a road going up a hill to the left, and at the top, the bright yellow crime scene tape had been strung up around the perimeter of John's property. Sgt. Hall's pickup was parked alongside the house. He had brought us a generator in case we needed light in the house while we worked.

I vaguely knew what to expect because Sgt. Hall had described the scene for me. He had told me that the killer(s) had totally ransacked the house. Not only that, the investigators had to displace things further in order to do their job. I agonized over the fact that John had clearly wanted to be left alone in his life, that he had been terrified of people, that he never let anyone into his house. First of all, to think about the murderer(s) going through all of John's things was horrific. Then to think of the investigators going through everything with a fine-toothed comb was almost as bad. And thirdly, to think of us – his family – coming and again going through his things was almost too much to bear. But worse than that was the thought of leaving his things there for just anyone to go through, take or destroy. I just couldn't let that happen.

Along with the privacy issue that was playing havoc with my emotions was, of course, the fact that my brother had been murdered in this house. It took a strong effort for me to force myself to walk through the door. Even though Sgt. Hall had warned me about the condition of the house, it was much worse than I had imagined. The smell of heavy smoke – the accumulation of years of cigarette smoking and the wood burning stove – was the first thing to hit. Added to this was the smell of the dirt and debris that had never been vacuumed from the carpet, which was accompanied by the pungent scent of cat urine or mouse droppings or a combination of both. (Sgt. Hall shared with me later that his little girl had asked him how come he smelled so bad when he came home in the evenings during this investigation.)

While my nose was taking in the smells at the scene, my eyes were taking in the terrible disarray of all of my brother's belongings. As I had been told, everything in his home had been ransacked in one fashion or another. The officers had made some attempt to sort out things that we might find of value: John's stamp and coin collections, some photos, some documents, several drawings. Other than that, there was not much in its place.

We walked through several rooms, and then Sgt. Hall pointed out where the body had been found. He had been lying near the door he used for entry and exit. On the door frame, I spied blood. I asked if that was John's blood, and I was told, "Yes." I felt as if my knees would buckle. I asked Sgt. Hall why there would be blood there as I had been told earlier that he had died from being beaten, and I was then told that he had been hit on his head and that there had been some blood from that wound. The officers had checked the blood to make sure it was John's and not someone else's.

It was hard to get my mind around what had happened in this place. Further, it was hard to get my mind around how he had been living in this house. It was frigid without the wood burner going, the house's sole source of heat. It was filthy. It was dark, as it was boarded up as only a paranoid person would do. What lay around me looked predominantly like junk, but it was precious to me because it had been my brother's. We had to start focusing, and quickly, about how to get it all out of there. We had only the late morning and the light of the afternoon until approximately 4:00 p.m. to get it done. We made arrangements with Sgt. Hall to come back later in the afternoon to pick up his generator, and then we set to work.

My son and I began to work together looking through the small things, discarding broken items or those that had no value as we went. However, we kept most everything, throwing items into plastic bags, because it was my main concern that all things that were personal to John were removed from that house and brought to safety with me. We wanted to have the time later to go through everything for clues about his life and possibly clues about his death.

The city dumpster sat in the street next to John's house, making it very easy to dispose of things too far gone to even transport. Still, there wasn't a whole lot that we dumped because we wanted to go through it more carefully, and because there were heirs who would need to be made privy to what was there. So, mostly we crammed everything we could into the U-Haul truck. There were basically only two rooms of furniture to take, but lots and lots of boxes and other items. We knew that ultimately the majority of it would be thrown out, but we had no time in which to make such decisions that day. Sgt. Hall had also told us that they had taken approximately a pickup full of items to the sheriff's office for investigation that would be released to us at a later date.

It touched me deeply that John had collected small bric-a-brac that was meaningful to him, the kind of things that other so-called "normal" people would collect. He had tried to make a "home" for himself even though he lived in terror of people every day of his life. I found pictures of his cats and the actual toys that he had bought for them. I found that he had made donations to the ASPCA. Because I love animals, and cats in particular, finding that John also loved cats really touched my heart.

John had pictures neatly hanging on his wall. Sgt. Hall had set aside some large sketches they had come across that John had himself drawn. John had bought himself many different kinds of dishes, probably at garage sales judging by the incomplete sets. He had a TV/VCR player and other electronics that he used when he hooked up his generator. He had lots of books, and that again touched me deeply as I love books and majored in English. He had games that he must have somehow played against himself. He had some music, some videos. He had garden tools. All of these things allowed me some insight into the kind of life he must have led. I would learn more when I could spend time with these belongings, and with the additional items that would be released to me from the sheriff later.

Sometime during the day, several townspeople approached us. We met Dean Gordon and a fellow Ethel citizen (I wish I could remember her name); they wished to express their condolences. Dean told me how he and his family would sometimes drop off meals for John, predominantly on holidays. John would only come out if he knew the person, and even then he didn't always come out. Dean said that there were several times when John had attended the nearby church. He said that John had drawn a picture of the altar and then donated it to the church when the pastor said that he liked it.

Dean said that he himself had probably been the reason that John had moved to Ethel because he was the realtor that sold John the Ethel property. Dean had tried to talk John into moving into a better home, one where he would have electricity and water. (I am unsure why Dean didn't advise that he just establish these things in the house he already had there, but I didn't learn until later how bad the shell of the house actually was.) He said that John had gone to see a realtor in another town and wanted to buy a particular house. The realtor just looked at John, who essentially looked like a vagabond, and dissuaded him from talking about it. As I would later discover, John could easily have bought the house he had looked at – for cash.

At one point Dean had told John that he would not be considered as a buyer unless he took better care of his house and yard and unless he got rid of some of his cats. John bought a lawn mower, but I am unsure how often and how well he kept the yard mowed. My son did find a few cat skulls out in back of the house, and hopefully John did not feel he had to kill them. That would have been particularly sad since it certainly appeared as if he had enjoyed having them there. Hopefully those found simply died of natural causes. Either way, it meant that then the mice thrived.

As we were wrapping up the personal property removal, my son came across a room that had not yet been searched. It appeared that no one had really gone through the possessions it held. That fact was later corroborated by Sgt. Hall who said that they had no further time to explore and that nothing had been ransacked in that area; therefore, no clues would have been found there. My son ventured forth into this new area that had been sectioned off by John from the rest of the house. In it, he discovered several boxes of John's art work. That is exactly what I was hoping to find, as I remembered the paintings he had done prior to his move to Missouri, so this find was the very most precious to me of all. These drawings and paintings gave me more insight into John's soul than anything he might have bought and owned.

Even though it was a cold day, I didn't really feel it. The task at hand was much more important than how I physically felt. Unfortunately, there wasn't even a restaurant in Ethel where we might grab some lunch or some hot coffee. We had a few juice boxes and a bit of trail mix, as I recall. That sufficed for the day. The day went fast, and we finally had everything loaded into the truck. We double-checked that we had not left anything important behind. We even had space at the end of the truck that we filled in with wood from the pile that had been delivered shortly before he was murdered. This would prove to be supremely ironic because we learned later that the wood that we took had been delivered by John's murderer.

I called Sgt. Hall about an hour before we finished up so that he could meet us at the house to pick up the generator. He was kind enough to offer to escort us to the funeral home in Macon. He also was kind enough to offer to take us somewhere for dinner. We followed him to a restaurant that was outside Macon, again seemingly out in the middle of nowhere.

The time during the ride to the restaurant gave me time to become very apprehensive about going to the funeral home. During the day's activity, I had been able to put that aspect of our trip out of my mind. Now the knowledge that I would soon be seeing a brother that I had not seen for over 20 years was hitting me head on. As was the fact that he lay dead in the funeral home.

Our food, though mediocre, sat well on our stomachs since we were beyond hunger. It felt great to get a cup of hot coffee as well. It also felt good to be sitting there with Sgt. Hall, who could hopefully answer some of our questions. And, if he could not answer, he could at least offer an ear to our concerns and frustrations. He informed us that they had just taken someone into custody that they were sure was the person responsible for John's murder. He could not share much with us due to the confidential nature of an ongoing investigation. We were elated with this news, but he cautioned that arresting someone is one thing, but actually indicting someone and ultimately convicting someone was a long and arduous process. Additionally, he told us that the person had been arrested for another crime altogether and much criminal investigatory work lay ahead to try to tie the person to this crime. But, he continued to say that he was 99% positive that this was the perpetrator of the crime.

I remember distinctly that during our meal Sgt. Hall asked if I enjoyed hunting. I told him, "No." He then asked if I owned a gun, and I replied with an emphatic, "No." He didn't out and out ask me, but I presumed he was trying to find out if I would come back and try to shoot the person who had killed my brother.

After our meal, it was time to head to the funeral home. We had called Brian to let him know approximately when we would arrive to make sure he would be there since there was no service, only our family visitation – and a small family visitation at that. My two remaining brothers had no interest in viewing our dead brother.

I still cannot express the thankfulness I continue to feel for Sgt. Hall offering to actually drive us to the funeral home so we could leave our U-Haul parked in the restaurant parking lot. During such great times of stress, it is extremely comforting to have someone be so caring of our emotional and physical needs. It's hard enough traveling in a new area under normal circumstances. In our situation, it would have been highly stressful to find our way around an unknown community in a huge U-Haul that essentially carried my brother's very life in its bowels while searching for the funeral home that held his bodily remains.

Walking up the steps to that funeral home was a totally surreal experience. I could not believe that I was in an unknown-to-me Missouri town on my way into a strange building to view my murdered brother's body. It was all I could do to put one foot in front of the other. A woman greeted us, who said that she would find Brian. I had talked quite extensively with Brian on the phone and so he seemed very familiar when we actually met him. He immediately put me as much at ease as was possible at the time.

During our phone conversations prior to this trip, Brian had asked me about John's appearance, and he had been given a photo of John from earlier days. I can't honestly remember how he acquired the photo, though it was probably through Sgt. Hall who had discovered all of John's photographs. I remember asking him if they had found any decent clothes to put on John. He told me, "No," but added that he had actually donated some of his own. That touches me greatly still – that he would think of putting his own clothes on John to prepare him for our viewing and to make him look as good as he possibly could. (I recalled viewing my father prior to cremation, and he was simply covered with a sheet.)

It was now time for Brian to escort us into the viewing area, after asking several times if I was ready to do so. Sgt. Hall came into the room with us, but he and Brian hung to the back of the room while we walked forward. Again, my mind told me to move forward step by step, but I could hardly make my legs move. When I looked in the casket, my breath caught, and my legs started shaking uncontrollably. I wondered if Brian and Sgt. Hall could see that fact. And, I started crying, spontaneously.

My brother – my blonde, blue-eyed, beautiful brother – who was once on top of the world and had everything going for him was lying there old and grayed and dead. And he looked so very, very small and fragile. There was a bruise across his head where he had been hit, although it had been covered up fairly well. I could only think about how small he was and that he had been beaten and hurt so badly. (Later I learned that John's ribs had been broken, which punctured his lungs, and then he had suffocated.)

I touched his face, and I touched his chest, and I wished with all my might that I had a chance to talk to him again in this lifetime. It was just not fair that such a thing could happen to him. Why in the world had someone so beautiful and smart been targeted with a mental illness that took him away from everyone and everything that mattered to him? What in God's name made it fair for someone to live in terror and isolation for over 30 years? And what in the hell made it all right for someone to come and take his life away when all he wanted was to be left alone? I wanted to pick him up and carry him home with me – to safety. Or, at the least, to hold him in my arms to mourn him. I could do neither.

Our son, my husband, and I probably only spent 15 minutes viewing the body. I sometimes regret not having stayed longer, but what good would it have done? His image is forever imprinted in my brain. Brian, thankfully, had done an excellent job of having John's hair cut and styled as he himself had styled it many, many years before. His scraggly beard was shaved. He was dressed in clean, attractive clothes. It meant the world to me to see him at least halfway between what he had been as a young man and what he had now physically become.

After viewing John, however, there was one more task to accomplish before we left the Greening-Eagan-Hayes Funeral Home. I had to choose an urn. Because my brothers had not been interested in seeing John – just as they had not wanted to see their own father after his death – I had decided to have John cremated so that transfer of his remains to Illinois would be easy. I had made arrangements for his urn to be buried next to my mother's grave after a brief memorial service for family members only.

We drove all the way back north to Kirksville to spend that night, again because of the fear of staying anywhere in the vicinity of where John had been murdered. It would, however, have made much more sense to stay in Macon after such a long and stressful day. At least we were able to do a relatively quick drive north up Highway 61, a road that didn't have all those horrible hills, curves and drop-offs of Highway 149.

Upon our return home, KTVO-TV3 reported that following the autopsy by the Missouri State Medical Examiner's office, "the death of 58-year-old John Wolff of Ethel, Missouri, has been ruled a homicide." However, "authorities will not reveal the cause of death at this time for fear it will interfere with their investigation." Thus, at that time, I still did not know exactly how John had died.

Two years later as I wrote the above paragraphs (which have sat yet another 12 years unpublished), the urge to bring John home with me was just as strong as it was that night. The urge to cradle him as a mother would. The need to make up to him perhaps for all that his family could not do for him during all those years of isolation. I still feel the same.

Chapter 21

I couldn't help resent the fact that I was again involved in planning funeral events for a loved one. Although I was not in charge of my mother's funeral after her death, I had sat with her to plan it while she was ill and death was imminent. We had spent weeks sorting through her belongings piece by piece and designating each to go to the appropriate recipient. When my father died, I was making decisions long distance with the aid of my aunt in Florida. And, now here I was, without the support of my remaining brothers, making all the decisions on how to handle my murdered reclusive brother's remains. Just what in the world prepares a person for undertaking such a task?

The most helpful turn of events for me during this stressful time was learning through funeral director Brian Hayes that there was a Crime Victims' Fund available through Missouri's Department of Labor and Industrial Relations. (I think John would have smiled to think that he "won" more compensation through a government agency. And without a lawsuit, no less.) The Greening-Eagan-Hayes Funeral Home would receive a Crime Victims' Compensation check to pay for John's viewing and funeral expenses. Brian would make arrangements to have John's cremated remains delivered to the Marengo-Union Funeral Home for subsequent interment at the Marengo City Cemetery. (Our stepdad offered up a burial plot next to my mother's grave since he lived out of state.) The Crime Victim's Fund would also cover the expense of a clergyman, the grave opening, an obituary, and monument installation.

Because of my brother's estrangement from us for so many years, I knew that it would only make sense to plan for a simple service for the family members here in Illinois. My remaining aunts and uncles living out of state were too old to easily make the trip, and I did not want to burden them with asking them to do so.

There was only my immediate family, my brother Jim and his family who were in the area, my brother Charley and possibly his daughter, and my eldest brother's (deceased 5 years before) children. Probably only half of these family members would even bother attending a service. Additionally, there were two cousins in the area – one from our mother's side and one from our father's side, who I felt might be willing to serve as their family's representatives at the service.

I was happy that my stepdad, who lived in Texas, had told me about that empty cemetery plot; it saved me from deciding where I might scatter his ashes. As mentioned before, I knew that my brothers did not wish to view John's body, so that made cremation and transport from Missouri to Illinois simpler. I called the local cemetery and made the initial arrangements for the service.

I still believe that my brother's schizophrenia was brought on, at least in part, by his forced military service. Possibly it developed due to the stress of giving up his life back home; the stress of having to learn to be a soldier, which was so clearly against his gentle nature; the stress of all he heard and saw while in Vietnam; or by the fact that he undoubtedly had exposure to Agent Orange while there. Whatever the exact reason, my brother deserved to be honored as a veteran. I made arrangements with a local vets organization to have someone come and play taps at the service.

Although I had distanced myself for the previous year or two from our church, I felt that a minister should conduct a graveside service for my brother. John had been raised a Lutheran as had I; he had attended a parochial school; and I knew that he had attended the church in Ethel at least several times, which indicated some kind of continuing belief in God. Our minister readily agreed to perform the service, and I wrote up a very brief eulogy since he had no idea who John was. In reading it now, it was such an insubstantial tribute to my brother. In my grief, I did not get my ideas across clearly. I guess it sufficed at the time, and no one made any negative comments about it. I do recall the minister asking me pointedly if I'd like him to read it. Either he was questioning whether I myself wanted to read it or perhaps he was inferring it really should be a more solid piece. If the latter was the case, he really didn't let on, probably recognizing that I was not in my best writing mind.

My niece, who worked for a nursery floral shop, kindly offered to bring a funeral wreath for the service. I planned to pick up a single rose to place on his grave.

I arranged for the funeral home in Missouri to have my brother's cremated remains arrive before the funeral service scheduled for December 13, which date had been set based on the minister's availability. I made sure that the local funeral home would transport the urn to the graveside, and that the grave would be open. I also made sure that the trumpeter would arrive at the appropriate time to play taps. I made arrangements for a veterans marker to be placed at his grave when the ground was thawed enough to make it possible. I contacted all relatives to let them know the day and the time and that we would be serving refreshments at our home following the service. I made arrangements for the food and was very thankful for my sister-in-law's help.

Almost two weeks had passed since the investigating officer had shared that offensive (to me) ID photo of my murdered brother. Now I was in the midst of planning his funeral and putting together a collection of what few photos I had of him. Again, it all seemed surreal. There were several photos of him during grade school days with blondish brown hair and wide-gapped toothy grin. These evolved into pictures of a very handsome young man, dressed to the nines – starched shirt with dark-colored suit, highly polished dress shoes, neatly manicured nails, a golden tan, and well groomed hair. I included the picture that he had had taken of himself at a local studio back in 1980. I also included the very last picture that was to be found of him, standing in his back yard, extremely thin and fragile, with sad eyes and a longish beard, but on that day clean-looking.

The day arrived – a very cold and windy Saturday. It reminded me of the day of my mother's funeral, which had been in January. I had only visited her grave once after her death – not because I didn't care, but because I knew she was not there – and I was a bit apprehensive that I would not be able to find it now. Luckily my husband had a much better memory for such detail, and he knew right where it was located. It was too cold to stand around, so we sat in our vehicle and waited for others to arrive.

After my brother had returned from his tour of duty in Vietnam and his mental illness became increasingly evident, he had made those threats against one of my brothers. This brother had subsequently been estranged from John thereafter, and I was not absolutely sure that he would even come to the service. I was very happy when I saw him arrive with his wife, and his two daughters and their husbands. I was also happy to see half of my eldest brother's children, plus my Wauconda cousin and her husband. All our children attended the service. My other brother – who I *had* expected would attend – did not appear.

The service itself went as you would expect a graveside service to go. I broke down when the minister gave me a comforting hug; it was good to have his presence there. It was even more emotionally difficult for me when I was presented with an American flag by the veterans who presided.

Before we left the cemetery, I placed a rose next to John's urn along with a butterfly sticker, to signify a new and peaceful life for John. My son and I had found many butterfly stickers when going through John's things, as well as quite a number of other items with butterflies. For whatever reason, they must have had great meaning for him.

I can't be sure how my brother Jim really felt as he stood at the service that day. He did not let on that he was overly upset by the events that had transpired. It was enough for me that he was actually present at the service and at my home afterwards. It let me know that he at least felt that he should honor John as a brother whether he really felt like being there or not. My other brother was a very different story.

I knew that my brother Charley cared deeply about all of us, but his behavior towards us seemed to depend on the amount of alcohol consumed that day. On the phone in the days prior to the service, he had expressed his concern. Yet this had been coupled with questions about the amount of money John may have had. On the day of the graveside service, he did not appear at my home until late in the day. My niece had called warning me about his over-consumption before his arrival, but I was still unprepared for his behavior when he finally did arrive.

First of all, he scorned my hug of empathy upon entering our home. He said, "I'm okay. It's no big deal. I'm okay," as he more or less pushed me away. Obviously no thought had entered his head as to what I might be feeling or what I might need emotionally at that time. He then proceeded to tell me just how much money he figured John must have saved up and speculated how little he must have spent on himself, living as he did in hermit-like fashion. I was totally appalled, and when he finally started talking about the "bad" things that John had done and how it really didn't matter that he was gone, I finally asked him to just leave. I could not believe that he was not expressing any sadness at the loss of our brother, particularly since we had previously lost two of our older brothers.

After he left, I called my brother Jim to relate this sordid-seeming event, which had surely served to intensify my already-frazzled emotional state. Thankfully, Jim spoke out against this very hurtful incident – against our brother's drinking – against our brother's unseemly behavior.

Thus the day came and went, and I was glad it was over. I felt I had done as much as I could possibly do to honor John's memory under the circumstances.

John's obituary ran in the local paper on Monday, December 15, 2003. I did not hear from anyone who might have known him.

An exciting bit of news was highlighted on December 17 and 18, 2003, in the Macon Chronicle-Herald. The headline read, "$5,000 Reward Established for Conviction in Ethel Murder." I learned subsequently that a fellow veteran had posted this reward. I also learned subsequently that the Major Case Squad was really not happy with the reward being posted because they did not want anyone coming in and trying to get the money by making up false information.

Now the work of handling my brother's estate began in earnest. Neither of my brothers would undertake the task; one because he simply did not want to, one because he was not capable at the time of doing so.

I was extremely happy that John had been a pack rat with documents and that we had brought all of those documents back with us to Illinois. Documentation of his banking accounts dated all the way back to the 1960s. I was able to identify four banks that he had dealt predominantly with during the five years prior to his death. The documents allowed me to track the movement of his monies from bank to bank, as well as to figure out bank name changes. Any letters dealing with transfers had one or more copies for me to review.

I also had access to Social Security records, which were extremely important. I had to make sure that they were apprised of his death so that his monthly disability payments would cease. That process, thankfully, turned out to be quite simple, and they made sure to cover payments to him until the date shown on his death certificate.

Another of my very first tasks was to find out if my brother had hidden a will anywhere. The investigators did not find a will on the premises, but I thought it was possible that he had placed one in a safe deposit box. Investigators had found records from several banks in various towns nearby Ethel amongst items they had held for evidence. I called all of these to see if he had a safe deposit box at any one (or more) of them, knowing full well they may or may not share such information since I had not yet been recognized by the courts as the estate's personal representative.

The banks thankfully shared more information with me than I initially thought they would. He had a safe deposit box at one of them, but had closed it. I did find one existing box that I was able to check out during one of our Missouri jaunts. No luck finding a will; I found three nonsensical items.

I knew that I could not administer John's estate through an attorney from the state of Illinois. This fact, however, made things extremely complicated because I would need to contact an attorney in Missouri totally unknown to me about a legal process that was just as totally unknown.

I called Sgt. Hall for guidance, and he told me of an acquaintance of his who practiced in a town nearby Ethel. Because I had become emotionally reliant on Sgt. Hall – who I relied on for information about the murder suspect and a hopefully subsequent trial – I decided to go with his recommendation. Working with an out-of-state attorney, however – and I'm fairly well convinced it wouldn't matter which attorney – was exceptionally difficult for me.

To me, the Missouri attorney seemed totally unsympathetic to the situation. From the very first conversation, he made it clear that he only cared about the law; that he was clearly not interested in any personal information. In the state of Missouri, if there is no will, the estate is divided equally between heirs, as in most states. However, in Missouri, these heirs – with equal decision-making status - would include not only John's living siblings, but all of my dead brother's children – six of them. I tried to make it clear to the attorney that my brothers and I did not feel as if these six children could possibly have as large a say in how the property would be distributed as the three of us remaining siblings.

In hindsight, I can understand the attorney only being concerned with strictly following the rules of law. However, he seemed not to have a clue as to the emotions involved with such a process. I tried to make him see that I had no problems with these heirs getting any money that would be due them, I was only concerned that they not have a say in John's personal property.

I felt that the attorney did not acknowledge my role as an independent personal representative even though all heirs legally signed off that I take on that role. It seemed to me that the attorney seemed to think that I was going to bilk the estate for my own gain, and at times he seemed to try to bollix my decisions and force me to file documents with the court that simply were not required of an independently administered estate. Instead of just providing legal guidance, it felt like he essentially took on the role of my personal adversary throughout the whole two years of the estate process. It was an emotional enough process for me without him giving me cause for more worry.

Chapter 22

On January 12, 2004, the Macon County Sheriff's Department announced release to me of items they had taken from John's house for further investigation. Previously shared with me was the fact that these items had completely filled a pickup. I, therefore, had to figure out how to now get a pickup load of possessions home. My Honda CRV would certainly not hold them. Luckily, my husband had a pickup, and he was able to locate a cab top that he finagled to fit. Since this would be a two-day trip, we had to make sure that it was tight enough to lock up for the night. I had no intention of losing John's things to another thief in a hotel parking lot on my way back home.

Our live-in son (who at that time was thankfully unemployed) agreed to accompany me on a late January journey. We were anxious to get the balance of John's "stuff" in the hopes of finding important documents that would not only help me administer his estate, but that also might help us learn how he had spent the past 20-some years. And, we still harbored secret hopes of finding a fantastic clue that would help nail John's killer.

Neither my son nor I felt comfortable entering the Macon County Jail that January 23. We had learned that my brother's alleged murderer was being held there on a check forgery charge from the state of Kansas. Before we braved our visit to the jail, we stopped in to say hello to Brian, the coroner. He filled me in on details of the current investigation as he had heard them. We then took a deep breath and headed over to the sheriff's office.

I remember the feeling of trepidation as I walked up those stairs. We were supposed to meet Sgt. Hall, and that thought was somewhat comforting. When we went up to the barred service window in the vestibule, we were told that Sgt. Hall had gone to lunch with Sheriff Dawson and that they'd be back shortly. We decided to wait outside in our vehicle. We watched people come and go and wondered if they had anything to do with the case. We watched a car stop underneath a barred second-story window and heard the driver calling up to a prisoner up above. We wondered whether the prisoner was John's murderer. And, we wondered how the driver was so bold as to do that and why no one in the sheriff's department paid any attention.

After about 20 minutes, Sgt. Hall pulled up with Sheriff Dawson. We immediately were uncomfortable with the Sheriff, who did not seem to want to look us in the eye. We were taken around the side of the building, down a short set of stairs, and into a dungeon-like "holding" room.

I was shocked to see the red evidence tape wrapped around the boxes holding John's things. Case Number 03-000777. It was very disturbing to again have it boldly pointed out that my brother had been murdered, like a punctuation point to my grief.

Sgt. Hall had every box clearly numbered according to what room the items had been found in. Before we could take a box out, Sgt. Hall had to find it on the list, check it, and then mark it as released. There were numerous boxes and as many free-standing items.

What struck me most about the free-standing items was how many safes there were. More evidence of my brother's paranoia. The money that had been found in the house - $3,152 to be exact, plus another $25 found in his coat pocket - was also released to me that day. I hate carrying cash of any amount over $50, so I was very uncomfortable having to safely carry that amount on the journey back to Illinois, particularly because we would be spending the night in Kirksville (again) and not going directly home.

Finally, all items – 18 boxes, misc. papers and tools; $3,177 cash; 2 suitcases; chest; 2 lock boxes; 2 safes – had been checked and marked off the list, and we were free to leave. I was very happy that Sgt. Hall was the one to release the items to me. He shared much information about where the items had been found, which increased my knowledge of how my brother lived. He also shared information about the significance of the evidence found. Sheriff Dawson more or less stood in the background through this whole process and jingled the change in his pocket. We seemed to make him feel uncomfortable, and he still never really made eye contact with us.

Sgt. Hall had shared with me that there seemed to be some competition between the Major Case Squad and the Macon County Sheriff Department. Perhaps the Sheriff felt that since the crime occurred in his jurisdiction he should have been in charge of the investigation or at least played a more major role. Or perhaps it was just that he felt his department was not getting enough recognition for the part that they *were* playing. And maybe he just didn't know how to approach a murder victim's family. Whatever contributed to his behavior that day, however, only served to heighten our own unease during the whole procedure.

Ah, the brain fingerprinting production. How can I explain the feelings that welled up when I found out about it? I think a blend of dread and outrage probably describes it best.

In May 2004, five months after learning about John's death, three months after going through all his personal belongings, and after those months of trying to make sense of things, to learn what we could about the investigation and to hope that they had the right guy behind bars while not yet even charged with John's murder, the phone rang. My son's friend called to tell him that he had had insomnia the night before and that he had decided to get up and watch TV. After his PBS show of choice was over, he had continued to let his VCR record while he began listening to the next program. He became fully alert as the narrator started talking about a murder in Ethel, Missouri. It sounded familiar, and as he listened further, he realized that it was a show that had begun to focus on my brother's murder!

The show was a PBS documentary, "Innovation, Episode 8: Brain Fingerprinting," about a new scientific method of reading brainwaves to determine whether or not the details of a crime were embedded in a criminal suspect's mind. If they were, it offered proof that they indeed had committed that crime. Dr. Lawrence Falwell, the inventor, called his new methodology "Brain Fingerprinting." Even though the description of Episode 8 as found at that time on PBS's web site centered around the murder case of Jimmie Ray

Slaughter in Oklahoma, the first part of the program, about 10 minutes worth, had indeed focused on my own brother's murder in Ethel.

No one had apprised me that such a show had been taped, and I had certainly not been aware that it was running on PBS. My son's friend had made a copy for us to watch, and I sat stunned as I watched my brother's house come into view. They showed the scene as the investigators arrived and described the basic murder scenario, the one which had been released to the papers. Even worse, they proceeded to show John's alleged murderer being escorted into the "test" area by Dr. Falwell. The suspect's face was blurred out, but there was no mistaking how huge the man was in comparison to Dr. Falwell. There was no mistaking how he would have towered over my frail brother and easily overpowered him.

It also stunned me to see Sheriff Dawson being interviewed in the video. My immediate reaction was to think how totally stupid the law enforcement was in Macon to cooperate in such a video. Wouldn't the defending attorney be able to cry foul when the time came for the trial? Wouldn't they say that the jury was then prejudiced because they had access to the PBS show and the ensuing video that would be offered for sale? Even stranger was the fact that the narrator then reported that the defending attorney – the alleged murderer's attorney – was cooperating in this videotaping that ultimately depicted his client as being guilty.

As the theory was explained, if a person had committed the crime, then he/she would recognize pictures associated with the crime scene and their brain would produce a strong spike of recognition. Macon County Sheriff Dawson appeared, stating that his department was short of manpower so the major case squad had been called in. They then worked together and found a person of suspect. They, the Sheriff and the public defender, decided to have the suspect brain fingerprinted, which would hopefully indicate whether or not he really had anything to do with the crime.

The narrator reported that my brother, a Vietnam vet, had been found dead in his home on December 3, 2003. He stated that the details of the murder – the motive, the location of the body, the manner of death – had not been released to the public. And, that that was why it would make it "an ideal crime for brain fingerprinting."

One of the Sheriff's deputies stated that he had picked the suspect up for forgery, and the Sheriff told him that this person was also a suspect in John's murder. The deputy told the suspect about brain fingerprinting and that it might eliminate him as having a role in the crime. The suspect agreed to the procedure. The narrator added that a murder conviction would have made the suspect eligible for the death penalty.

Dr. Farwell placed a headband on the large black man's head and told him that he would be able to tell what information was stored in his brain. He asked the suspect if he had committed John's murder. The response was, "No."

Dr. Farwell asked further if the suspect would know any details of the crime. The suspect responded that he would not because he didn't know John, only saw him in the newspaper.

Dr. Farwell, to clarify, stated that the suspect, then, had never seen him at all except in the newspaper. At that point, the suspect said that was true because he had newspaper clippings.

He was then asked if he had ever been in John's house, to which he said, "No." But, he went on the say that he had been *at* John's house, but only on the outside when he delivered some wood.

Dr. Farwell had visited John's house in order to ascertain the "targets," items that would be recognized by the murderer. What he chose included a dumpster next to the house, the trees behind the house, the covered porch, and the wood pile. These targets would be displayed to the suspect, along with details that would only be known to the perpetrator of the crime.

The test was conducted over a period of two days after which Dr. Farwell went over the results with the suspect. Contrary to the suspect denying having known John or having been in his house, Dr. Farwell stated, "He did know a number of the most salient details about the crime. He knew where the body was lying, what the body was lying on, what the person was wearing, an unusual item that was taken from the crime scene at the time of the crime."

Even after finding out the results, the suspect continued to state that he had nothing to do with John's murder. No charges were filed at that time.

After viewing the program, I hurried to contact Sgt. Hall to see if he was aware of it. He was totally surprised and asked that I send a copy to him immediately. After viewing it, he assured me that nothing would come of it. The process would not be allowed in court. Further, he did not feel that the general populace in the area would view a PBS special such as this anyway.

Even though he told me not to worry about it, it was always in the back of my mind, throughout the actual trial.

Chapter 23

The Missouri attorney alerted (more like alarmed) me that it would be prudent for me to appear in person before the Macon County judge at a preliminary estate hearing on June 7, 2004, which would initiate the probate process. The attorney stressed that anyone would be able to walk into the courtroom and cause havoc for me in becoming the personal representative for the estate. I tried again to tell him that there was no one in our family who would contest such a thing, but he convinced me to be there or suffer the consequences if anyone turned up. Thankfully, I coaxed my brother Jim into accompanying me to Missouri since my son had already made two trips with me.

This would be the first and only time that I had personal contact with the probate attorney. It appeared to me that the judge was dismissive of an out-of-county probate attorney, and much less impressed with the fact that my brother and I were there; indeed, not even acknowledging our presence. It simply seemed to me like a good way for all legal entities to earn some extra fees. We were in and out of there in approximately 10 minutes. This cost the estate about $300 in mileage to my brother, since I did not see why he should bear the brunt of the cost – nor me – for this unnecessary trip of 760 miles and 14 hours of travel time round trip, not to mention lost time at our jobs.

Since I had not been privy to any details of John's life in Ethel, the information I found while more leisurely going through his private possessions, now that I had them at my home, helped me fill in that tremendously long 20+-year gap in time. It was extremely uncomfortable going through someone else's things, particularly John's given his privacy issues, but we knew it was essential not only in administering his estate, but also in the opportunity to come up with any clues to his murder that may have been overlooked by law enforcement. (Not having been through such an ordeal, we had no idea how very thorough his murder investigation had already been and would prove to be.)

Although I had been appalled at the sorry state of my brother's home, Sgt. Hall repeatedly told me that it seemed to him that John had had most everything in its place prior to the ransacking. So, even though all things were very dirty due to lack of running water to clean them and electricity to power a vacuum (although he did have that generator), it was comforting to know that his home had at least been set up in an orderly fashion.

The concept of orderliness now made sense as I thought about all of the decorative elements that he had hung on the walls in "normal" fashion. John had a pantry where he kept his clean dishes. He had a bookcase to hold his books. He had cupboards to hold his food items. He had chests and furnishings that could hold particular items. And, he had many safes in which to put his important papers, as well as loose cash.

While the probate court hearing on June 7 (which was approximately six months after my brother had been killed) had simply been a legality initiating the start of the actual probate process, it was the start of much heartache and many headaches for me personally.

I had been cautioned – months before – by the Missouri probate attorney that I should not disburse any of John's personal property. I had, however, sent my own forms for my fellow heirs to sign indicating that a) they were not interested in getting any his personal things, as listed on a separate inventory sheet, or b) that they wanted to come to our home on the date I had chosen to pick and choose what they would like. I figured that we would be able to equitably distribute things based on each taking a turn at choosing something until it was gone.

There were several things I held back that we felt were worth a bit more. These things would be advertised separately, and the money they brought thrown into the estate bank account that I had established. The heirs were free to bid on the items that were held back if they chose to pay for them with proceeds going into the estate account. I did let them know in a roundabout fashion that I was hanging onto John's artwork as I felt that I was more entitled to it. No one disagreed or contested this idea.

My feeling going into this was that I did not think that my nieces and nephew should be able to take anything of John's. I felt that John's possessions belonged to his siblings. I was told that this was not legally acceptable, however, so I felt coerced into hosting that "family choice day" as the next best option.

All heirs had signed off that any personal items remaining in my possession after the date we gathered to make our choices would become my own personal property to dispose of as I wished. I then held a garage sale and sold whatever I could of what was left and kept the minimal proceeds in payment of my husband and I having done all the work of collecting, transporting and cleaning everything up to begin with.

The only, what could be classified as, good news (though still extremely alarming to me) during this time frame appeared as a news item on the Missouri Attorney General's Office website on July 7, 2004. The headline read, "Attorney General, Macon County prosecutor file murder, robbery charges in connection with death of Ethel man." The press release read:

> Macon, Mo. – Missouri Attorney General Jay Nixon and Macon County Prosecuting Attorney R. Timothy Bickhaus today filed criminal charges of robbery and murder in connection with the death of John Wolff, an Ethel resident found beaten to death in his home Dec. 3, 2003. The Attorney General's Office is assisting Bickhaus on the case.

> Ivan Johnson (DOB – 11/7/59), of Macon, is charged with first degree murder and first degree robbery. The probable cause statement filed with the felony complaint alleges that Johnson bludgeoned Wolff to death and robbed him of approximately $1,500 sometime between Nov. 27 and Nov.

30, 2003. The probable cause statement also alleges that Johnson previously propositioned others to help him rob Wolff. The statement also alleges that Johnson told several individuals that he used a large metal pipe to beat Wolff and rob him for drug money.

Under Missouri law, Johnson is considered a prior and persistent offender. He previously has been convicted of the felonies of rape, sodomy, assault of a law enforcement officer in the first degree and second degree robbery. Bond for Johnson has been set at $500,000.

Murder in the first degree is a class A felony under Missouri law, punishable by either death or imprisonment for life without the eligibility for probation or parole. First degree robbery is also considered a class A felony under Missouri law, punishable by not less than ten years imprisonment. The charges against the defendant are merely accusations; as in all criminal cases, the defendant is presumed innocent until or unless proven guilty in a court of law.

But ... back to probate. All through the probate process, things were hung up while waiting for responses in signed paperwork from one niece or another or my nephew. It was infuriating to me to begin with that I had to even get their signatures on anything; more infuriating still that they were holding up the probate process. The legalities became frustrating as hell.

What was worse than dealing with the family paperwork was dealing with the Missouri attorney. As mentioned, all through the process, I felt as if I were treated as an adversary, as someone who was trying to pull a fast one on the rest of the family. Meantime, I was the one trying to save every penny that I could for the estate, so that we would all have more to split when the time came. And, mainly, I was trying to protect all of us from other legal entities who might be able to find a means to suck even more of the estate money away. Again, I had no problem with my nieces and nephew getting their fair share, only that they had been given an equal say to me and my remaining brothers.

In fact, I did all I could to preserve as much money as I could through an interest bearing estate account. I tried to gather all refunds that were possible from checks of small denominations that John had never cashed from various entities. I watched his various bank CDs and waited until the appropriate times to cash them out. I hauled his stamp collection to an appraiser in Rockford, getting virtually nothing because the collection was in sad shape and not worth a lot to begin with; proceeds went into the estate account. I called an appraiser about his antique fishing pole and was told that it would be worth $25 at best. Since I had already had the sale, I simply let my brother Charley take it. When I found loose change or a stray bill pop up amongst John's belongings as I went through them, I deposited every penny into the estate account.

The most helpful documents I found amidst John's belongings pertained to all of the land purchases that he had made since the late 1970s. My brother – due to his illness – seemed to be very gullible to magazine advertisers touting wonderful, cheap land deals. Aside from maybe Missouri and most likely Florida, there was no evidence that he visited these sites prior to purchase. After the fact, he had visited the Bahamas, as confirmed by his having kept a copy of his airline ticket from December 1982.

Over the course of five years, as detailed chronologically earlier in this book, my brother had purchased property in Missouri (two different towns), Florida, the Bahamas, Australia, Colorado and New Mexico. There were signs that he had looked into other property in Texas and Wyoming, but there were no discoverable deeds. His parcels of property caused me hours and hours of time, aggravation and research as I had to learn if they were all still in his name, how much they were actually worth, what the process was that I would need to follow in order to sell them, and how that all tied into what was necessary for the probate attorney in Missouri.

Unfortunately for me, each state ended up having a different process. I knew that he still owned the properties in Missouri, Florida, Colorado and New Mexico because there was tax documentation (although he had not paid his taxes in Florida for five full years, which would cause its own problems). I found out land values as best I could via the Internet. Other than Missouri, I found names of attorneys and/or escrow agents in the aforementioned states on-line.

The Bahamas and Australia would be problematic because I did not want to use up John's estate for outrageous legal costs. Research on-line showed me a process whereby I could check ownership in Australia for a very low fee. That was wonderful because it turned out that the plot was now in a bank's name, not John's. If I wanted to check further – to make absolutely sure – it would mean hiring an attorney in Australia. That would mean more money for most probably the same result.

Based on correspondence from an Australian property owner next door to John from October 1982, it was clear the property was not worth much anyway as it was so small in comparison to what would be needed to generate any income in the outback. The Missouri attorney and I decided that the Australian property would fade into the background. The final estate documentation contained a copy of everything I had discovered about the property, with a recommendation that it was not worth anything to the estate.

Researching the Bahamas property meant months of back and forth faxes and letters trying to find out the exact process I would have to follow to find out who held title to the property. I would send inquiries to one particular department, and would then be asked me to submit more forms, which when submitted would go unacknowledged. I finally discovered a department that could help. Thankfully, it turned out that the lady responding was actually an attorney who knew the rules.

So, I paid the $250 it would take to learn whether ownership was still in his name. It turned out that it was. However, he owed back taxes which could wipe out anything that we could sell it for, and, indeed, the estate could also be charged a fine for taking so long to pay up. At the time John had purchased the property, there had been no real estate taxes in the Bahamas. But, I had found a letter from Grand Bahamas Properties apprising property owners that the Commonwealth of the Bahamas instituted taxes as of the year 1977. It stated that John would owe taxes beginning in 1982 because his Conveyance was dated in 1981. I found no tax payment documentation in John's things.

Before I went any further with that property, I decided to try to find out its real value. If it were in a growing area, perhaps it would be worthwhile to go through the whole ordeal of selling. If it were in an undesirable area, however, I did not want to open a can of worms with their government.

I finally found a realtor who was very helpful in ascertaining its worth. Unfortunately, it was not in an area that was particularly growing or attractive. She apprised me that the real estate sales costs would essentially obliterate what the estate would take in. And, we would still have the possibility of those government fines hanging over the whole deal. In the end, I turned in final estate documentation that would show the judge how the attorney and I had come to the decision to let the property lie as it was. Someone else could buy it up for unpaid taxes.

If you have gone through administering an estate that has out-of-state properties to sell, you'll understand the frustration I went through. It was especially frustrating because I was a novice to the whole estate process to begin with. Thankfully, selling the property in New Mexico was a piece of cake. I dealt strictly with an escrow agent who didn't charge much, and New Mexico law does not require that an attorney be involved in the process. The property was worth hardly anything, and I just wanted it sold.

Colorado proved tougher than New Mexico, and the state did require that an attorney *or* an escrow agent be involved in the process. I found a realtor/escrow agent on-line, and I thought she sounded pretty straightforward. Later on, she seemed to drag her feet, which was highly irritating because I needed the process over in order to settle up the estate. It didn't seem to me like she made much of an effort to find a buyer for the property, and it almost seemed like she was holding out in order to take less on the property. Of course, that doesn't seem to make sense as she would then be getting a lower commission, but it turned out that she herself was considering buying the piece. Even though the name of the buyer on the final real estate documents was not hers, I still feel it was someone she was in partnership with. Ultimately, though, it was sold and done with.

Sale of the Missouri property would have been easier had my one brother and I not decided to sell it to my other brother. This brought forth major documentation that had to be signed by all heirs – including my nephew and all those nieces that we, the siblings, thought shouldn't have a say in things to begin with. Several of these heirs just couldn't seem to understand that their signing such documentation – even though they told me flat out that they didn't care – was essential. Back and forth and back and forth between heirs and the attorney. I would finally be forced to call my one niece, who was extremely cooperative, to help me out with the others. I did not like having to bother her with the situation, but I didn't know how else to move the process along.

The Missouri property was the last piece of John's holdings to be sold because of all that commotion. The upside was that this property was in the state where John had been a resident, so it was easy for the probate attorney there to handle the paperwork and process.

Worse than Missouri, worse than all of them, was selling the property in Florida. Florida dictates that there must be a separate probate administration in Florida for all deceased property owners. This is not cheap. Even though essentially not much is involved, the attorney gets a hefty fee. And, then there was more documentation that had to be signed by all heirs and the sometimes seemingly impossible task of getting everyone to sign and send back the documents. And, it meant working with another out-of-state attorney's office, one that didn't offer me much in the way of civility, empathy or expediency.

The Florida property was the only property that held any real value because of its location in a growing area in the Panhandle. It was very expensive getting a survey conducted, and it took a long time to find a surveyor who would do the work. Thankfully, I located a real estate agency that was straightforward that did their best to get me the best price possible. In this case, I ended up with a better price because it did take so long to process the deal. The longer it laid there, the more money people were willing to bid on it.

I handled all of these sales basically on my own without the Missouri attorney's help. In the few times I went to him for advice, it ultimately seemed as if it were to my benefit to just take things on myself, saving the estate lots of money. However, my taking on these duties took a whole lot of time and energy on my part. If I had not handled things, the entire estate could easily have been drained by out-of-state attorneys and courts.

I cannot imagine how I would have been able to handle all of the above without the use of the Internet and email. It would have taken years – and large sums of money - if I had had to conduct my research and sales process through phone calling, regular mail, and/or traveling to all of those locations.

Chapter 24

On August 10, 2004, Ivan Johnson was arraigned – the first formal presentation of charges. We chose not to be present. A KTVO-TV3 transcript of the event stated that "Johnson arrived at the Macon County Courthouse in shackles, maintaining his innocence in the murder of John Wolff. 'Because of my past record, they feel that I'm a criminal to society, I do have a right to change and better myself,' said Johnson." Johnson, who had already been reported as a repeat and persistent offender, one who had committed and been convicted of rape, sodomy, assault of a law enforcement officer in the first degree and second degree robbery, still had the audacity to say, "I have morals and respect about myself. I could never bow down that low to kill a man, or whatever or to rob."

The Macon Chronicle-Herald reported after the arraignment that Johnson's preliminary hearing had been set for October 5. His attorney would be Kirk Zwink with the public defenders office in Moberly. Kevin Zoellner, a prosecutor with the Missouri Attorney General's office had been assigned to assist Macon County prosecuting attorney R. Timothy Bickhaus. Bond was set at $500,000.

I did not find out about the Ethel remembrance event for John until well after the fact, but I was so touched with what the residents had done and with their thoughts about John. A newspaper article appeared in the Macon Chronicle-Herald on September 29, 2004, entitled, "Town Remembers Man Who Lived a Reclusive Life: Ethel Residents Say, 'John Wouldn't Have Hurt A Fly.'" A photo of Ethel Postmistress Linda Lile in front of John's house accompanied the article.

"John would always remember my name when he would come to the post office," Linda Lile said. "He would call others by any name he chose, but he always called me Linda." She went on to say that "John's parents had brought him to Ethel when he was around 32 years old. He had one sister in Illinois and two brothers [he actually had three still living at that time]. I have talked to his sister many times over the years about John's welfare."

The article then made several errors in their reporting. The first was in stating that Linda told them that I had told her that John "had managed a pizza place several years ago." He had indeed managed a pizza place, but that had been over 30 years prior to his death, prior to his tour of duty in Vietnam. She then said that John was a "tunnel rat" in Vietnam. I have no idea who had told her that, but it was not the truth. He surely was in Vietnam, and he had gone out on a rescue mission or two close to his base camp, but primarily he maintained helicopters.

Ethel resident John Hawkins said that John talked more when he first moved to Ethel. "You could ask him a question and he would give you a short answer."

Ben Williams, another Ethel resident, said that John's appearance tended to scare people. "I knew who he was so he didn't frighten me. He would come to fire [department] suppers sometimes. I would see him along Highway 149 where he walked a lot." Several residents would give him rides to Macon or Brookfield, Linda Lile amongst them.

"When I had a general store in Ethel," Linda remembered, "John would come in and order a pineapple sundae …always pineapple sundaes. I would be playing 60s music and he would listen to the songs and that was the only time I saw him smile."

On September 16, 2004, a potluck dinner was held to honor law enforcement for their work on John's murder case. "In my 33 years in law enforcement, I have never seen anything like it," Ron McAffee, Missouri State Fire Marshall, said. "It was so nice for the people of Ethel to put this dinner on for us."

Ethel Mayor Janice Lea shared, "You have to drive out of your way to come to Ethel. We are not located where you would just pass us by. There are a lot of man hours accumulated on John's case. We just wanted to show our appreciation for the work being done for John …"

The article summed it up by saying, "Everyone in Ethel agrees they don't want people to think John was crazy… 'He was just our John.'"

On October 5, 2004, a preliminary hearing was held to determine if there was adequate evidence to bring John's alleged murderer to trial. I was very apprehensive about going to this hearing, but I absolutely knew that I wanted to be there and was very happy that my son agreed to accompany me. This was to be held in the same Macon County courthouse where I had attended the preliminary probate hearing. That fact did not make me feel any more comfortable in approaching the building on that particular day.

Having – thankfully – never been through such an ordeal before, I did not know what to expect. The prosecuting attorney, Kevin Zoellner, who had met with me and my son in the Chicago suburbs prior to the preliminary hearing, told me that it was like nothing you saw in the movies. Actually, he was a bit wrong about that. It definitely did have the flavor of things shown in old movies that took place in the deep south. The courthouse itself seemed antiquated, with no modern amenities. The wooden pew-like seats ran around the perimeter of what reminded me of a "bull pen" where the accused and their defense and prosecuting attorneys sat or stood and expounded.

What I was totally unprepared for was actually seeing the accused. I had seen the back of his head and his height and his shape on the PBS video, but I had not seen his face before this day. It was shocking to me to even be seated in the same room as this person, if one could call him a person. It was even more shocking to listen to testimony from the doctor who had conducted John's autopsy and to listen to the clinical report of what he found. His testimony made me cringe with the pain that John must have felt as each blow fell. I had not known before that day exactly what he had gone through. I had still been under the impression that it was perhaps a bit "accidental," as the Sheriff had initially tried to imply.

What really boggled my mind, and my son's, was the fact that this criminal could walk cockily across the room to the section where we were seated – right in front of our faces – and try to "come on to" the few women who sat in the benches not far from us. I couldn't understand how this was acceptable courtroom behavior and why none of the court-appointed people said one word about it. And, why was he allowed to even come anywhere near us? For that matter, why wasn't he advised by his counsel to NOT even look us in the eye as he did several times. We both shot our individual eye daggers of death his way, and he did turn away from us, but the audacity!

We also were not prepared for hearing the witnesses, who essentially served up facts that made the defendant look guilty. These were his supposed "friends," who were now turning on him. The fact that each and every one of them, approximately a dozen of them, came forward to testify against him could not possibly be lost on him. And we learned that without a doubt it was the woodcutters – who we initially suspected of the crime – that indeed brought this person into John's very-private world. Johnson had helped deliver wood to John's residence several months earlier and apparently could not get it out of his head that he was told that John held large sums of cash in the little Tupperware containers out of which he would pay contractors.

Johnson had tried to talk maybe five of his so-called friends into helping him commit the crime. The best he could do was get several of them to drive him near the residence, although one of those people could not be found. Later we learned that one other "friend" had been in John's house with him the day of the murder. This friend was never arrested or tried, and it was most probably the person who mysteriously "vanished."

And, finally, we were not prepared to see so many of those witnesses arrive in shackles themselves because they were serving drug, forgery and/or robbery charges of their own. It was like a surreal circus. It was a world I personally resented being drawn into. However, it did open up a new window of information about how other people live in this world. I felt like I had been totally sheltered, even though I consistently listened to the media and had seen plenty of movies and TV shows about the criminal element. It was much different when seeing it in person and knowing that people like this had caused my brother's death. In their own way, all of them were involved. Any one of them could have blown Johnson's cover *before* the murder was allowed to take place. However, they were all too busy saving their own hides from drug and other felony charges.

As the two sides addressed the facts, it became apparent that the judge clearly considered the possibility that the defendant was guilty, and it was decided that a trial was in order. I was never so glad to "get out of Dodge." I felt unclean, as if our near proximity to these people had allowed their criminality to enter our very bodies. I knew that we would one day have to face all of them again, and I did not look forward to it.

On a brighter side at that time, finally things were winding down with probate. The Colorado property was finally set to go after weeks and weeks of back and forth exchanges with no real progress. Because I was out of state and had no legal representation to back me, the buyer ended up getting the property for a song. I was just happy to finally sign the papers and get the property sold.

The Florida sale was also coming to a close. The realtors there were straightforward and reputable, and they got the highest price they could for us. In fact, as time slipped by, the price did go up, which was clearly to our benefit. Unfortunately, I could not hold onto it even longer in the hopes that prices might soar because the estate needed to be closed out. And, a number of the heirs had made it quite clear that they were looking for their money.

To be honest, I myself was looking forward to getting my personal rep fees because I had essentially given up the past year and a half of my life to put all the pieces together. My beloved gardening had gone on hold, my writing had gone on hold, and my masters program had gone on hold. It took a very long time to rebound after such a fantastical thing as murder touched my life that December day back in 2003, and some of the pieces would never be put back together.

The day arrived, however, when I could write out the final checks. The attorney in Missouri forced me to send the checks to him for disbursement, and I can see how it would be his duty to do so. Still, at the time, it felt like he thought I was trying to abscond with John's estate money. The only thing left thereafter was to make sure that estate taxes were filed for the year 2004. Hallelujah!

Chapter 25

It seemed somewhat appropriate that the trial week would include our oldest brother's birthday. So many memories of family and everything that had gone down between my brothers lay there open for contemplation. And, bottom line, there they were … both murdered brother and birthday brother, dead.

If I was not prepared for the preliminary hearing in Macon, I was definitely not prepared for the actual trial in Columbia. Attorney Zoellner had kept me posted on any details that preceded bringing the case to trial. I can't express my thanks enough to him for this. Since I pretty much was hanging out there on my own with no sibling support, it meant more to me than ever. My husband accompanied me to the trial, and I cannot imagine being there without him for moral support.

Again, it did seem much like what I had seen in movies, except that with John being a recluse, the courtroom was not filled with relatives and friends and acquaintances. The few people from his home town of Ethel, the closest things to friends that he had, were actually witnesses. Thus, they could not sit and listen to the trial, and so there were no people from Ethel in the benches with us. I did get to speak with several of the townspeople before the trial began, and I know that they were very concerned that the accused be brought to justice. I appreciated that very much.

So, there my husband and I sat, basically alone in the spectator seats aside from the victim's advocate who had been assigned to me, several other court-associated people, the defending attorney's wife, and a reporter who sat way in the back. This is how it would be for the next three days. I believe my legs shook for the entire time I sat in that courtroom. The trial started on a Tuesday, and we were told to expect that it would not end until Friday. It seemed like eternity.

If the trial were a Clue game, the playing board would need to be huge to accommodate all possible players. Not to mention running out of colors for your chosen token.

Ivan Johnson, was, of course, the major player that day in Columbia, Missouri, since he was the accused murderer. Attorneys for his defense were Public Defender Kirk Zwink and Assistant Public Defender Manuel Tatayon, both working as attorneys for the State of Missouri. For the prosecution: Kevin Zoellner and Andrew Scholz, both Assistant Attorneys General for the State of Missouri. 152 exhibits (pieces of evidence) would be presented during the trial:

Exhibits 1 – 10:   Diagrams of the interior and exterior of John's house and its relationship to roads

Exhibits 11 – 23:   Photos of the exterior of John's house – in all directions

Exhibits 24 – 88: Photos of the interior of John's house focusing on the layout, where the body was found, body itself, personal belongings, entry logistics, tools used, and state of disarray

Exhibits 89 – 93: Personal belongings with ties to the case

Exhibits 94 – 96: Footwear casts

Exhibit 97: Binocular case, Room #2

Exhibits 98 – 114: Tools which had been used during the robbery and safes and metal boxes broken into with said tools

Exhibits 115 – 117: Gelatin lifters of footwear

Exhibits 118 - 120: Defendant's clothing and shoes

Exhibit 121: Defendant's buccal swab

Exhibit 122: Defendant's jacket

Exhibit 123: Photo of defendant wearing Exhibit #122

Exhibit 124: John's death certificate

Exhibit 125: Two wooden doors, which had partial fingerprints

Exhibit 126: Latent print

Exhibit 127: Whiskey bottle with partial fingerprints

Exhibit 128: Defendant's ten-print card

Exhibit 129: Victim's ten-print card

Exhibits 130 & 131: Defendant's clothing

Exhibits 132 & 133: Victim's clothing

Exhibit 134: Sheet and body bag

Exhibit 135: Victim's blood standard

Exhibit 136: Defendant's buccal swab (also shown as Exhibit 121)

Exhibit 137: Kleenex with blood

Exhibit 138: Carmex

Exhibits 139 – 141: Photos of footwear imprints

Exhibits 142 & 143: Exhibits of personal items indicating where found

Exhibit 144: Advice of Rights dated July 15, 2004

Exhibit 145: Shoe chart

Exhibit 146: Walmart records

Exhibit 147: Advice of Rights dated December 12, 2003

Exhibit 148: Videotaped interview of Defendant

Exhibits 149 & 150: Rights Waiver

Exhibit 151: Letter to Sam Smiley

Exhibits 152 & 153: Left blank on court list

Exhibit 154: Metal file box, Room #3

Exhibit 155: Justin Blain written statement (court list indicates this was neither offered nor admitted)

The prosecuting attorneys would bring forth 37 witnesses who were examined and most of these were cross-examined. The defense attorneys would bring forth a mere 6 witnesses, one of whom had already testified for the prosecution. I could only feel that Kevin Zoellner had spared no time and energy in his attempt to bring justice to my brother John. A paranoid schizophrenic hermit's case could have simply faded away, as happens in so many other instances where the victim is not an outstanding member of society. But the Major Case Squad and the prosecuting attorneys did an exemplary job in making sure the murderer came to trial and that all evidence possible was used to convict him.

I also felt that the attorneys, along with the Honorable Senior Judge Frank Conley who heard the case in the Circuit Court of Boone County, Missouri, did an admirable job in choosing their jury. As found in court transcripts shared with me thereafter, Judge Conley conducted a very thorough preliminary examination of potential jurors. Many pertinent questions were asked, and answers discussed, that encompassed the issues of age, county of residence, criminal history, legal licensure, medical hardships, caregiver hardships, history of being a criminal victim, and former jury duty. The jurors chosen had indicated that their past – whatever it was – would not affect their serving on a jury in this murder trial.

Following Judge Conley's examination, the State's voir dire (preliminary examination) was conducted by Andrew Scholz. Scholz closed his session with a question about who amongst the potential jurors was a veteran of any branch of armed services. In reviewing this information, it made me happy to know that there were potentially five fellow Vietnam Vets sitting on John's jury. It was not really possible to determine from the court transcript which of the questioned vets, if any, were actually chosen for duty in the trial.

A roll call of the jurors selected was taken. Jurors stood and took their oath, being sworn in by Deputy Clerk Sheri Vanderhoof. The judge then instructed the jury that he was going to read them their instructions "concerning the law applicable to this case and its trial." He told them that thereafter the State would make an opening statement regarding their evidence, but that the "attorney for the defendant is not required to make an opening statement then or at any other time." Judge Conley said further, "At the conclusion of all the evidence, further instructions in writing concerning the law will be read to you by the Court after which the attorneys may make their arguments. You will then be given written instructions of the Court to take with you to the jury room." Before they broke for lunch at noon, Judge Conley cautioned all jurors not to talk to anyone about the case or to let anyone talk to them about it.

At 1:12 p.m., Defense Attorney Zwink approached the bench and wanted to "invoke the rule regarding witnesses." The Judge retorted, "It is a little late, isn't it?"

Attorney Zoellner said, "Judge, the only witness we have in the room is Mary [Wolff], that's the victim's sister." Attorney Zwink then decided he did not have an objection, and Attorney Zoellner said he would keep his witnesses out – all but me.

Chapter 26

Attorney Zoellner's State's Opening Statement is offered in full as it will not only provide a factual account of the murder, but it explains how all of the many witnesses – the players in this "reality" game of Clue – are interwoven. Additionally, his statement provides the details of the physical evidence that all together ultimately point to the conclusion that Ivan Johnson was indeed my brother John's killer. Attorney Zoellner spoke:

"John Wolff went outside his house to get some wood. He was keeping his fire on so he would be safe and warm. Instead he got killed. He got killed because someone wanted his money. That someone would be Ivan Johnson.

"Now, before we tell you exactly what happened that night, let me tell you a little bit about John Wolff and how he wound up in [Ethel]. John Wolff grew up over in Illinois. Eventually … was in the Army, was in the Vietnam war. When he came back, he had some problems because of that I think. Had some mental issues. And ultimately wound up buying little pieces of property all over. But he ultimately wound up in [Ethel], ultimately wound up buying a small house. John lived, we sort of called him a hermit. He was like a hermit. Lived by himself. Didn't have anything to do with anybody else in town except for one or two people. And he lived in this little bitty house. We call it a shack. And he had all his earthly possessions in that shack. He was a pack rat. It was packed with stuff.

"When John had to go out, it was for very limited things. The first of the month he was getting an SSI check. There's a couple of people in town he befriended and they would pick him up and they would usually drive him down to the post office. He'd pick up his check, maybe go to the bank and cash it, deposit some money. He'd go get some groceries, he'd go back to his place, and there he would stay. He wouldn't come out except for very limited times and he didn't bother anybody. That's the life John Wolff led.

"But the problem with that life, if you want to call it a problem, was that people started talking. You know, we probably all grew up with some person like this in our neighborhood. I remember we had a house in the woods kind of where we lived, everybody talked about, oh there was a witch, don't go there. And all these stories. We all probably had someone like that. Well, John was that person in the community of Ethel which is north of here an hour or so. Real small community. People talked about him. They talked about [him] and thought he had lots of money in that house and stuffed all his money in mattresses and that's what people thought. And one of the reasons people thought that is because people saw him with money on occasion.

"Wilford Broadway, you're going to hear Wilford's name a lot. And he's going to testify in this case. Wilford was a man who lived over in Bucklin. He's a little bit of a character too. But Wilford Broadway was ... a Vietnam vet also. Somehow got to know John Wolff and befriended him. He would deliver to him wood on occasion so he could heat the stove. [In] the little shack, in the house, the only heat he had was a wood burning stove. He didn't have running water. He used a bucket of water from the pond as a bathroom. He kept his food in a little cooler in a room. Wilford and John became friends. Wilford would occasionally take him to town. But Wilford would also deliver wood. On one of those occasions when Wilford and his nephews had chopped up wood and brought a load of wood to Mr. Wolff, on one of those occasions, Ivan Johnson came along. And on that occasion, as they're throwing wood from the road up into the yard because John was the one that would always stack his wood, as they're throwing it, Ivan is able to see that John is up there with Wilford. He's got a Tupperware container, some type of box and he's paying money out. But unfortunately for Mr. Wolff, unfortunately for John Wolff, Ronnie Broadway is along on that trip too. Ronnie didn't do anything wrong. But he did say something that led to the events you're going to hear about. ... He told Ivan Johnson about how John Wolff had lots of money in that house. And you will hear over the next couple days how that set into a progression John Wolff's murder. Because what Ivan Johnson then did, you'll find out, is he then went to everybody that he knew, just about, everybody he could and he told them about John Wolff. He told them about the money. But that's not why, he wasn't just telling them to pass along neighborhood gossip, he was asking them to rob John Wolff. He was needing help. He needed a car, he needed a way out there. He wanted to rob John Wolff.

"You're going to hear from Bobby Smith. Bobby Smith is Wilford Broadway's nephew, one of his nephews. And Bobby Smith will tell you that he was present when Ronnie made this statement about John Wolff having money and Ivan having heard that. But he will tell you a little while later – this is all before Thanksgiving of 2003 – a little while later there was an occasion where Bobby was driving Ivan in Bobby's car. And he will tell you that as he drove along, Ivan told him 'I want to rob the old man in Ethel.' What he said he wanted to do was hide in the woods or shed around the house, and when he came out of the house he wanted to jump him, he wanted to mace him. He wanted to tie him up and he wanted to take his money and he wanted Bobby to help him. He wanted Bobby to drive him out there. Bobby will tell you he didn't.

"But it wasn't just Bobby that Ivan went after for help. He also talked to Wayne Bridgewater. Now Wayne Bridgewater is the son of James Bridgewater. The Bridgewater's are all close family or friends with the Broadways. The names, I've been working on this case for a year and a half and they still confuse me. Wayne Bridgewater, who is in jail for a burglary of his own, he'll tell you about that. Wayne Bridgewater will tell you that when this was all going on prior to Thanksgiving, Ivan approached him and wanted Wayne to steal his father's car. Wanted him to drive Ivan out there so they could rob the old man and murder him. And Wayne Bridgewater's reaction was, 'I'm not in for no murder.' And Wayne Bridgewater didn't help him. You will also hear from Wayne Bridgewater, and I'm jumping ahead a little bit [to] when this was all over with, when Mr. Wolff had [already] been murdered, when he had been robbed by Ivan, Ivan had called him from jail and told him he had done it.

"But Bobby Smith and Wayne Bridgewater weren't the only ones that Ivan tried to get to help rob this old man. There's two girls that are going to come testify, Dinisha Fraley and Maggie Nelson. They're friends. One of them was dating Ivan Johnson's friend called Charles Douglas. He goes by C-Dog. If you can keep track of names. Ivan was living with C-Dog at that time or staying there at least part of the time. There were multiple occasions. He'll tell you at least two or three times prior to Thanksgiving of 2003 that Ivan Johnson would approach them and talk to them about the old man. He called him 'Wolffy,' the old man in Ethel, told him the old man in Ethel has got lots of money. He keeps it in boxes. He doesn't believe in banks. He told them, 'I just want to mace him. I just want to take his money, I need a ride. Will you give me a ride, will you drive me, I'll give you money.' Both of these girls will tell you they listened to him repeatedly but they always told him no and they wouldn't drive him out there.

"Now, Bobby Smith, Wayne Bridgewater, Dinisha Fraley, Maggie Nelson will all tell you, so will Anthony Minnis, another friend of the defendant's. These are all his friends. Anthony Minnis will tell you that Ivan talked to him about wanting to rob an old man in Ethel. Now we've talked about Bobby Smith. We've talked about Wayne Bridgewater. We've talked about Dinisha Fraley, Maggie Nelson, Anthony Minnis. That's not all.

"David Reynolds and a fella named Jerry Pickens ... are individuals that Ivan also approached about robbing Mr. Wolff, prior to Thanksgiving this occurred. But not only did those guys get approached by Ivan Johnson about robbing Mr. Wolff, those guys actually tried to help him. If you can picture these three men, Ivan, Jerry, David, driving around the town of Ethel in the middle of the night. Now they tried to tell law enforcement, they'll try to tell you that we're looking for girls in this small town of Ethel in the middle of the night. They'll tell you they drove up and down the roads but they'll tell you it was Ivan who told them he was out there to rob an old man.

"Fortunately that night, Ivan couldn't find the house. And all of those people were approached by Mr. Johnson prior to Thanksgiving of 2003. Thanksgiving always happens on a Thursday. We know then [that] Friday,

Saturday, Sunday is the weekend afterwards. But you'll hear that there's a fella that lived in that town of Ethel named Dean Gordon.

"Dean Gordon will tell you – Dean unfortunately has had a stroke since this has all happened. He's all there mentally but unfortunately has trouble communicating. But Dean will tell you that over the years, because they befriended John Wolff, that one of them would always take a plate to John Wolff. He will tell you that on that [Thanksgiving] day, [in] late afternoon, three or four in the afternoon, that he himself was the one who took the plate to John Wolff that day. And John Wolff when he left him was alive. John Wolff was well.

"Now, I don't know, and I can't tell you the exact date that John Wolff was killed. But we know his body, and you'll hear evidence, was found December 3rd. Now, how his body was found is this: When he didn't come [out], there were certain townspeople that looked out for John, cared about John. One of those people was a lady named Linda Lile who is a postal worker, worked at the post office. She knew [that] John on the 2nd of December, 2nd of every month, would make arrangements with someone to get to town to get his check, to get to the bank, to get his food, and [to] go home. On December 2nd, John didn't show up. In fact, on December 2nd [believe he meant December 3rd here since his body was found on the 3rd], John didn't make those arrangements and she became worried and she called law enforcement. And the police went out to his house. And you'll find out [that] in [his] shack that he kept it boarded up, he kept it locked up with multiple locks. I'm gathering from what you will see of these pictures that he was very paranoid and he was very private. And they had to break their way into that window, [and] they found him laying on a pile of wood and he had been beaten to death. He had multiple bruises about the head and face. He had been beaten about the head. He had ribs both in the front and back broken. He had his arm, his humerus which is a very strong arm bone, and you'll see this, this is important because he was a very frail man, he suffered from emphysema. But no matter how frail he was, the doctor will tell you who did the autopsy that the humerus is a very strong bone, and it would take something, not a fist, not a foot, it would take some type of object to break that bone. He was hit with something, a tire iron, a crowbar, sledge hammer, a piece of his own wood. He was hit with something. And you will hear that those rib fractures caused his breathing to become labored and caused him to die.

"They found in that house, when they began looking in that house, an utter mess. You'll see on the walls pictures. John kept a nice house. It might not have been clean. My wife is always on me about this. I'm kind of anal, I've got stuff in the same spots everywhere. It's not clean. I've got dust around it. That's sort of how John was. It looks like he played a board game with himself to keep busy. He had art supplies, he would do art. But his house was dirty, had dust everywhere. Ash from the wood stove. He had a room in the back where he was doing, building some kind of sand thing, had a little aquarium. But his rooms I think you could assume had at one time been clean because nobody had been in there, nobody was allowed in there but John. But when the police got in there, you'll see that entire house had been ransacked.

"Ivan Johnson went in there, and we'll establish he went in there with someone else. I believe it was David Reynolds. But he went in there with someone else and he murdered John and then they spent I don't know how much time trying to find the money. Now I'm willing to bet they found that little Tupperware container with a little bit of money in it. Ivan Johnson later told people he got $1500 out of the robbery. But what they didn't find, and I don't even know if they're aware, but despite those rumors about John having a lot of money in his mattress, those weren't true. John had a lot of money, but he was smart enough to keep it in the bank. He had about $160,000 in the bank. And Mr. Johnson and his friend didn't get it. But they spent their time. They got in there, and they needed tools because when they got in there or confronted this private man, [he] had all these safes. He had all of these file cabinets and everything was locked up. He had a tool box. And that tool box you'll see was broken up and tools, sledge hammers, crow bars, pry bars, screwdrivers were all taken out. Mr. Johnson and David Reynolds went about beating everything they could open and going through everything they could looking for that money. And there's papers and all of his earthly possessions are just spread out all over the house.

"Now, the question is, and we'll establish to you that Ivan Johnson is [there], the question is when did it happen? You'll hear that Ivan Johnson [was in] this Macon area, Ethel area outside of Macon, [and] Ivan left that area on Thanksgiving night. But he went to St. Joe, where he apparently went frequently but by his own words, own admissions, he came back that Friday morning. And he was next seen Saturday morning by a girl in Ethel named Amber Haun. He was seen banging on her grandmother's door. And he said he was looking for some place or looking for a fella named Art Sellick. And then in fact she pointed him in the direction of Art Sellick's house. But he didn't go to Art Sellick's house. He went to Ronnie Broadway's house, the relatives of Wilford we mentioned earlier. They live in Ethel. He winds up there around 10 or 11 in the morning and winds up sleeping off and on until four in the afternoon. The reason he's tired, the reason he's there, he's been up all night waiting for John Wolff to come out and get his wood. And he didn't come out that night. He's cold because he's [been] out all night. He sits there and warms up [and] they eventually throw him out. He leaves again alone, heads to Macon, [and] he eventually hooks up somehow with David Reynolds. They wind up out there, I believe you'll find that [to be] Saturday night, waiting for John to come out and get his wood. When he comes out, what you'll see is he had to unlock his door so the lock is right inside the house. When he got out and got the wood, I submit to you that's when he was confronted and taken back in that house and either beaten to death right then or when they couldn't find the money. When they were in this fury because they couldn't get these safes open and find the money, and he wouldn't tell them where the money was at, he put up a fight and he was beaten to death.

"Now, when this murder is over with, when this robbery is over with, Ivan Johnson immediately heads back to St. Joe. And [on] Sunday night he heads back there. December 3rd he's actually at a house where the police go to arrest some other people, and he is also arrested. He's arrested by Howard

Judd and Mike Wilkerson. And what they eventually learn is that he had beenin town for a couple days. And the first thing he did when he got into town was he hooked up with a girl named Christy Nichols. ... When he had committed this crime, Amber Haun, the Broadways, will tell you he was wearing this greenish gray, bluish gray flannel jacket that people in that town had seen him in. But the first thing he does when he gets to St. Joe is he asks Christy Nichols to go steal him a black Carhart jacket. When she does that, he switches that jacket out so he can hide his appearance and whatever evidence may have been on that jacket. The next thing he does [is to] eventually wind up at some people's house named Brenda and Shane Proper. They're watching one of these criminal shows that's on TV, that's talking about murder. Ivan tells them for whatever reason, 'I was just in a house with a dead guy, I was in this house and I was in there just to steal copper, trying to take some copper out to salvage and steal, and I saw a dead man.' He's talking about John Wolff.

"Now, as I mentioned to you earlier, this is what's going on in St. Joe. By December 3rd, John has been found. And the police are there looking through the evidence. And they're trying to sift through this mountain, this mountain of mess. And they'll tell you that there wasn't very much blood, and they'll tell you that they didn't find any fingerprints although they looked. And they didn't find any DNA. But what they did find in that house amongst all that dust and ash were footprints belonging to two people. So they had a footprint to go on.

"You'll hear that Ivan Johnson when he was arrested was wearing a pair of shoes called Earth-Bandits, size 13 boot. You can get them at Walmart. They're made specifically for Walmart. Ivan didn't buy that pair. He had gone [to a Walmart] about two months before [and] stole a pair, size 13 pair, Earth brand shoes. When he's arrested, he's wearing size 13 Earth-Bandit boots. That footprint that was in the dust was compared to those boot prints, those boots. And they are the same in every respect, size, shape, sole design. Somebody from the crime lab will describe that to you. And he will tell you they are consistent with a size 13 Earth-Bandit boot. And there's an employee from Walmart [who] will tell you that there [are] under 7,000 of this type of shoe and this size of shoe sold in the United States. And Ivan Johnson, the week of the murder, the week after he had been trying to get people to help him rob and murder this guy, is found wearing that very pair of shoes.

"Now, Ivan immediately tries to blame other people. First of all he tells the cops I've never been to Macon, never been to that area, because he's trying to distance himself from the murder. Tells Howard Judd and Mike Wilkerson that. But he's then interviewed by David Hall. Not really interviewed. David Hall approaches him because they're hoping there might be some DNA on the clothing. There wasn't much blood to begin with, but they're hoping. When David Hall describes to Ivan, 'I need to do a buccal swab to test your DNA, stick a Q-tip in your mouth and swab the skin cells on your cheek, I need to do this to see if you've got some DNA left behind at the crime scene,' Ivan Johnson's reaction was, 'If you put something in my mouth, I'm going to bite it off.'

"David Hall decides to ask him about that jacket. Says, 'Hey, what about this greenish blue flannel jacket that we now know people saw you in on the very day when this murder happened, that you immediately traded once you got to St. Joe, what about that jacket?' Ivan says, 'I don't know what you're talking about, I don't own a jacket like that, I never had a jacket like that.' But you'll learn that not only did he own it, not only did he have it, there's an actual picture of it taken in Macon County in the sheriff's department files of him wearing that very jacket that he denied owning.

"The next police officer that interviews him is Sheriff Dawson, Macon County sheriff. And you'll get to see videotape of this interview. But what Ivan does first, his first ... reaction, now he's caught, is he blames a fella named Leslie Wright. He says Leslie did it, that Leslie needed a change of clothes right after Thanksgiving, that he approached me about the change of clothes. Said he had gotten down and dirty with somebody. Blaming Leslie Wright for this murder, this robbery of John Wolff. But he doesn't stop with his story there. He's then interviewed later on by Mark Dochterman and

David Bower of the Highway Patrol. His story has now changed, it's not Leslie Wright that did it, it's the Broadways, it's Wilford Broadway and James Bridgewater. They did it. His story is now changed because he knows they're telling law enforcement what they know about his activities, his involvement in this crime. He's now blaming the Broadways. But Ivan as you'll see, he talked to, remember Bobby Smith, he talked to Wayne Bridgewater. He talked to Dinisha Fraley, Maggie Nelson, David Reynolds. He talks to all these people. He can't stop talking apparently because when he's in jail he keeps talking. He talks to an inmate friend of his named Tracy Freeman that he's known for years. And he tells Tracy Freeman details that only the murderer would know about this case. He tells Tracy Freeman that he went in and robbed this old man for money. He describes to Tracy Freeman how filthy the house was, how dirty, how the old man had to use a bucket of water from the pond for a bathroom. He'll describe how the old man put up a good fight. But he didn't stop talking to Tracy Freeman. As the trial got closer, as his day in court approached, he knew what was coming. He knew justice was coming so he had to do something about that. He talked to a guy named Justin Blain, another inmate. What he tells Justin Blain is, 'I need you to go lie, I need you to go lie to the prosecutors, I need you to even lie to my own attorney, and I need you to tell them David Reynolds did it.' Justin Blain, I think, will come forward and tell you about those conversations. But that's not all he did to stop this day in court from coming. That's not all he did to avoid justice."

At that point, Attorney Zwink interrupted and said, "Objection, Judge, that's argumentative. He's been wanting this day."

Judge Conley, the Court, responds, "The objection will be sustained. Continue."

Attorney Zoellner resumes:

"The next thing he did was talk to another inmate named Sam Bailey. What he tells Sam is, 'The Broadways are going to testify against me.' And he knows [that] Sam is in for, I think it was some piddly assault charge or something, probation violation; Sam is getting out. And Ivan knows that, and

Sam is from up in that area. [Ivan] says, 'When you get out, I need you to call the Broadways.' Gives him a phone number and letter. 'You need to tell them that if you testify against me, you're a done deal.' Sam asked him, 'Well, what's a done deal?' He said, 'What happened to Wolffy, the old man, that was a done deal.' He's threatening the Broadways. Then when Sam gets out, he calls Sam from the jail and asks Sam, 'Did you call them?' Sam says, 'No.' Ivan then threatens Sam and threatens Sam's girlfriend for not having cooperated in threatening the witnesses against him.

"Ladies and gentlemen, I know there's a lot of little pieces here. But when this trial is over in a couple of days, we'll get to come back and talk to you and help you put the pieces together if they aren't already there for you. But what I want you to know when you get to that point, there's only one person [who] knew John Wolff had money, there's only one person [who] spent all his time talking to people about wanting to rob John Wolff. There's only one person [who] was asking people to go out there and rob John Wolff with him. There's only one person [who] tried to find his house in the middle of the night and couldn't. There's only one person walking around with that green jacket on during the time frame John was killed. There's only one person [who] got rid of that jacket and then denied ever owning [that] jacket … when we've got a picture of him wearing it. There's only one person with a size 13 boot that was found at the crime scene. There's only one person [who's] guilty. He sits right there. His name is Ivan Johnson."

Chapter 27

Judge Conley: "Opening statement for the defense."

Attorney Zwink commences:

"You find out somebody in jail is charged with murder and it's a prime opportunity. A prime opportunity when you're facing charges like manufacture of meth and you have several convictions in your past, and you know that this person is accused of murder, and all you have to do is say, 'Ivan came into my cell and he said I trust you, I just want to tell you this, I did it.' It's a prime opportunity after the police have come and talked to you, now that you have me in custody, I want to tell you Ivan called me up and confessed. I can go over all these statements the State is saying Ivan made. There's no doubt Ivan talked. You're going to hear all the things that people are going to say he said. But you need to wait to hear that. Because there's something about this case that just doesn't make sense. It doesn't make sense. John Wolff was a person that stayed secluded. If you want to call him a hermit. He was a person that kept to himself. He was kind of a strange guy in the sense that sometimes people would come by and he would say, 'Hi,' and talk to them, and sometimes he would just turn away. But for the most part he stayed in this house that you're going to be seeing pictures of. And he kept it locked up and secure. And he kept it boarded up. And you're going to find out it was so boarded up, all the windows were so boarded up that the house was almost pitch black even in the daytime. And when the police came to the scene to investigate this, they first started to film the inside of it. This is in broad daylight. They realized there isn't ample enough light. They had to actually bring a generator and put lights in there. It's a house that has no electricity. It's a house that has no water. John Wolff wouldn't open that door for people. People would come, some people would come. People who were trying to help would come, they would knock on his door. He would come and look out the window to see if he recognized you. But even if he recognized you, most of the time he wouldn't come out. Somebody brought food to him [who] had just seen him in a restaurant, knocked on the door, they're out there with food. Somebody from Ethel. Somebody he has seen before. He looks out and shakes his head no. Now, some people he would on occasion open the door for; Dean Gordon was one of them. But even [then], and Dean made a habit of coming over there and bringing Thanksgiving food; Christmas, he'd bring Christmas food. And his grandson or granddaughter would come over there on occasion. But one time his granddaughter goes over, and she had been gone for a couple years so she had grown, and John wouldn't even open the door for her. He was fearful. He was fearful. He was paranoid. And you'll see that. He would not open the door for anybody.

"Ethel is a small town. 100 people. Basically everyone knows where Macon is. You go over about 10 or 15 miles, and it's about 10 miles north. Out in the middle of nowhere. There's a highway, Highway 149 that runs through it. Runs up and over these railroad tracks and then it cuts back to the west and then back through town. There's 100 people in this town. And before you get to the railroad tracks as you're coming in, there's a part of town, there's a couple streets that come up out here that have, I don't how many for sure, [maybe] 20 houses on one side of the railroad tracks. Across the railroad ... tracks, turn left ... and you've got a couple of businesses, a gas station, a restaurant on one side, and on the other side, kind of the center focus of town, is the post office where Linda Lile works. From that post office she could look out the front door and up this hill, and at the top of the hill [is] ... where the restaurant is, and up behind there is John Wolff's house. And if you were to go up to John Wolff's house, you'll find there's a road that goes towards the east with houses back over here. There's a house right ... past it, and there's a series of houses all around here. Behind it is a hill that goes down with a wooded area. This is wintertime, no leaves on these trees. Into a pond area. No one knows when John Wolff is going to come out.

"Look at Ivan. We all can look and see that Ivan is a big black guy. Big black guy in a town that does not have any black people living there. And on Saturday, November 29th, Ivan is seen on the wrong side of the tracks that are away from John Wolff's house. He's looking for Art Sellick's house, and he's knocking on a door, and a woman approaches. It's the granddaughter of this woman's house that he was knocking on the door. She said, 'Can I help you?' He said 'I'm looking for Art Sellick's house.' She tells him where Art Sellick lives, which is down the street up a little ways, and there's a house and Art Sellick's house is right behind that. Railroad tracks are right next to it.

"The police come to the scene. Actually there's a concerned citizen call, haven't seen John Wolff, could somebody come out and check this out. Police come to the scene, actually just one person, this deputy Michael Johnston. He takes a person by the name of Bernard Jones, who is also somebody who actually helps John Wolff. Bernard takes him shopping come the 3rd of the month. Has done that for approximately a year. So Bernard comes out. Bernard is one of the concerned people, along with Linda Lile. They go up together and get to this house, they look around, they don't see anything wrong with the house. All right. Deputy Johnson, who is there because these citizens are concerned, can't see anything about the yard or the presence of the house, window wise, door wise, anything that to him suggests somebody has been killed. No forced entry. Knocks on the door, nobody answers. Walks around knocking on windows trying to peer in but he can't see in because most of the windows are barred up. Eventually after checking out whether he's able to do it, whether he's able to actually break in because of this, they end up prying open a door and coming into the scene which you're going to see. ... You're going to see pictures ... where pry bars, screwdriver, hammers, this scene where people have tore into this and reached into different filing cabinets and so forth. Ripped drawers, these metal drawers, ripped them up. And remember, this is a house without any electricity. This was a house that's extremely cluttered with stuff. This is a house without any forced entry. And they collect the scene and while they're doing that, the police do what they call a canvass, which is just talking with people that live around [there] to find out if anybody saw or heard anything, and not one person, not one person on John Wolff's side of the tracks ever said, 'Hey I saw this big black man hiding right there out in front of the house where we all could see him.' Not anybody ever said that. He was seen Saturday morning at 10 in the morning. This is Saturday after Thanksgiving. You think about it, this is a day that the post office is open. Basically the hub of the town, kind of a center of entertainment. This is how small the town is but just where people gather. Where people are driving by. Not one person said they ever saw Ivan Johnson on that side. But the sheriff's department, police officers, you know, all do the same thing. They do the thing that we would all do which is they start trying to figure out what happened and start thinking about who might have done this. And the sheriff's department was aware that Ivan Johnson was in town, and Ivan Johnson was the first name that popped in their head before there was any evidence that suggested Ivan might have been. Ivan is their number one suspect before, from the beginning. And Ivan was arrested in St. Joe.

"Now, Thanksgiving night, Thanksgiving Day, food is delivered to John Wolff's house. Saturday, the day Ivan Johnson is seen in Ethel on the opposite side of the tracks where John Wolff lives, that day John Wolff, that night John Wolff was seen by a person outside by the name of Geoff Christy. So he was still alive Saturday evening. Ivan was arrested because he had an outstanding warrant out of a different town, out of Kansas. He was arrested when the police came to this scene to basically, called a knock and talk, just talk with people there and get names and discovered that Ivan had this warrant. That he is when he was arrested. Once he was arrested on the 3rd, the sheriff's department in Macon, actually that was where the warrant was out of, he had a warrant for bad checks out of Macon. And he said he had never been to Macon, and they realized this because he's got this warrant that he's telling them he had never been to Macon. Because the second he finds out he's a suspect, he's totally telling them, 'Yes, I have been to Macon, in fact I live in Macon.' So he's telling them that. Sheriff Dawson calls the Buchanan

County sheriff's department. Talks to Lieutenant Colley and says look, we suspect Ivan was involved in this murder, burglary/murder. And because we suspect that, what I want you to do, we've got torn up filing cabinets, ripped up metal, you need to go look at Ivan and see if he's got any injuries. See if he's got any injuries. And so I'm not sure if he was a detective, Officer Wilkerson and another officer go under a pretext, have Ivan take off his shirt. And they look over him carefully. And you'll see with all the, all these tools, all this torn up place, operating supposedly in a house that has supposedly no light and cluttered like it is, they will tell you there was not a single injury that they could see on Ivan, not a single scratch, not a single cut, nothing. Nothing on Ivan.

"The State tells you that [John Wolff] was killed when somebody was waiting outside for him to come out so they could then take advantage. They want you to believe that Ivan sat in the middle of this town, out in the middle of nowhere where no black people live, just waiting.

"They start investigating and they start talking to people. One of the persons they talk to is David Reynolds. And the State is telling you that David Reynolds did this with Ivan. David Reynolds is not charged with any crime. I don't even know if David Reynolds knows that the State just told you that. But David Reynolds tells the police that he took Ivan Johnson to St. Joe on Thanksgiving evening with Anthony Minnis. They both say the same thing. And Ivan says it. And then because David Reynolds was with Ivan, they start questioning David Reynolds, questioning David Reynolds. And now they're going to tell you that David Reynolds had something to do with this too. First I hear of it. But Wayne Bridgewater, I could go through all of these, and I'm not going to go through all of these, but I'm going to do this with at least one person, and you'll see what I'm talking about. None of these people that the State is telling you that, 'Ivan, oh, yeah, Ivan talked to me about wanting to rob this guy.' You'll find out when Ronnie Broadway said, 'Hey, you know that old man has a bunch of money,' when by the way everybody in Ethel thought that, Linda Lile the postal worker, she's not going to be willing to admit to that because it's rude, but you'll see that everybody in town had this idea that this guy had a lot of money. When Ronnie Broadway said 'Oh, hey, you know that old man has a bunch money,' Wilford Broadway says, you know, 'Shut up. You just got that guy killed' because of these 15 or 16 criminals that were around at the time that it was said.

"Wayne Bridgewater who doesn't say anything about Ivan calling him up and confessing gets locked up as a juvenile. Now he's in detention two months later finding out that Ivan thinks that Wilford Broadway did this. His relative. He says, 'Oh, no, Ivan talked to me and he confessed.' Which you'll find out when they go first talk to Ivan and they ask, 'Have you talked to anybody since you've been in jail?' The first thing he said was 'Yeah, I talked to Wayne Bridgewater. I talked to Wayne Bridgewater,' He's not going to say, 'But you know I confessed. I talked to Wayne Bridgewater.' That's the first person he confessed to. So a couple months later Wayne Bridgewater is … in custody saying, 'Oh yeah, Ivan confessed he did this.' Never said anything about, 'Oh he tried to ask me to help him.' You'll find that out. He doesn't do that until later when he's in custody for something else.

"So I could go through all these statements in opening. I'm not going to. But when a person is charged with murder, you're going to find out how the people that are sitting in jail facing the loss of liberty are going to take advantage of it. And the thing is that this does not make sense. And as you listen to this and watch the evidence come in, it is clear that Ivan didn't do this. And you will have to come back with not guilty.

"Thank you."

Chapter 28

So, there you have it. Two opposing theories of the same event. I know which one sounded the most plausible to me from everything I had been told by law enforcement and read about in newspapers and heard about not only in the preliminary hearing but thus far in that very courtroom. But now, I had to get through the actual trial, and I was anxiety-ridden about being called to the witness stand.

Judge Conley: "Evidence for the State. Call your first witness."

Attorney Zoellner: "Mary [Wolff]."

And so it began, the first trial day of three. I was the very first witness, trying to speak about John as to the person he was before he became hermit-like. I tried to portray him in a favorable light for the jury, to help the jury see John as a "person," not simply as a paranoid schizophrenic person with no life value. I tried to highlight his value as a Vietnam vet, to provide a window of understanding of the mental illness that might ensue such service. In my emotional state, however, Attorney Zoellner had to ask some very leading questions in order to pull out any kind of detailed response from me. I know I did not do a good job at showing them the John that I had known and loved. Perhaps my obvious state of distress spoke for me better than my words could have.

Dean Gordon testified next. In the interim between meeting Dean in Ethel when we cleaned out John's house and the day of the trial, he had suffered a stroke. He had been very upset when I briefly talked with him and his wife outside the courtroom before the trial began. Dean struggled to convey his feelings, and he had a hard time controlling his tears. I thanked him profusely for coming forward that day. His testimony was drawn out in basically simple yes or no answered questions.

What follows are brief summaries of testimony from all "players'"
and how each of them had participated in John's murder drama. Both the
State's and the Prosecution's Opening Statements are undoubtedly even better
at depicting their exact roles, the roles that led to John's murder and the
solving thereof.

Day 1 – November 1, 2005

I had testified first and Dean Gordon second. Mr. Gordon testified to
the fact that John seemed to trust him, and he helped and essentially cared
about John. That said, he let jurors know that even he was not allowed entry
into John's home.

Linda Lile – Ethel Postmistress. Ms. Lile testified that she kept an
eye on John from the post office and could be considered his friend. She
testified that there was no smoke coming from the chimney and that John had
not picked up his check as usual, thus she alerted law enforcement (along
with Bernard Jones).

Michael Johnson – Head of investigations for the Macon County
Sheriff. He and Bernard Jones went in the house and discovered John's body.
Mr. Johnson took Mr. Jones along because John would talk to him.

Brian Hayes – Macon County Coroner. He testified as to why
December 3rd was used as the date of death, and he testified as to the cause of
death.

Edward Adelstein – Deputy Medical Examiner who conducted
autopsies in cases of suspicious deaths. He testified as to how John was
dressed and how the assault had injured him. He also testified regarding time
of death issues.

Kurt Mueller – With the Missouri State Highway Patrol, Division of
Drug & Crime Patrol. He collected evidence and took photos during the
autopsy.

Wilford Broadway – Testified that he had heard from others about
the "Wolffman." He started giving John rides to the store because he was a
fellow Vietnam vet. He then started to deliver firewood to him. He stated that

John had an "old plastic container. There was a lot of money in it."

Bobby Smith – Wilford Broadway's nephew. He heard his cousin Ronnie Broadway talk about John "having money hid away somewhere." Mr. Smith testified that Ivan told him that he wanted to rob John.

Ronnie Broadway – Another of Wilford Broadway's nephews. He helped deliver firewood to John, and he testified that he told Ivan that "the old, the man had money." He also testified that Ivan was in Ethel on Saturday around noon and that he had binoculars. [I found, as had the investigators, a binoculars box in John's house, but no binoculars.]

Errol Coder – Wilford Broadway's cousin, who met Ivan in Macon. He took him to Wilford Broadway's to help him build his house. He was in jail with Ivan Johnson after Thanksgiving 2003. He testified that Ivan asked him to remind the Broadways that he was at their house on Friday of that Thanksgiving week.

Anthony Minnis – Friend of Charles Douglas (C-Dog) with whom Ivan Johnson lived in Macon. He testified that Ivan said, "Something that he was going to get a pump from a dude in Ethel … an old man or something."

Wayne Bridgewater – Incarcerated at the time of trial. His father was Jimmy Bridgewater (already deceased at time of trial). He was a friend of Wilford Broadway. He testified that he knew Ivan through his dad, basically his whole life. Ivan had asked Mr. Bridgewater to drive him to John's house to steal money that he could use to post bail for his charges in Kansas. Mr. Bridgewater testified that a day or two after Thanksgiving, Ivan called and told him "he went over to the guy's house and he beat him. And took his money so he could bail out of jail in Topeka, Kansas."

Day 2 – November 2, 2005

David Reynolds is now missing and thus not available to testify.

Dinisha Fraley – Also a friend of Charles Douglas (C-Dog). She testified that Ivan Johnson wanted her to give him a ride to John's so that he could rob him. Ms. Fraley testified that Ivan said, it "would be easy … no neighbors … didn't think he even had any family. Nobody would know."

Maggie Nelson – Testified that Ivan had virtually the same conversation with her as Ms. Fraley had. Ms. Nelson stated that Ivan had wanted a ride out to Ethel to rob John for "something about a bond he had to pay in another county." She stated that Ivan asked her this on two occasions.

Jerry Pickens – In jail at time of trial. Mr. Pickens testified that he was with Ivan Johnson and David Reynolds (Wayne Bridgewater's brother) when they went to Ethel where Ivan said they went to meet some girls and to look for John's house. Mr. Pickens testified that Ivan had said he wanted to rob "this old man," but, "Ivan couldn't find the house."

Amber Haun Griffin – Testified that she saw Ivan in Ethel on Saturday after Thanksgiving. Ms. Griffin also testified that she had seen a vehicle that she did not recognize on the night before (Friday). She said that Ivan – on Saturday – had knocked on her grandmother's door to ask directions to Art Sellick's.

David Hall – Criminal investigator for the Missouri State Highway Patrol. Sgt. Hall gave lengthy testimony regarding the crime scene and the evidence presented. He focused on Ivan Johnson's denial of owning clothing that he had been seen wearing and was photographed as wearing, specifically his denial of owning the shoes that were later proven to be his and proven to be at the crime scene. Sgt. Hall also testified as to Ivan's unwillingness to provide his DNA sample.

Christy Nichols – Testified that she stole a black Carharrt jacket for Ivan in exchange for drugs. The black jacket was found, through evidence presented and other testimony, to be a replacement for the jacket Ivan Johnson wore when perpetrating the crime.

James Battick – Ms. Nichols' boyfriend; Ms. Nichols being the mother of his child. He testified that he saw Ivan Johnson in St. Joseph the Saturday or Sunday after Thanksgiving.

Shane Proper – Testified that he had been at his aunt's house watching a murder show on TV a few days after Thanksgiving with Ivan Johnson, and his aunt had wondered what they would do if they found a body. Mr. Proper testified that Ivan said, "Well, I found one once before, too." Ivan had said that it was when he went to strip a house of copper.

Brenda Proper – Shane Proper's aunt. She testified that a few days after Thanksgiving Ivan Johnson had said he was getting pipes out of a house and stumbled over a dead body.

Michael Wilkerson – With the Buchanan County Drug Strike Force/Narcotics. He found Ivan Johnson hiding in a house in St. Joseph where drugs were dealt. At that time, Ivan Johnson lied about his birth date. Detective Wilkerson had found out about a non-extraditable warrant out of Macon and a felony warrant out of Kansas.

Howard Judd – Worked alongside Detective Wilkerson on the Buchanan County Drug Strike Force. Detective Judd testified that he found a dark plaid jacket with hood, which Ivan Johnson "emphatically denied ever owning such an article." Ivan told him that he had never been to Macon. During a second interview, another date, Ivan Johnson told him that he did live in Macon with Charles Douglas and also with Jimmy "Pops" Bridgewater who was like an uncle to him. Detective Judd testified further that during this particular interview, Ivan contradicted an earlier statement about being at the Bridgewaters *before* Thanksgiving because he mentions that he was there having Thanksgiving leftovers.

Tracy Freeman – In jail with Ivan Johnson for several weeks. He testified that Ivan told him he was suspected of killing an "old man" somewhere around Macon. Ivan told him about the conditions of John's house. Mr. Freeman testified that "[Ivan] did say it was in the daytime," and that he came up the back way. Ivan told Mr. Freeman that "the old man gave him a run for his money."

Sam Smiley – Also in jail with Ivan. Sam testified that Ivan Johnson had given him a letter and told him that when he was released he was to call Wilford Broadway to say, "He better not show up for court … or he would be done like Wolff." Mr. Smiley testified that Ivan kept calling him and "screaming, threatening, yelling" because he had given the letter to the State's Attorney. He finally blocked Ivan's calls.

Justin Blain – Incarcerated at the time of trial. He testified that Ivan

Johnson wanted him to lie and say that he (Justin) had been in a bar with David Reynolds and that Reynolds talked about killing somebody. Ivan told Mr. Blain to tell that to the prosecutors and Ivan's own attorney.

Thereafter, testimony ensued regarding the existence of physical evidence or the attempts to get such. The evidence was presented piece by piece.

Stephany Louk-Denney – With the Missouri State Highway Patrol Crime Lab. Ms. Louk-Denney gave a description of the fingerprinting that was done on items taken from John's house (whiskey bottle and safe), and how she had had no luck getting usable evidence.

Kimberly Hardin – Also with the Missouri State Highway Patrol Crime Lab. Ms. Hardin testified that she found "no prints of value" on the pair of wooden doors, the sledgehammer, the hammer, or the binocular case. She testified that she had found some partial prints, but there was not enough detail on the door locks of the wooden doors.

William Randle – With the Missouri State Highway Patrol Crime Lab working as a trace evidence examiner. Trace evidence includes hair, fiber, paint, explosive materials, soil, and foreign substances. Mr. Randle testified that the dirty environment of John's house was problematic. He had checked John's clothing, but Ivan Johnson's clothing was not examined until six (6) days after the body was found. He checked all clothing for pepper spray, which might have been used in the robbery, but did not find any. He did find one green fiber in the boot gelatins taken at the crime scene, but he was unable to match it to anything.

Stacy Bollinger – With the Missouri State Highway Patrol Crime Lab as a DNA analyst. Ms. Bollinger testified as to where they had found blood that was tested, basically on Ivan Johnson's jeans and on a Kleenex taken from the crime scene. She visually saw five (5) small stains on the back cuff near the bottom of Ivan's jeans, about the size of the clicking end of a pen.

After that testimony, a sidebar took place in the Court about bringing FBI test results in. Attorney Zwink was concerned that there would be testimony regarding results from samples that Ms. Bollinger sent to them.

Attorney Zoellner said it was sent to the FBI because "they can do mitochondrial DNA work, because they can do the smaller work." He continued, "The FBI was able to determine there was a mixture but they don't know whose because with mitochondrial you can't take it any further." Attorney Zwink is concerned with this because "he's [Zoellner's] going to want her to testify to the fact, besides the fact it's hearsay objection, but testify to the fact mixture of two, mixture of two individuals. But they don't know whose it is." Mr. Zoellner then says, "Basically that they determined there was a mixture of two person's DNAs there and that's it. Because of the nature of the testing, they're not able ..." The Court determines, "I'll permit you to show you sent it to the FBI but I don't think that what their results were needs to come in. That they weren't able to ..."

And so, Ms. Bollinger testifies that the sample had some DNA, but "we were not able to make enough copies to make a DNA profile."

Mike Coppedge – Walmart store manager in Macon. Mr. Coppedge testified about the theft of the Earth-Link boots from his store. He said that Ivan Johnson had come in with someone else, but they then split up. Ivan went into the restroom with a shoe box and came out without it. Ivan then met up with the other man and left the store. Mr. Coppedge's employee had alerted him as to what was happening. Ivan had left his old shoes in the box in the store.

Linda Renburg – Worked in the shoe department at the Walmart in Macon. When she saw the theft occurring, she called a Code 1200 over the intercom, which is a shoplifting alert. Ms. Renburg identified the shoes that should have been in the box – Size 13 Bandit, a hiker boot. Ms. Renburg also identfied Ivan Johnson as being the man who shoplifted the shoes that day. She said that she had thrown away the old tennis shoes that he had left in the Size 13 Bandit box.

Robert Dawson – Macon County Sheriff. He had a December 17, 2003, interview with Ivan Johnson videotaped after he had given Ivan his Miranda warning. This videotape was played in Court. During the interview, Ivan blamed Leslie Wright for the murder. He said, "Les Wright had called and wanted somebody to bring him some clothes, said he got down and dirty." Sheriff Dawson had tracked down Mr. Wright and found no evidence linking him to the crime. Ivan also talked about the Broadways during this interview, but he did not suggest that they murdered John.

Also during the interview, Ivan said that he had been in Ethel either on November 28th or November 29th (the Friday or Saturday after Thanksgiving). He said that he visited Dean Broadway and Art Sellick; he wanted to buy pot from Mr. Sellick. He said that he had been in Ethel a total of three (3) times. The first, Ivan said, was when he helped deliver wood in September. The second time was when he went with Dave Reynolds and Jerry Pickens to get pot. And, Ivan said the third time was a day or two after Thanksgiving when he went to see Mr. Broadway and Mr. Sellick. He said that on Thanksgiving eve, he had gone to St. Joseph and the day after had hitchhiked back to Macon.

Day 3 – November 3, 2005

Mark Dochterman – Criminal investigator with the Missouri Highway Patrol. Sgt. Dochterman conducted a July 15, 2004, interview with Ivan Johnson, after giving him his Miranda rights. Ivan Johnson told him that he had delivered wood to John's house with Wilford Broadway and had seen him go into John's house to be paid. Ivan then stated that Wilford Broadway was having money trouble and was unable to borrow more from the bank. Ivan went on to talk about how on the Friday after Thanksgiving he had hitchhiked from St. Joseph to Ethel to get pot. He said that Art Sellick then dropped him off in New Cambria. From New Cambria, Ivan said he went back to Macon and then to St. Joseph. Sgt. Dochterman asked him why he needed to buy new clothes in St. Joseph. He told Sgt. Dochterman that "he works out a lot and in fact he told us he works out three to, about three times a day, six hours workout and he sweats a lot and did not want to smell."

During the interview, Ivan told Sgt. Dochterman, "I know who did it. I know the facts." Sgt. Doctherman went on to testify, "He stated that in September and also in October and also the day before Thanksgiving that

Wilford Broadway, Mr. Broadway, who he was living with, stated that they wanted, and he used this saying that I won't forget is, 'I want to hit a lick in Ethel.' I thought, 'Well what does a lick in Ethel mean?' He said, 'To make a robbery for money.' And he stated that Mr. Broadway asked him about it in September and October 2003 and the day before Thanksgiving that they wanted him, also along with a person by the name of who we called Pops, who we found later on his last name is Bridgewater. And they were going to drive to Ethel to where Mr. Wolff lived and hit this lick by robbing Mr. Wolff, stating that he had approximately $2,000 that he had in some type of container." Ivan also went on to clarify that he had not gone to St. Joseph on the Sunday or Monday he previously testified to in an interview. Ivan said he actually went to St. Joseph on Thursday night (Thanksgiving night) and again on Sunday. Ivan clearly says that he was in Ethel on Friday, but the Sgt. was unsure about Saturday.

Todd Garrison – Another witness from the Missouri State Highway Patrol Crime Lab. Mr. Garrison gave very lengthy testimony regarding footwear impressions – the photos and gelatin lifters – how they are made and what information can be deduced from them. Attorney Zoellner wraps up the testimony regarding Ivan Johnson's stolen Size 13 Bandit boots from Walmart by asking, "So with respect to individual characteristics, you can't exclude or include these boots at all, can you? Answer: "That's correct." Question: "Would it be fair to say based on your observations at the scene and your examinations of those boots that ... these boots are consistent with having created those impressions." Answer: "They're consistent with the class characteristics I had seen represented by those questioned impressions in the photographs and lifters." Question: "Based on your training and experience there's nothing about those boots that is inconsistent with what you found at the crime scene?" Answer: "That's correct."

And then came the final, crucial piece of testimony upon which Johnson's guilty verdict was hinged. Thank God for those footprints and for Johnson's theft of the Walmart shoes.

Brad Schaffner - Final witness for the State. Mr. Schaffner is a shoe buyer for Walmart Stores, Incorporated, the corporate Walmart office in Bentonville, Arkansas. He is the prime witness who can directly tie Ivan Johnson's stolen Bandit shoes to the crime scene.

Attorney Zoellner brings out State's Exhibit 118, the pair of Bandit shoes. Through questioning, Schaffner attests that he was in charge of the sales of that particular shoe, the Earth Bandit. He attests that Earth Bandits are proprietary to Walmart, and that their plant in Bentonville, Arkansas, designed the upper and the outsole and sourced it directly through a factory in China. Thus, it is only available at Walmart stores.

Questioning highlighted how the outsole is made of molded plastic, and that the molding would be different for each individual size of shoe, that a size 12 is different from a size 13, etc. Schaffner further testified that Earth Bandits were first sold in July of 2003.

State's Exhibit 146 was a report of how many Earth Bandits were sold from the time of the shoe's launch in the U.S. up through January 31, 2004, while State's Exhibit 145 was a chart to more easily relay the report's information.

Throughout the U.S., a total of 6,855 pairs of Earth Bandits had been sold in size 13. Only 211 were sold in Walmart stores throughout the state of Missouri. The records indicate that no size 13's were "sold" either in the Macon store or the nearby Brookfield store.

Attorney Zwink then commences a cross- and recross-examination which, to me, seemed to tie Johnson even more directly to the physical evidence found rather than exclude him. He asked Schaffner whether or not his records reflect the number of shoes that were stolen, and the answer was that it did not.

Q. "So there's no, you're not talking about, you do not know the number of those size 13 or any of the sizes basically that were stolen from Walmart?"

A. "No."

Redirect Examination by Attorney Zoellner:

Q. "Mr. Schaffner, if there was testimony in this case that there was one pair stolen by someone in the Macon store, we could put a number one there, couldn't we? In terms of distributed from your store?"

A. "I would guess, yes."

Q. "Okay. I don't have any other questions."

Recross-Examination by Attorney Zwink:

Q. "How many numbers, do you know how many numbers you could add then to that?"

A. "What's that? I'm not sure I understand that question."

Q. "He just said if you had, if there was testimony that one pair of shoes was stolen, you could add number one to that number, right?"

A. "One that left the store I guess, yes."

Q. "Yeah. And in terms of number that left the store not purchased you can't say?"

A. "For the other numbers, no."

Q. "Or any of the numbers for that matter?"

A. "I don't have a way to track what was stolen, no."

Q. "Okay."

At this point a sidebar commences to determine if all the evidence has been admitted. After concluding that all evidence has been properly admitted, Attorney Zoellner indicates that the State intends to rest. Attorney Zwink then says he'd like to file a Motion For Judgment of Acquittal, which is admitted. Before the Court allows Attorney Zwink a requested break before he calls his defense witnesses, the Court held an "off-the-record" discussion with Ivan Johnson to inform him of his right to be a witness in his own defense if he so chose. A 10-minute recess was then held.

The Court: "State rests?"

Mr. Zoellner: "Yes, Your Honor."

Witnesses for defendant

What follows is a summary of the defense witnesses. There is really no one who can substantiate any of the claims made by Ivan Johnson. And no one can give Johnson a solid alibi since there was no way to pinpoint exactly when the murder took place.

Bernard Jones – A fellow vet who gave John rides to the bank and stores. He testified basically that John trusted him. Attorney Zwink asked Mr. Jones to give a brief description of John to which he responded, "Well, he was a little different because of Vietnam. But he was smart, a very smart man." From there he testified as to what door John came out of when Bernard went to pick him up or check on him. Attorney Zoellner did a redirect examination of Mr. Jones in which he said that John would <u>never</u> let him in the house and he never saw that John had a lot of money.

Mark Lusher – Mr. Lusher was John's neighbor for about a year, he lived just down the alley from him. [As I recall from my initial visit to clean out John's house, it was not easy to actually see the Lusher house because of property line vegetation and John's old shed.] He testified about the location of John's house relative to its surroundings and how John basically did not carry on conversations with anyone. At one point, Mr. Lusher had asked John about the raspberry patch behind his house. "I asked him about picking raspberries. He kind of laughed a little bit. Said 'Have you got any whiskey?' I said, 'Oh, no, I don't drink.' And he told me I could pick berries. That was about the end of that conversation." He then testified that he had not seen Ivan Johnson around John's house over that Thanksgiving weekend.

Art Sellick – His sister is married to Wilford Broadway. Mr. Sellick testified that his wife said that Ivan came over on the Saturday after Thanksgiving, not on Friday as he himself had thought. He said that Ivan was there only one time that weekend, and that when he was there, he had a pair of binoculars with him. [Again, we had found the box for the binoculars amongst John's possessions, but not the binoculars.] Mr. Sellick further testified that he took Ivan to Ken's Junction store in New Cambria around noon that day.

Wilford Broadway – Had testified for the State. Attorney Zwink appeared to be grilling him on his not wanting to tell the police who his nephew was and about what his nephew had said. Mr. Broadway replied that he figured that his nephew should be the one to tell the police what he had said and heard. Additionally, he questioned him about whether or not he had money troubles, at which point Mr. Broadway pulled papers out of his pocket showing that he had substantial loans for expenses to build his house.

Aric Bowzer – Canine handler for the County of Macon. Sgt. Hall had wanted him to search for a wallet on John's property. Attorney Zwink simply wanted him to say that he had found no evidence. Attorney Zoellner cross-examined him to show that the dog was only looking for John's scent on any discarded evidence.

Geoff Christy – A high school student who said that when he went to get mail after school, he was able to see what was going on at John's house. He claimed that he had seen John on Saturday night, about 9:00 or 10:00 p.m., in the dark. "I think it was Saturday." Mr. Christy claimed that he talked to John for 5 or 10 minutes while he was doing something to a window or a door. [First of all, John wouldn't have talked with anyone in the dark, nor would he have talked as long as 5 or 10 minutes.]

Chapter 29

At approximately 11:15 a.m. on Thursday, November 3, 2005, the Defense rests. The Court recessed until 1:00 p.m. When the jury returned, Judge Conley gave them their instructions. This was followed by the State's Opening Argument by Attorney Zoellner.

State's opening argument

"The judge just read to you a bunch of instructions, and you take those with you. And he told you what the law is. But what he told you in there, if you listen carefully – and I think this is one of the most important things you should keep in mind – is that you should be guided by your common sense, your judgment and your years of wisdom and experience. Because that's what these cases come down to. It's sort of like the Republicans and Democrats. You may get that impression, trying to spin evidence. This is what it really means. What I want you to do is look at all of the evidence. I don't want you to cross apart and think you have to resolve all. Because there's a lot of evidence that you've heard that's conflicting. I mean, was Ivan Johnson in St. Joe on Saturday like some of these witnesses thought or was he in Macon like he said he was? People are mistaken. You have to sift through it and look at it.

"And what I'm going to hope to do is ... give you some idea of the things I would like you to consider as [you use] your common sense. And ... I'm going to start with those boots. Witnesses lie. Every witness who took the stand has a motive to lie. The defendant when he's interviewed by the police has a motive to lie. He doesn't want to go to prison. Evidence, the tongue in these shoes, they can't lie. There were 6800 of those shoes in United States sold in that time frame. 6800. Actually, if you remember that number is high because it includes two months after the murder. 6800 people are walking around with this pair of shoes on. Use your common sense. Mr. Johnson is seen stealing a pair of those two months prior to this murder. Mr. Johnson is arrested in that pair of boots six, seven days, whatever it was, December 3rd, after the murder."

Attorney Zoellner proceeds to focus on all of Johnson's lies. He lied about owning and wearing the size 13 Earth Bandit shoes. He claimed that he had borrowed them. He lied about having and wearing the green plaid jacket, which a witness saw him in, and which they had an actual photo of him wearing. In fact, he not only wore it, but that he then had somebody go out and steal another one for him so he could get rid of the green plaid one. Johnson lied repeatedly about who had committed the murder. First Leslie Wright and then Wilford Broadway. And, he lied repeatedly about where he had been when.

Zoellner attacks Zwink's supposition that it was too cold for Johnson to have been lying in wait outside John's house because of lack of winter clothing. "He had warm enough clothes to hitchhike halfway across the state, didn't he?" And he attacked Zwink's supposition that there was no struggle outside the house. " ... The person who committed this crime is sitting outside waiting for that moment for him to pick up those logs and to walk back into that house. And when he gets up near the doorway, he [John] gets bone-rushed and pushed inside that house. Use your common sense. That's what happened. There's no struggle outside the house. That may or may not be true. But because there's no sign of it as he indicated, doesn't mean he's not dead. Doesn't mean his house wasn't robbed. Just means we don't have a lot of evidence."

Zoellner further confronts the lack of what most people would expect to find at a murder scene – fingerprints and DNA. " I would love to have a fingerprint. But they told you we don't get these hardly ever. The important thing is we don't have a fingerprint there at all. What that means is either they're wearing gloves or because of the nature of the item as the people described to you just didn't leave a fingerprint."

"Same with DNA. It would be nice to have gotten some DNA off of the clothing belonging to Mr. Johnson. And we don't have that. But what I can tell you is there wasn't much blood in that house. There was very little. His injuries that killed him and his broken arm, they didn't bleed. Bled a little bit from the nose. But to have that type of evidence, you have to transfer it. And we just don't have that in this case. Well, that means nothing. Because when Ivan was in there, he took the money he stole. He didn't drop it on the way out like a popcorn trail. He took it. Whatever was taken out of that house was taken. And that's why we couldn't find any evidence outside the house.

"Mr. Zwink wants to confuse you by talking, oh there's no lights in the house. Well, I tell you what, John Wolff lived in the house and regardless of whether it was day or night, it would have been pretty much pitch black in that house. John Wolff had lights in that house or he had flashlights or he had something, he had something going, enough light he could get in there, he could play his little board game. Enough he could chop wood when he wanted to. That's more than enough light for Ivan Johnson to come in and commit this crime."

Zoellner stated that it would seem Johnson had plenty of light since papers had been thrown around while he was looking for money. And, that something had been used to beat John hard enough to break his arm, and the object very well could have been a mag light that Johnson had with him. " ... But the State doesn't have to prove what time he got in there, it doesn't have to prove how he actually got in the house, it doesn't have to prove that there were lights on. That's why we asked you early on whether you would make us prove things we don't have to prove. What we have to prove is that Ivan Johnson committed these crimes. And the issue isn't, if Mr. Zwink will acknowledge it, the issue isn't did these crimes occur because by golly they did. Mr. Wolff was robbed. Mr. Wolff was murdered."

"Ladies and gentlemen, there is only one person [who] spent the months and weeks leading up to this murder asking every person he could to drive him out there to commit this robbery. There's only one person [who] went out there with David Reynolds and Jerry Pickens to try to find the house to commit the robbery. There's only one person [who] has repeatedly lied about the boots that left the impression, about owning these, that was left in that house. There's only one person [who] was wearing this jacket that immediately upon committing this murder denied even owning this jacket. There's only one person [who] stole these boots two months before this murder. There's only one person who tried to blame an innocent black man, Leslie Wright. There's only one person [who] told Tracy Freeman that the man gave me a run for his money. There's only one person [who] tried to get Sam Smiley to threaten witnesses. There's only one person [who] asked Justin Blain to lie to the prosecutors and his own attorney.

"Ivan Johnson is that person. Ivan Johnson is the one that killed John Wolff. He's the one that murdered him. Use your common sense."

Zoellner went through the instructions given to the jury by the judge and pointed out that there were two counts – murder and robbery. "Now, the easy and obvious solution is ... Ivan Johnson committed murder in the second degree because he did it during the course of a robbery and somebody died. That's what we call felony murder. If you read, there's instructions that the judge read to you, you believe there's a robbery occurred and it's obvious that there is, and you believe somebody died, you believe Ivan did it, he's guilty of that crime. The issue, though, is really whether he committed first degree murder. And the difference is here, that means you kill somebody and you deliberate about it. You think about it. You plan it."

Zoellner postulated that, based on Johnson's knowledge of John and the surroundings and his planning of the robbery, that "Ivan Johnson is guilty of first degree murder. He's guilty of robbery in the first degree and you should find him guilty of that."

Closing argument for the defense

Attorney Zwink also focused on using common sense. He stated that it didn't make sense that the prosecutors didn't know exactly when John was murdered. He said it didn't make sense that Geoff Christy would testify seeing John late on Saturday night, while the State's theory was that John was killed before then, before Johnson had been seen in the area. He continued that it didn't make sense that the State didn't believe Johnson's drug-taking friends when they reported where Johnson had been during Thanksgiving weekend.

It didn't make sense to Zwink that Ivan being a black man had not been seen in Ethel. And he went on to say that it didn't make sense that Ivan would "sit outside in an area that is surrounded by houses, has houses around it, has people around it, and wait? [The view of John's house was blocked by trees towards the main road and to the east where the neighbor who testified lived. Across the street were unoccupied houses, and to the back was a tree line overlooking a steep drop to a pond.] I mean the only time that he would do something like that would be late at night. Late at night. And he would not know whether John Wolff is going to come out. He wouldn't know that at all. So why would he do that?"

Zwink continued that it made no sense that there was no physical evidence, no DNA, no fingerprints, no hairs left behind. (Johnson would have been wearing a heavy jacket, gloves, his head was clean shaven, and John's belongings were covered in soot, dust and debris.)

Also to Zwink, it didn't make sense that the witnesses didn't come forward earlier. (It was obvious to me that they would not because many of them were hiding from the law for their own crimes.) And, Zwink stated that it didn't make sense that law enforcement believed any of their witnesses because of this. He inferred that the State gave its witnesses special deals for making up stories to corroborate the State's theory.

"The thing that they can't tell you, they want to make a big deal about Ivan lying or appearing to lie about this clothing. But the thing that they can't explain is injuries. Injuries. Now, this thing with the light, no light in there. The pictures of all the destruction, the tearing up of these filing cabinets. You look at those pictures and you'll know that somebody is reaching in, somebody is tearing this stuff up, reaching in, supposedly got into this altercation with the person. Running around this house that has absolutely no lights. Trying to do all this. Using all these tools, sledges, pry bars, screwdrivers, hammers, chisels. Working around the sharp edges, they knew it was important." But, Zwink goes on, they only find John's blood, no one else's. And, they find no injuries when they examine Johnson. (Again, Johnson was wearing a heavy coat and gloves, so why would he have any injuries?)

And finally, it doesn't make sense, since the State only got partial footprints of a shoe, that it was definitively a size 13 (even though the Walmart buyer testified as to why it was so). And, it didn't make sense that they would know it was the pair that Johnson had stolen.

"It's what the State can't tell you which is important. You're required to find beyond a reasonable doubt that Ivan did this. Beyond a reasonable doubt. This case every step of the way is full of doubt. And Ivan didn't do it. And he's been adamant he didn't do it. And he's been trying and trying and trying to tell them he didn't do it. And he's been desperate trying to get them to look at someone else. He doesn't know who did it, but he didn't do it. And they haven't done it. He's not guilty. And I'm asking you to find him not guilty."

Attorney Zoellner had the opportunity to once again solidify the State's case in his Closing Argument.

Closing argument for the State

Attorney Zoellner: "Mr. Zwink is wrong about one thing. I did tell you all, and I'm sure you paid attention, and I told Mr. Zwink, he said he'd been waiting all this time to find out when the State thought Ivan killed him. We told you that on Monday morning or actually Monday afternoon, I told you then that Ivan killed him some time Saturday night, that he had been out there and he had gotten cold. The evidence, what the evidence supports is he was out there Friday night Saturday morning, some point got cold and started looking for a ride out of town, he needed to go somewhere. He was cold. Goes to Art Sellick's. Winds up at Broadway's. He winds up maybe in New Cambria if you believe Art Sellick. But he winds up back some time late that night in Ethel. And we know somebody else brought him there because he doesn't have a car of his own. And got driven back there because there's two sets of prints in there. Ivan didn't do it alone. By golly I wish we could prove who the other person is. We have our suspicions and so probably do you by this time. But someone drove Ivan back out there late Saturday night. So to sit here and ask Geoff Christy questions, ... a meaningless question. He says he saw Mr. Wolff. We take him at face value. If you listen to his history, do you know Mr. Wolff is going to be out. Maybe he's a strange man apparently. Maybe he's out there at nine o'clock at night fixing a window. Maybe that's when Ivan stumbled upon him and bone-rushed him, but we know he got killed some time late that night because it's the very next morning when Ivan says he went back to St. Joe. Mr. Zwink wants you to believe Ivan wasn't sure he was in town. He told Mark Dochterman point positive, 'I left Thanksgiving night, I left Sunday night and in between that time I was in Macon because that's when they set me up.'"

Zoellner tore into Zwink theorizing that if all that activity had taken place, that there would have been blood left somewhere that wasn't John's.

"Mr. Zwink is absolutely right. Somebody tore, excuse my language, tore the hell out of that place. ... It amazes me that a couple of insipid criminals like Ivan Johnson and David Reynolds didn't cut themselves and didn't give us a gift like their DNA.

" ... We know he was last seen by a very credible witness, Dean Gordon, on Thanksgiving night. We know he was found on December 3rd. Where in there did it happen? I can't tell you point positive. But the reasonable evidence is that it happened late Saturday night, early Sunday morning, and that Mr. Johnson hightailed it out of town with the help of whoever was with him because he doesn't have his own car."

As far as the idea that the State had bought off the witnesses, all of the witnesses testified that they had not. "Tracy Freeman told you I wanted a deal. I even demanded a deal. Said I wasn't going to testify. But why did you testify when you didn't get the deal you wanted? Because it was wrong what he did to that old man. Believe it or not, there's a code amongst some of these people. There's a code of some sort. They call it honorably thieves I guess. But these are his friends and the Broadways, did they act like people who wanted to blame him for a murder? Look at Errol Coder. He sat up and talked about what a great worker he was, how he helped build the house. Wilford looked over at Ivan and basically said how long have you known each other. These aren't people trying to blame him. These are people who know a little bit about a crime and are here to tell you about it."

"There's only one person [who] everybody in his life says he asked me to help him with a robbery or he did a robbery and a murder. There's only one person, I hate to keep harping on it. There's only one person [who] had those boots on that matched the evidence at the crime scene. There's only one person [who] switched out his jacket and told the feeblest of lies about that jacket. That person is Ivan Johnson. And the reason he continues to lie is because he's guilty of this crime."

Chapter 30

The Court: "Ladies and gentlemen of the jury, there are 14 jurors. And there are two of you that are alternates; if you'll remain in the courtroom. The remainder of you may go to your jury room and deliberate."

The jury left the courtroom at 2:14 p.m. to begin deliberation. During their deliberation, my husband and I went to a find a place nearby where we could grab a coffee. We ended up sitting near a table that filled with people associated with the trial. Most notably, there was Sheriff Dawson, the person who had escorted Ivan Johnson into the courtroom during the preliminary trial in Macon and then again into the courtroom in Columbia, and Attorney Zwink joined the party for a time.

We actually ended up sitting with this group (sans the defendant's attorney) as they talked about how they felt about Ivan Johnson's guilt or innocence. Every man there thought Ivan Johnson was guilty, without a doubt. Listening to them talk openly, frankly, made me appreciate each of them more for their roles in the whole murder/trial scenario. My earlier impression of Sheriff Dawson changed as I now found him approachable and talkative, overall friendlier.

Still, I wasn't sure that the jury thought the evidence was compelling enough. I was thankful that the Court came to find us approximately 3 hours after the jury left to deliberate, but that in turn made me afraid that they were going to find Johnson innocent.

The following proceedings were held in the courtroom, in the presence of the jury, commencing at 5:25 p.m.

As the jurors filed back into the courtroom, there were several who looked at me with what seemed to be looks of compassion. This led me to believe that they were going to find the defendant guilty of murdering my brother. My legs continued to shake, even at this late stage of the ordeal.

The Court: "Would you deliver your verdict forms and the instructions to the bailiff, please.

"Members of the audience that are present in the courtroom, once I read these verdicts, you will be in the courtroom until the jury has left the courthouse. So if there's anyone that wants to leave, you leave now. Otherwise you will be with us probably for 10 or 15 minutes.

"As to the Count I, we, the jury, find the defendant Ivan Johnson guilty of murder in the first degree as submitted in Instruction Number 5. And the verdict has been signed by your foreperson. Is this your verdict and so say each member of this jury?"

The jurors responded affirmatively.

The Court: "As to Count II, we, the jury, find the defendant Ivan Johnson guilty of robbery in the first degree as submitted in Instruction Number 10. And the verdict has been signed by your foreperson.

"Is this your verdict and so say each member of this jury?"

The jurors responded affirmatively.

What a relief to have it over and done! I envisioned that this would be the end of it for me. I would be done dealing with ALL of the players, and I would be able to move on and pick up my life that had been on hold for just shy of two years. How very mistaken I was. I would question everything about my life and about life and death in general. I would end up divorced. But at that moment, I was relieved. I wouldn't call it a state of happiness, just a sense of relief and justice and incredible thankfulness to Attorney Zoellner, Sergeant Hall, and the jury.

Judge Conley and the two attorneys scheduled the final disposition for December 16, 2005. The trial adjourned at 5:38 p.m.

On December 16, Judge Conley fixed punishment at life imprisonment on Count I and 20 years on Count II. The sentences were to be served consecutively.

Chapter 31

The way back to Ethel was just as I had remembered it to be from my first terrible trip. In fact, since I had been in shock the first time, this return trip along Hwy. 149 seemed perhaps even more treacherous. This time the continuous steep inclines, excessively sharp curves with accompanying drop-offs were expected, so trepidation had already set in. Added to my foreboding was news from Ethel that the slow-moving Amish with their horses and buggies might appear at a moment's notice as we cleared the top of a hill. Nothing bad happened on the return, however. We (my new partner and I) drove slowly, giving the landscape and the Amish their due respect. On our first day, we drove into and through Ethel just so I could take a look and remember how it had all been in 2003. (It certainly doesn't take but a minute to drive all the way through Ethel.) My first reaction was that it all looked cleaner somehow. Of course, there was no ominous crime scene tape looming from up on the hill where John's house had stood. All of the trees and brush had been cleared to the south and west of my brother's former property so that the community center stood out proudly at the top of that hill. The city garbage dumpster was no longer present on the northwest side of the property; a parking lot had taken over its space. A house or two had been taken down at the start of W. Commercial Street, so it was a very open view up to the new Ethel Community Center.

We stopped and took a few pictures without alerting anyone to our presence. Indeed, it seemed as if we were the only people in town, except for a school bus that disembarked a child or two and then moseyed off into the hills. Otherwise, I don't recall seeing a soul.

We then drove through New Cambria on the way to Macon. I had thought the distance to New Cambria to be further than it was. In early 2004, we had gone to the bank there to open the safe deposit box that held those several strange items that only John understood. The bank looked the same. As we drove on to Macon, we saw the sign for the Long Branch Restaurant, and I remembered how Sergeant Hall had accompanied us there after our long day of house cleaning. Further down the road was the ominous looking hotel – one clearly never renovated since the 1960s – that my son and I refused to stay in after the preliminary hearing in 2005. As then, we drove on to the Comfort Inn where I had made reservations, I remembering how nice it was after that first Macon court ordeal.

It was no problem finding the Comfort Inn again (I had forgotten my paperwork at home so had no address in the car). It was in clear sight as we neared the intersection of 36 and 63, right where I thought it was. It was a welcoming sight, just as it had been in 2005. We asked the hotel clerk about a good place to eat and she put us on to AJ's, which was just up the road. We got some great sandwiches and some fantastic onion rings. Afterwards, we went back to the hotel to relax.

Even though I had emailed several Ethel and Macon residents a number of times in the months preceding my journey, I was still apprehensive of my reception the next morning. I had carefully planned who I would talk with, but I had not prepared any kind of script, so I didn't really have a clue how to start a conversation with anyone. Thankfully, they were somewhat prepared for me, and all that was necessary to get us off on the right foot was a smile, a hello, and a brief introduction of who I was.

First, we stopped at the post office, where I had been told that Ethel residents normally gathered. Again, it all seemed much cleaner somehow. In fact, the post office was in great shape, and Linda Lile, who had testified during Ivan Johnson's trial, was very friendly and accommodating. It was to her that I first showed the photo collage of John that I had brought to present to the community center. I very much wanted the Ethel residents who had known John to actually see him as a total person, as someone who had indeed had a "normal" life, a worthwhile life, prior to becoming mentally ill and winding up in Ethel, Missouri, as a virtual hermit for the remainder of that life. Linda seemed to appreciate the pictures of John and the brief story of his life that I had written to accompany it.

Linda called Lynn Mason, the pastor of the Ethel Christian Church, as she had requested be done when I arrived. Lynn and I had never met, but had only emailed back and forth after I had contacted her to see if John's drawing still hung in the church there. The pastor to whom John had presented his drawing was no longer there, and Lynn had said in an email that she had never seen it. She had never met John. Lynn was very friendly to us, and she waited as I continued the conversation with Linda and with Gary Allard and his son, who had walked in to get their mail. Gary told us that prior to Bernie Jones giving John rides from Ethel to New Cambria, Marcelline and Macon, Gary had sometimes done so. Gary also had run what became Ken's Country Junction, which John had left grocery notes about. It was fortuitous to meet yet another person who could share a bit of information with me about John's life in Ethel.

From the post office, Lynn walked with me up the hill to the community center, while my partner drove the car up. She gave me more background about the surrounding houses and area and escorted me further up the road so that I could actually view the pond that sat down the hill behind John's old property. It was an area where the police dogs had been sent to search for evidence but found none. The view was actually quite pretty, and I could understand a bit of why John decided to stay in Ethel. I walked up behind the community center and remembered my son telling me that he had found cat skulls back there when he was taking pictures of the house perimeter in December 2003. I was unable to walk all the way around the building to view the side yard, but I noticed that the small shed had been taken down, along with all the perimeter shrubbery.

Nadine Wooden then came out of the building to introduce herself to me. She also had been kind enough to share emails beforehand so that I learned about their community initiative to put the center together so that Ethel residents would have a gathering place. I was very impressed with what they had accomplished: a small grocery store upon entering the building, a small gift shop, a large meeting hall with dining tables, an expansive kitchen to cook community meals, and an additional room that was to be turned into a library. Indeed, there were quite a number of books already neatly arranged in racks in the large room. As I walked through the rooms, however, I distinctly remembered the layout of John's house and how I had felt walking through it. Now, it eerily seemed as if I were entering the front of his home where his body had lain. It seemed a bit surreal, but very fitting that a community center should now sit where his home had been. And fitting that his photo collage would be able to look down upon it all – and hopefully approve and be at peace with it.

Bernie Jones patiently waited outside of the community center while I chatted with several people, including Gordon Dean's wife Ursula. Ursula was pleased with the photo collage and said that she remembered John as he looked in one of his older photos, one that had been taken a few years prior to his moving to Ethel. Several others had told me the same thing. She commented that John had been a very handsome man, and I shared that he had had many girls after him in his younger years. She said that she missed him. That is still a bit hard for me to take in given his paranoid personality. It's wonderful to think that some people there actually cared about John, but hard to imagine them missing him since he really communicated with them so very little. I'd like to believe, though, that they did.

I had shown John's picture to Bernie prior to taking it inside, and he was the only one who said he remembered John from the last photo that John must have taken of himself. That last photo was of a gaunt John with a long beard and sort of ghostly expression, wearing a waffle knit blue henley shirt and blue jeans.

Bernie gave us a tour of Ethel. I had not previously driven through the "town." I had only read about the layout in the court transcripts where Attorneys Zoellner and Zwink highlighted the treks that Ivan Johnson had made. I was surprised to see that all streets, save Commercial and Hwy. 149 through town, were narrow and graveled, and that some had such treacherous slopes. I don't think our rented car would have gotten up the one street that

Bernie's 4-wheel drive vehicle was able to navigate.

We went on a larger perimeter tour of the town, and Bernie showed us where he resided on its outskirts. He took us through areas where it would seem the poorest of the town's residents lived, and he took us through areas where the more well-off residents lived. He showed us the private lake where he would set up camp and fish for crappies. After hearing some stories of his background and previous states of residence, I had a hard time understanding why he would choose the Ethel area, and so I asked him. He said, "I came to visit 15 years ago and fell in love with the rolling hills and decided to stay."

Along our route, Bernie shared details about his relationship with my brother John. First of all, he shared that he would always pick John up on the 3rd of the month because that was John's payday (his disability check) and also his own. He had come that 3rd and John did not come out of the house when Bernie had pulled up as usual and honked. He noticed that the wood was not stacked, and that was totally unlike John because he would always stack it after delivery. "I blew the horn, but no John. And, there was no smoke."

Bernie said that he asked Linda to call the Sheriff. The Sheriff and Bernie were unable to get into the house, but they could see through a slit in the window that John was lying there. They called in Donald Salva, with the Ethel Fire Department, to break in the side door. When the door was open, the Sheriff stepped in first, then Bernie, and Don was behind them. When the Sheriff saw that John was lying there dead and that there was a safe with a screwdriver sticking out of it, he said that they all needed to move back out.

Bernie shared that there was only one time that John ever got mad at him. It was when John had insisted that he wanted Bernie to drive him to Arkansas, and he refused to do it. John kept asking him why he wouldn't do it, and Bernie said because he didn't want to. John couldn't figure that out since he told Bernie that he would pay him.

We turned down 149 towards New Cambria, and Bernie pointed out the wooden fence on the corner where John always stood when waiting for rides. Bernie said that John would never take a ride from anyone unless he knew them.

"John would give me $50 for every trip to the store." Bernie told him that he was giving him too much money, but John insisted. Every pay day he would take John to the bank in Marcelline, then to the smoke shop for John to get tobacco and/or cigarettes, and sometimes to the Sav-a-Lot. Bernie said, "I couldn't go in with John when shopping, he thought you were spying on him."

Every Christmas, John would give Bernie $100. Bernie would give John cigarettes and tobacco. Bernie said that John was always trying to give him money, but he didn't need it and would refuse. He told us how he used to make numerous loaves of zucchini bread to share at community or church meals, and that John liked his zucchini bread and also his chili.

There were several times that John told him that the aliens were after him. Bernie told me that John somehow slept under his house, under the floor boards. We had not discovered any floor boards that would come up, but we had not looked for them. It's possible he could get under them from the strange back room of the house. It didn't surprise me to hear that he would become that paranoid that he would feel the need to sleep in that fashion. It most likely reminded him of being in a bunker in Vietnam, just as closing himself into the closet under my dad's stairway undoubtedly did. It's unfortunate that under the floor boards is not where he was sleeping the night that Ivan Johnson and his accomplice laid in wait.

Sadly, Bernie passed away a few years back. I was very fortunate to have been able to meet him when I did and learn of his relationship with John. Bernie had also shared during our visit that he was the vet who had put up a reward to find John's murderer. I thanked him then, and I am still thankful that he thought enough of John to do so.

After our Ethel visit, we headed back through New Cambria on our way to Macon. This time we headed for downtown Macon, and I figured it would be relatively easy to find a place to eat. Since I had left my paperwork at home, I didn't have the names of the spots that Coroner Brian Hayes had recommended. We drove back towards our hotel, arguing about a few of the fast food spots, and then we happened to spot a Mexican restaurant. Mexican beer, chips and guacamole, an enchilada and tacos hit the spot. Back we went to the downtown area.

Earlier, I had spotted the Eagan - Hayes funeral home and also the Macon County courthouse. However, we had also passed a funeral home of another name on Rubey Street, which sure looked like the one where Brian had readied John for viewing. I had mentioned to Brian that I wanted to take a few pictures and that I would also say hello if he was going to be around. I wasn't sure what "home" he would be at, so we went to the Eagan – Hayes site. The woman there told me the office was on Rubey Street, and she thought that Brian might be there. On Rubey Street, I was told that Brian was elsewhere officiating a service, so I did not get a chance to say my hello. There really wasn't anything else I could have talked to him about; we had talked over everything that tied us together back in 2003 and 2004. As mentioned elsewhere in this story, I will never forget his kindness to me during those very trying days. What I did do was take pictures of the Rubey Street funeral home, which was more like a grand old home that must have hosted many parties in its day.

From Eagan – Hayes, we wandered over to the Macon Courthouse. I had gotten an idea about trying to get pictures of the courtroom where the preliminary trial had been held. It was almost serendipitous that the law enforcement officer who was stationed there that day, when questioned, told us that he himself was from Ethel and he was well aware of the John Wolff murder. He told us that we should be able to take pictures of the courtroom after they finished up their hearings for the day, which he figured to be in around half an hour. He said we were welcome to wait around. I asked him if Dawson was still the sheriff there, and he said, "Yes." He pointed out where the sheriff's office was, which happened to be on a different corner than I remembered. When I saw it, though, I remembered it quite well.

As my partner and I wandered over to the building, I shared remembrances of when my son and I had parked in front of it, watching as a car drove around the side of the building, parked, and then the driver hollering up to an inmate behind the barred window up above. That was not happening today. We walked into the building, which seemed familiar. We were told that Sheriff Dawson was not in, but the officer speaking to us was very gregarious. I had not met this person before, but he shared a lot about the County criminals and the current goings-on. He presumed we were from the area, but we hadn't a clue about most of the local information he shared.

I took a few pictures of the inside of the entry area, and then the officer offered to let me do so in the back room. I tried to tell him that I had never been into the back area, but he wasn't listening. So, I took a picture of the chair with leather straps that sat in the corner of the one room. The officer told me to be careful of my picture taking because there was someone in the holding area adjacent to the chair, but I had not seen anyone and certainly didn't want to take their picture. The chair looked like one that would be used to strap someone in for electrocution, but in actuality it was used to strap people down who were high on drugs. I then asked if I could take pictures of the stairwell out in back that led down to the evidence room. He said sure, but he told the officer behind the barred window what I was doing just in case I accidentally triggered the alarm from wandering too close. I remembered the stairwell as being rather ominous when we were led there to obtain that truckload of John's belongings being held in evidence. It still looked ominous, though I couldn't get too close to actually look down that dark stairwell.

It must have been a full half hour, so we walked back over to the courthouse. I had not remembered the courtroom being on the second floor until I took a closer look at the stairway. Then, I remembered how some of the locals had lounged against the railway as we had to walk past them on our way out while they made comments about how we looked. I suppose we did look like misfits coming from a Chicago suburb versus a rural Macon/Ethel culture, me in my business clothes with not a hair out of place and them all in their jeans. I took pictures of the stairway from below and from above, and I had plenty of time to do so because I was told it would be yet another half hour before court was done for the day.

Attorney Zwink, whose office I had seen downtown earlier in the day and who had been the defending attorney for Ivan Johnson, wandered out of the courtroom. I introduced myself, and it took him just a moment to remember the case. He said, "He's still in jail." I responded, "He'd better be." The half hour turned into an hour. It would have been interesting to stand in the courtroom and remember that preliminary hearing day in 2005, but I was not willing to give up any more of my time since our wait had already stretched into an hour and a half.

All the while we drove around Macon, and considering Ethel and its environs, I was still having a hard time understanding the attraction of the area. I know that it all depends upon where a person is born, the geography they are familiar with. Being in the Chicagoland suburbs for so many years, I am spoiled by all of the conveniences and attractions that abound. I am used to lots of activity and life around me. I mentioned to my partner, "All of the population of Ethel about equals the number of people that work in my office every day." I was ready for my return visit to Missouri to end and to be on my way back home.

Chapter 32

Prior to my final trip to Ethel and as previously mentioned, I had emailed back and forth with Nadine Wooden, with Pastor Lynn Mason, and with the Gordons. Ursula had been kind enough to pose my questions to her husband Dean and had then responded on his behalf because of his stroke. Their answers fill in a bit more of the puzzle of John's life.

Ursula: "We didn't know John very well, just tried to talk with him whenever we met him at the post office, etc. For some reason, he would always accept a meal from us when I was cooking for our large family and sent him a plate. We only did this occasionally but he generally seemed glad to accept it. Always, on Thanksgiving when we were in Ethel, we tried to not forget that he was probably alone and sent something up. I used to run a little quilt shop, The Buttercup, and made homemade cinnamon rolls in the mornings. John would often come in and ask if I had any left. He really enjoyed the rolls."

Some of their answers below seem to contradict what Dean had told me when I was in the Ethel for the very first time. Perhaps, however, I had not correctly understood what he said at that time considering the stress I was under.

Question: You had mentioned to me that you feel that it was you who influenced John into buying in Ethel. Why do you feel you talked John into moving to Ethel?

Answer: No, Mary. Dean had nothing to do with John's decision to move to Ethel. John inquired into Ethel on his own. Don't know what influenced him except I recall he saw an ad for some property here. Where, I don't know. It may have been through United Farm Agency because John said a United Farm agent told him to contact Dean. At the time, Dean was a farm real estate broker here. (He mostly sold farms, not houses). He asked

Dean what he thought the property was worth that he was interested in. Dean gave him a ballpark figure of property values here but that was the end of the contact. We were fairly new to the community at the time also.

Question: What year was it when you tried to get John to update his house or to move to another community? You had mentioned that he actually tried to look elsewhere for houses at one point in time. Brookfield, perhaps?

Answer: Dean didn't try to get John to move to another community but the opposite. John had gone over to Brookfield without any encouragement that I know of and inquired of a real estate agent about a house that was for sale there. Neither of us can remember the date but probably sometime in the mid 1990's. This agent (a lady) came to Dean and asked him if he knew John, which he said he did but not very well. She may have been concerned that he would not qualify for the house. Then, I believe John asked Dean about it and Dean recommended him not to move because people in Ethel kind of watched out for him, and Dean was actually concerned about him living in a community that was larger and where people didn't really know him. [In hindsight, that was probably true because it was not anyone from Ethel who harmed John but someone from another town.]

Question: You mentioned that you encouraged John to clean up his place – mow his grass, do something about so many cats. Was that to prepare for the sale of his home? So, that a lender would look favorably on him? You mentioned in that conversation that it appeared that he had gotten rid of most of his cats after your talk with him. [Prior to that I found evidence that he actually liked those cats – there were many pictures of them and receipts for purchase of items specifically for the cats, such as toys and tunnels. Yet, in the two times I visited the property after his death, I only saw one cat.]

Answer: Neither one of us were ever in John's house so we don't know exactly what improvements needed to be made. But, he may have been encouraged to improve his house for his own benefit by someone. Dean doesn't remember encouraging him in this area. But it seems to me that he may have asked Dean about how he could improve his property. I don't know for sure but I do remember someone saying something to him because he cut his grass after that. He was evidently trying to improve his property. As I said above, Dean was actually concerned for John's welfare for him to move somewhere else. However, that doesn't mean that John had given up the idea of moving. There is no way of knowing. I don't know about the cats. It may have been someone was complaining about them. There was a dumpster right outside his house and they were all over the dumpster most of the time when people took their trash. This is just a guess, Mary. Everyone knew he was fond of cats because he seemed to have several. I wouldn't doubt that he took in strays because there are always stray cats in Ethel. I think John had a kind heart. I have no idea what happened to his cats. I don't ever recall the city complaining to him but perhaps I wouldn't know that. I know now they will insist that people cut their grass if it gets very long. Most of what I have said is just conjecture on my part.

Question: You and Ursula both mentioned that John would accept food from you at Thanksgiving. How many years did you provide this for him? Would you take it to the house and he would come out and accept it? (I want to heartily thank both of you for doing that for John.)

Answer: I don't really recall how many times, Mary. Not nearly enough, I can tell you that. We should have paid more attention to him. Ralph and Sandy Clark who owned the inn occasionally took it on Thanksgiving also. Perhaps three or four years on our part. It seems that I also took it a very few times on other occasions. He came out in the yard and got it and always thanked us for it. As far as I know, they were never inside the house either.

Question: Did John actually ever communicate (talk coherently) with anyone in the community?

Answer: There were times when John would say hello. Other times, he would not speak at all but just stare at you. If he wanted something, he would ask for it, I think. He came into my little quilt shop a couple of times and asked if I had any cinnamon rolls left. That was late in the morning. Then there was once when I took some left over up to his house and knocked on the door and he either was not at home or would not answer the door.

Question: To your recollection, did John ever bother anybody in Ethel?

Answer: Not that I know of. Actually, I think people were rather fond of him. Dean's mother who was scared of her shadow was not a bit afraid of John. She prayed for him a lot.

Question: Are there any incidents that you remember specifically about my brother that may not have been mentioned in answer to those questions?

Answer: Only one. Once before I knew who John even was, I picked him up in a snowstorm on Highway 36 heading toward Macon. I really had to talk to myself on that one because he is the only hitchhiker I have ever picked up in my life. However, it was freezing and I was very concerned that he might not get picked up by anyone else and perhaps be stranded. I took him into Macon and he got out on the street corner. The only question he asked me was, "Are you married?" I had to chuckle at that one. It seemed on the way, I did ask him where he lived and he told me Ethel which made me feel more at ease.

Chapter 33

While a promising new community center marked where John's home had been in Ethel, Missouri, a transitional home in Hebron, Illinois, now marks where John had lived when first trying to make his way after his return from Vietnam. The old Hi-De-Ho Motel is now transformed into New Horizons: Transitional Living for Homeless Veterans. It is very unfortunate that the services offered through the organization called Transitional Living Services (TLS), offering services to McHenry County, Illinois, veterans in need, were not available to John as he struggled with his own initial mental illness.

New Horizons/TLS opens its doors to homeless veterans who are struggling with addiction, alcoholism, trauma, mental illness, unemployment, underemployment, chronic illness, and other misfortunes. The organization offers all of the services that could have made a real difference in how John lived out his life – a stable living environment for up to two years, mental health counseling, job search assistance, and an aftercare program once a veteran is able to transition to a more independent living arrangement.

Another uncanny coincidence is that TLS was headed by Alan Belcher (psychologist, now retired), who had helped found the local chapter of VietNow back in the early 1980's, the group I had referred John to for help and an opportunity to get involved with the Vietnam veterans' Agent Orange class action suit. This is the same Alan Belcher I had talked with on several occasions about John's circumstances and about the possibility of his schizophrenia being triggered by his experiences in Vietnam and his possible exposure to Agent Orange.

Chapter 34

The existence of New Horizons built upon John's old Hi-De-Ho Motel residence and the existence of the Ethel Community Center, built on John's Ethel home site seem very fitting. It's almost as if the circumstances of his life had come full circle and good had blossomed from the bad. What is sad is that he would never know about it.

What is even sadder is that not enough was known at the time he first became ill about how to deal with mental illness. There were no mental health support groups for him or for his family. There had been no development of drugs that would have been more beneficial with fewer side effects so that the suffering individual might actually want to take them and ultimately realize the benefits. There were no transitional veterans homes for anyone in John's condition.

John was stuck with a family and friends who didn't know how to deal with him, and who essentially ended up shunning him. Even the ones who truly cared and wanted to help didn't understand how to do that, including me. Much has since been published about the country's politically-charged climate to which the Vietnam veterans returned and that there was no special help there for any of them, let alone those who had developed mental illness, in reintegrating back into society.

Under the circumstances, it's surprising that John was able to carry on until his 58th birthday. And, he could have carried on longer had not Ivan Johnson chosen to end his life during that Thanksgiving holiday back in 2003.

Chapter 35
Epilogue to John

Well, John, I guess you were right. People can obtain something if they really want it and are willing to work hard to get it. The road there may take you places you wouldn't have thought about, and there may be many more obstacles than you ever anticipated, but if you have the determination, you can get there. Look at me. I just – finally - finished this book. So I want to say thank you for all of the encouragement you gave me through the relatively short time that we could share together. I hope that you are at peace. I am still not yet there, but I continue to try. Perhaps I can now let your lessons help lead the way.

One thing I think you would be pleased about is that now a community center with a small grocery section sits just where your house used to sit in Ethel. It was crazy how I learned about it. While I was doing research for this book, I was simply looking into Ethel in general. When I clicked on one of the Yahoo links for "Up With Ethel," I was all of a sudden staring at your house at 111 Commercial Street. I couldn't initially figure out just why a picture of your house would be showcased on this site. As I clicked on the links associated with that page, I ended up viewing short videos and many pictures of how your house was torn down and then bulldozed. It made me sad to see it. To know you would most likely have still been there had Ivan Johnson just left you alone.

As the pictures progressed and I read some of the text, it became evident that there was a group of Ethel residents trying to erect a community center right where your house used to be. I have now visited that center and met the people who run it. I think you would be pleased for them. Had there been a grocery store right in Ethel, you would not have had to ask for so many rides to the stores. And you would not have had to start out walking to get there before you got a ride. Had there been a community center there, I actually think you would have stopped in even though you did not communicate much with anyone in the town. If they were having a dinner or music, I think you would have sat and listened and maybe even smiled, as Linda Lile said you did while listening to Motown music in the small restaurant that used to be there.

I think it would make you happy that right on the site of the old Hi-De-Ho Motel where you first stayed in Hebron, when you were first trying to function with your mental illness, there is now a transitional home for veterans. The men and women who stay there are probably a lot like you. They are homeless for one reason or another. They may just have hit hard luck. They may be suffering from an addiction. Or, they may have some sort of mental illness. It is a place where you would have been given a chance to get your life back in order. Where you might have learned to manage your illness and remain a part of society. Where you wouldn't have been so alone.

I think you would be exceptionally happy to know that you had a profound influence on a former employee of yours at the Coachlight with whom you had shared some invaluable advice that helped guide her through her life. She shared a story with me several years back of how when working for you, she had gone through a traumatic break up with someone. She said that you had been wonderful in helping her through a tough time. She said that you were always very caring, making sure that she made it to her car safely after work, worrying about her welfare. She shared that you told her one thing in particular that helped her through many periods in her life, helped her to do things that she never would have thought of doing otherwise. At her lowest point, you told her that she could either be a victim or a survivor – it was up to her. She said that she chose to become a survivor.

Another thing I think that would make you happy is that even though you were not able to communicate with the Ethel residents as you did with people prior to your illness, they still spoke of you fondly. They graciously accepted the photo collage of you in various stages of your life (hopefully depicting the "real" you), along with the flag that I received from veterans when we held your brief graveside memorial service. The flag, I might add, rested in a beautiful cherry wood case that your friend Warren had given me. I was told that the photo collage and the flag will be displayed in your honor in the Ethel Community Center.

Additionally, your old friend Bernie asked if I would share a copy of one photo in particular that I had included in the collage – the one you had taken at DeWanes in 1980 wearing your army shirt and sporting a full beard. He said that he did not have a photo of you and wanted it to remind him of you, of the person you had been in Ethel, the friend who he had helped on his journeys.

I can still see you trudging up to my house, wearing that jacket, sporting that beard, and bringing me those lovely irises. And, I still miss you, my brother, and I still feel the same regret and pain for not being there when you needed me most. So saddened, as I have been many times during the writing of your story when I think of the song "He Ain't Heavy" by the Hollies, that you weren't able to let us in and help you with your load.

WORKS CITED

Ascher, Barbara Lazear, "Landscape Without Gravity." Penguin Books, May 1, 1994.

Astor, Maggie and Jacey Fortin, "50 Years Later, It Feels Familiar: How America Fractured in 1968." *New York Times*, www.nytimes.com. Accessed January 16, 2018.

Compassionate Friends, https://www.compassionatefriends.org/adults-grieving-death-sibling/ (Accessed 2006; information no longer available on that site.)

Dyregrov, Atle, "A Murder in the Family," *International Critical Incident Stress Foundation*, www.icisf.org, 2006.

Farwell, Lawrence. "Brain Fingerprinting," *Innovation*, Episode 8. WNET/New York, WNET New York, May 2004.

Gordon, Dean and Ursula. Personal Interview. February 14, 2011.

Hansen, Malene Breusch, "Head Injury Can Cause Mental Illness," *Science Nordic*, www.sciencenordic.com. January 3, 2014. Accessed 27 December 2017.

KTVO TV. Www.ktvotv3.com:
> "NEMO Authorities Investigate Apparent Murder." December 4, 2003.
> "Death in Ethel, MO Officially Ruled Homicide. December 9, 2003.
> "Suspect Charged in NEMO Bludgeoning Death." July 7, 2004.

Macon Chronicle-Herald, Macon, MO:
> "Law Enforcement Investigating Ethel Man's Death." December 4, 2003.
> "$5,000 Reward Established for Conviction in Ethel Murder." December 17, 2003.
> "Ivan Johnson's Preliminary Hearing Set for October 5." Terri Hackett, August 8, 2004.
> "Town Remembers Man Who Lived a Recluse Life." Terri Hackett, September 29, 2004.
> "Citizen Recalls the Day John Wolff Was Found." Terri Hackett, September 29, 2004.

Missouri Attorney General's Office, press release. "Attorney General, Macon County prosecutor file murder, robbery charges in connection with death of Ethel man." www.ago.state.mo.us/newsreleases/2004/070704.htm. July 7, 2004.

Moronell, Mark. *Sharecare,* www.sharecare.com/health/schizophrenia/what-flat-affect-for-schizophrenia. Accessed 27 December 2017.

Pedersen, T. (2016). Flat Affect. *Psych Central,* https://psychcentral.com/encyclopedia/flat-affect/. Accessed 27 December 2017.

Rettner, Rachael, "Head Trauma May Boost Schizophrenia Risk." *LiveScience,* www.livescience.com/15659-traumatic-brain-injury-increases-schizophrenia-risk.html. April 19, 2011. Accessed 2 January 2018.

Rohn, Alan. "Vietnam War Timeline." https://thevietnamwar.info/vietnam-war-timeline/, December 2, 2012. Accessed 27 December 2017.

U.S. Department of Veterans Affairs. www.va.gov/oaa/pocketcard/vietnam.asp. Accessed 27 December 2017.

Wikipedia. "1968 in the Vietnam War." https://en.wikipedia.org/wiki/1968_in_the_Vietnam_War. Accessed 27 December 2017.

Wray, T.J., "Surviving the Death of a Sibling: Living Through Grief When an Adult Brother or Sister Dies. Harmony, May 27, 2003.

About the Author

Mary Lee Wolff graduated from Columbia College, Crystal Lake, Illinois campus, with a major in English and a minor in psychology. Upon graduation she was an administrative assistant and gardening columnist for *Fifty & Better,* a startup senior publication, and then moved to its parent newspaper, the *Northwest Herald,* in an administrative capacity.

Upon leaving the newspaper, she wrote feature stories and edited for several telecommunications and horticultural trade magazines. Thereafter, she worked for a federally funded program assisting unemployed individuals, and after earning several masters levels certificates in career counseling, she was promoted to an assistant director position. Within her management role she wrote internal policy, grant proposals and web site content.

www.ingramcontent.com/pod-product-compliance
Lightning Source LLC
Chambersburg PA
CBHW070013110426
42741CB00034B/1317